D1519669

NATURE RED IN TOOTH AND CLAW

Nature Red
in Tooth and Claw:

Theism and the Problem of Animal Suffering

MICHAEL J. MURRAY

OXFORD

UNIVERSITY PRESS

OXFORD
UNIVERSITY PRESS

Great Clarendon Street, Oxford OX2 6DP

Oxford University Press is a department of the University of Oxford.
It furthers the University's objective of excellence in research, scholarship,
and education by publishing worldwide in

Oxford New York

Auckland Cape Town Dar es Salaam Hong Kong Karachi
Kuala Lumpur Madrid Melbourne Mexico City Nairobi
New Delhi Shanghai Taipei Toronto

With offices in

Argentina Austria Brazil Chile Czech Republic France Greece
Guatemala Hungary Italy Japan Poland Portugal Singapore
South Korea Switzerland Thailand Turkey Ukraine Vietnam

Oxford is a registered trade mark of Oxford University Press
in the UK and in certain other countries

Published in the United States
by Oxford University Press Inc., New York

© Michael J. Murray 2008

The moral rights of the author have been asserted
Database right Oxford University Press (maker)

First published 2008

All rights reserved. No part of this publication may be reproduced,
stored in a retrieval system, or transmitted, in any form or by any means,
without the prior permission in writing of Oxford University Press,
or as expressly permitted by law, or under terms agreed with the appropriate
reprographics rights organization. Enquiries concerning reproduction
outside the scope of the above should be sent to the Rights Department,
Oxford University Press, at the address above

You must not circulate this book in any other binding or cover
and you must impose the same condition on any acquirer

British Library Cataloguing in Publication Data
Data available

Library of Congress Cataloging in Publication Data
Data available

Typeset by Laserwords Private Limited, Chennai, India
Printed in Great Britain
on acid-free paper by
Biddles Ltd, King's Lynn, Norfolk

ISBN 978–0–19–923727–2

1 3 5 7 9 10 8 6 4 2

To Eleonore Stump
mentor and friend

Acknowledgments

This project was initially spawned through conversation with a relentless group of undergraduate students in an introductory philosophy of religion course at Franklin and Marshall College in 2001. I promised them that if those conversations ever led to a book, they would be credited by name. I hereby discharge that obligation: Brooke Anderson, Amoreena Bua, Chris Casalenuovo, Erin Colgan, Virginia Dearborn, Carolyn Erb, Keith Gibbs, Katherine Kimber, Rachel Kovenetsky, Seth Modesto, Maryam Namdari, Tim Patterson, Brett Rubin, Gerald Stoltzfoos, Samantha Strickler, Kelly Trefaller, Kristen Valpreda, and Sean Welski.

In addition, a draft of the entire manuscript was discussed by an astute undergraduate audience in an upper-division seminar at Franklin and Marshall in 2005. Their feedback was invaluable and I would like to acknowledge them by name as well: Jeff Baron, Ben Burghart, Ben Donahower, Brad Eagle, Andrew Goldberg, Tim Liu, Dan Oakes, Bryan Small, and Hailey Strobel.

My colleague Glenn Ross joined this blossoming discussion in the summer of 2001, and shortly afterwards we co-authored an essay which became the backbone for Chapter 2 of this book. I am deeply indebted to Glenn for long hours of conversation and argument which led to that chapter and which further helped me work out some of my own thoughts that formed much of the core of Chapter 1. I further wish to thank him and the editors at *Faith and Philosophy* for allowing the reuse of some of the material from the original co-authored article here. That article appeared under the title 'Neo-Cartesian Theodicies of Animal Suffering' (*Faith and Philosophy*, 23 (April 2006), 169–90). We would jointly like to thank many who offered constructive criticism of that paper at various stages of development, especially Bennett Helm, Peter van Inwagen, Nicholas Wolterstorff, Michael Rea, Carl Gillett, Fred Crosson, Todd Long, and Kevin Timpe. In addition, we are grateful to the audiences at the 'Persons and Freedom' conference at Indiana University in 2002 and at the Notre Dame Center for Philosophy of Religion Reading Group in 2004 for spirited discussions on earlier versions of the paper. Finally, the initial spadework on the historical background for that chapter (and indeed much of the rest of the book) was carried out by Franklin and Marshall student Sarah Berson, who was generously supported in her endeavors by the Franklin and Marshall Hackman Scholars Program. Daniel Garber, Roger Ariew, and Tad Schmaltz also provided me with helpful guidance concerning material on this topic from the modern period.

The bulk of the first draft of the book was written during 2003–4, while I was in residence at the Notre Dame Center for Philosophy of Religion. I am deeply indebted to the Center and the University for their generous support during that year. Research during that year was also supported through sabbatical funding by

Franklin and Marshall. Their unwavering support for faculty research is a model for liberal-arts colleges.

Early versions of Chapters 3 and 6 benefited significantly from questions and comments of the audiences at two venues at which they were presented: the Evangelical Philosophical Society Annual Meeting in November of 2005 and a colloquium at Purdue University in March of 2005, respectively. An early version of Chapter 4 was presented at Westmont College in February of 2006. I am especially grateful for helpful comments from Jeffrey Schloss and David van der Laan at that time.

I owe a special debt of gratitude to Daniel Howard-Snyder, who offered extensive and relentless criticism of the penultimate draft of the book which led to a substantial overhaul of many of the chapters and indeed the very structure of the book. Michael Rea and William Hasker also provided helpful comments on earlier drafts of the entire manuscript.

Finally, I am indebted to my family, Kirsten, Sam, Elise, and Julia, for putting up with a year-long move to South Bend in order to allow me to complete the work on this book. Without their gracious willingness to endure a new house, new schools, and new health clubs (and new pizza shops!), this project would never have come to completion. Their adventurous spirits keep me going. For their sake let me add: Go Irish.

Contents

List of Abbreviations   x

Introduction   1

1. Problems of and Explanations for Evil   10

2. Neo-Cartesianism   41

3. Animal Suffering and the Fall   73

4. Nobility, Flourishing, and Immortality: Animal Pain and Animal
   Well-being   107

5. Natural Evil, Nomic Regularity, and Animal Suffering   130

6. Chaos, Order, and Evolution   166

7. Combining CDs   193

Bibliography   200

Index   207

List of Abbreviations

CD	*causa dei* (i.e. argument in defense of God)
CTO	chaos to order
GE	gratuitous evil
HOT	higher-order thought
PAP	pre-Adamic pain and suffering
SCE	strong cognitive ethology
UE	undefeatable evil
WCE	weak cognitive ethology

Introduction

In academic and popular discourse about the relationship between science and religion scholars and pop-cultural commentators alike seem to agree that while science and religion offer us important perspectives on a variety of crucial matters, the two modes of inquiry do not, and cannot, overlap. Science, we are told, treats matters of fact that are subject to discovery through sensory observation or direct empirical testing, while religion trades in nothing more than nonempirical matters of meaning and morality. And yet, at the very same time, it is common to find covers of *Time*, *Newsweek*, and other major news periodicals which tell of scientists who claim that some discovery in cosmology, biology, or physics has finally 'found God'. News that the universe appears fine-tuned for the possibility of life or that cells contain 'irreducibly complex' structures that point to a designer is trumpeted as (at least potential) evidence in favor of a cosmic creator or designer.

Which is it? Are science and religion isolated domains of thought and inquiry—'Non-Overlapping Magisteria' (or NOMA) to use the phrase coined by Stephen Jay Gould—or does science vindicate religion? Some say it is neither, of course. Rather, defenders of this third alternative take it that science is hostile to religion—if not outright demonstrating its falsity, at least providing us with powerful evidence against its truth. This stance is on display, for example, in a recent essay by philosopher of science Philip Kitcher, entitled 'The Many-Sided Conflict Between Science and Religion'. In the essay, presumably intended as a survey article (appearing as it does in a general reference work on philosophy of religion[1]), Kitcher doesn't squander his efforts discussing the merits of Gould's NOMA, intelligent design, scientific arguments against belief in the miraculous, or other standard fare in the academic study of the relation between science and religion. Instead he focuses his attention on a topic that, by his lights, goes straight for religion's jugular. The topic, one that is surprisingly rarely discussed in science and religion circles, is one we might call 'the Darwinian problem of evil'. There are a number of ways in which Darwinism might be thought to raise problems of evil for theists. For Kitcher, the Darwinian problem consists in the vast and unquantifiable array of nonhuman-animal suffering that is endemic to the evolutionary machinery—machinery which has been winnowing unfit

---

[1] William Mann (ed.), *Blackwell Guide to the Philosophy of Religion* (Malden, Mass.: Blackwell, 2005).

organisms from the planet (often kicking and screaming) for nearly three billion years. In light of the evolutionary carnage, Kitcher finds it incredible that theists can sustain belief in an all-wise, benevolent creator:

[Were we to imagine] a human analogue peering down over a miniaturized version of this arrangement—peering down over his creation—it's hard to equip the face with a kindly expression. Conversely, it's natural to adapt Alfonso X's famous remark about the convolutions of Ptolemaic astronomy: had a benevolent creator proposed to use evolution under natural selection as a means for attaining his purposes, we could have given him useful advice.[2]

Acknowledged tensions between theistic belief in an all-good, all-powerful, and all-knowing providential creator and the palpable and pervasive reality of animal suffering are not new of course. Authors of the biblical texts as well as philosophers and theologians in the various theistic traditions have struggled with the phenomenon of pain and suffering for as long as they have struggled with the problem of evil itself. Many of those thinkers felt that the explanation for nonhuman-animal suffering was in one way or other to be found in wrongdoing by human animals, most notably Adam and Eve in the Fall. But by the early nineteenth century, as theists began to grapple with increasingly potent evidence that animals preexisted humans, explanations of evil that appealed to the Fall rang hollow. With the publication of Darwin's *Origin of Species* in 1859 these concerns only intensified. While most theists had by that point made peace with an understanding of creation that required a less than fully literal understanding of Genesis, the claim that organismic complexity and diversity was best explained by appeal to phenotypic variation and natural selection was a theological bombshell. Not only did Darwinism embrace the notion that animals—with all of their predation, pain, and death—preexisted human beings, but predation, pain, and death were now viewed as among the very instruments of creation. It thus appeared that the natural order was hatched via a mechanism fraught with evil at its very core. As Darwin himself explained the problem, 'the sufferings of millions of the lower animals throughout almost endless time' are apparently irreconcilable with the existence of a creator of 'unbounded' goodness.[3] Such sentiments led Darwin to utter his famous quip, 'What a book a devil's chaplain might write on the clumsy wasteful, blundering, low, and horribly cruel works of nature!'.[4] Consequently, in the half century after the publication of the *Origin of Species* Christian apologists who adopted the evolutionary account of biological origins were forced to grapple with the pervasiveness of animal suffering and death required by Darwin's view.

---

[2] Mann (ed.), *Blackwell Guide*, 268.

[3] See Darwin's letter to Hooker of 13 July 1856 in *More Letters of Charles Darwin*, ed. F. Darwin and A. Seward (Murray: London, 1903), i. 94.

[4] *The Life and Letters of Charles Darwin*, *ii*, ed. F. Darwin (New York: Appleton 1901), 105.

Many Christian thinkers of the period attempted to come to grips with the problem, as we will see later, by highlighting those facets of Darwinian evolution that seemed rather more indicative of providential wisdom, power, or concern. For example, many pointed out that despite its unpalatable by-products, the biological world was created in such a way that it was capable of producing creatures which were progressively more conformed to the image of the creator, culminating in the appearance of human beings themselves. Still others saw the creation of living things by means of the 'natural law of variation and selection' as testimony to the wisdom of the creator in much the way that the machines used in industrial production testify to the wisdom of their designers. The popular nineteenth-century preacher Henry Ward Beecher noted, in an 1885 sermon, that while looking at an Oriental rug at a rug factory we might remark:

Well, that is a beautiful design, and these are skilful women that made it, there can be no question about that. But now behold the power-loom, where not simply a rug with long, drudging work by hand is being created, but where the machine is creating carpet in endless lengths . . . Now the question is this: Is it an evidence of design in these women that they turn out such work, and is it not evidence of a higher design in the man who turned out that machine . . . which could carry on this work a thousand-fold more magnificently than human fingers did?[5]

As Beecher summed up the underlying sentiment, 'design by wholesale is grander than design by retail'.[6] In other words, for Beecher, the processes of evolution gave the universe the appearance of an intricately and divinely designed assembly line.

Wealthy industrialists who filled the pews of Beecher's Brooklyn church were surely nodding their heads at his insightful (if somewhat sexist) remarks. But others found this line of reasoning to be profoundly unsatisfying. For as insightful as these attempts at explanation might have been, they failed to explain why the evolutionary process must be attended by the evident horrors it contains. It was failure of this sort that led Borden Bowne to exclaim in frustration:

If evolution is the law of life, of course the present must seem imperfect relative to the future, and the past imperfect relative to the present. . . . [But this] does not meet the question of why this progress might not have been accomplished at less cost of toil and struggle and pain. In truth, it is only another way of saying that the system is to be judged only in its outcome and the outcome is assumed to be good. The fact that evolution in any way diminishes the Creator's responsibility for evil is really somewhat infantile. . . . Why might not pain have been dispensed with as a means? Why might not everything have been made perfect at once? Things may be as good as possible, but if there is an omnipotent goodness at the root of things, why are they not better?[7]

---

[5] H. W. Beecher, *Evolution and Religion* (New York: Fords, Howard, and Hurlbert, 1885), 116.
[6] Ibid. 115.
[7] B. Bowne, *Philosophy of Theism* (New York: Harper, 1887), 227, 232.

Indeed, after continuing to wrestle with the problem, Beecher himself was finally led to admit:

The weak go under. When the lowest, the foundation forms of existence begin to spring up—both plant and animal in their lower conditions—the struggle for existence begins, and still the weak go under, the strong prevailing. It has been said that this is an evidence of benevolence. So that in the end they who remain will all be strong; but this is a poor consolation to any man asking, 'why were they any weak? Why were they not all strong to begin with?'[8]

Such sentiments led many to conclude, in Beecher's words, that God's purposes in nature lie beyond our ken, and that 'neither in Nature nor in Providence are His ways like our Ways'.[9]

By the close of the nineteenth century many felt that explanations for animal suffering had largely eluded Darwinian Christians. Disciple of Herbert Spencer John Fiske summed it up as follows:

A scheme which permits thousands of generations to live and die in wretchedness cannot . . . be absolved from the . . . charge of awkwardness or malevolence. . . . it is impossible to call that Being good who, existing prior to the phenomenal universe, and creating it out of the plenitude of infinite power and foreknowledge, endowed it with such properties that its material and moral development must inevitably be attended by the misery of untold millions of sentient creatures for whose existence their creator is ultimately alone responsible.[10]

Complaints about the compatibility of theism and the suffering of animals are not, however, confined to the writings of nineteenth- and twentieth-century philosophers. Numerous scientists have sounded a similar alarm, perhaps none more forcefully than Oxford biologist and ardent opponent of theism Richard Dawkins, who merits quoting at length:

If Nature were kind, she would at least make the minor concession of anesthetizing caterpillars before they are eaten alive from within. But Nature is neither kind nor unkind. . . . It is easy to imagine a gene that, say, tranquilizes gazelles when they are about to suffer a killing bite. Would such a gene be favored by natural selection? Not unless the act of tranquilizing a gazelle improved that gene's chances of being propagated into future generations. It is hard to see why this should be so, and we may therefore guess that gazelles suffer horrible pain and fear when they are pursued to the death—as most of them eventually are. The total amount of suffering per year in the natural world is beyond all decent contemplation. During the minute it takes me to compose this sentence, thousands of animals are being eaten alive; others are running for their lives, whimpering with fear; others are being slowly devoured from within by rasping parasites;

---

[8] Bowne, *Philosophy of Theism*, 339.

[9] Cited in J. H. Roberts, *Darwinism and the Divine in America: Protestant Intellectuals and Organic Evolution, 1859–1900* (Notre Dame, Ind.: University of Notre Dame Press, 2001), 135.

[10] John Fiske, *Miscellaneous Writings, iv. Outline of Cosmic Philosophy* (New York: Houghton, Mifflin, 1902), 225.

thousands of all kinds are dying of starvation, thirst and disease. It must be so. If there is ever a time of plenty, this very fact will automatically lead to an increase in population until the natural state of starvation and misery is restored. Theologians worry away at the 'problem of evil' and a related 'problem of suffering.' On the day I originally wrote this paragraph, the British newspapers all carried a terrible story about a bus full of children from a Roman Catholic school that crashed for no obvious reason, with wholesale loss of life. Not for the first time, clerics were in paroxysms over the theological question that a writer on a London newspaper (*The Sunday Telegraph*) framed this way: 'How can you believe in a loving, all-powerful God who allows such a tragedy?' The article went on to quote one priest's reply: 'The simple answer is that we do not know why there should be a God who lets these awful things happen. But the horror of the crash, to a Christian, confirms the fact that we live in a world of real values: positive and negative. If the universe was just electrons, there would be no problem of evil or suffering.' On the contrary, if the universe were just electrons and selfish genes, meaningless tragedies like the crashing of this bus are exactly what we should expect, along with equally meaningless good fortune. Such a universe would be neither evil nor good in intention. It would manifest no intentions of any kind. In a universe of blind physical forces and genetic replication, some people are going to get hurt, other people are going to get lucky, and you won't find any rhyme or reason in it, nor any justice. The universe we observe has precisely the properties we should expect if there is, at bottom, no design, no purpose, no evil and no good, nothing but blind, pitiless indifference.[11]

Despite the evident difficulties that the long course of evolutionary history raises for theism, the compatibility of animal suffering and divine goodness has received strikingly little attention in recent philosophy of religion. This is surprising for a variety of reasons. First, the course of evolutionary theory over the last hundred years or so has made most of the halting nineteenth-century attempts to explain animal suffering even harder to defend. The notion that variation and selection is an inevitable tool for securing biological progress, for example, has long fallen out of favor. And the notion that evolutionary development has any teleological character at all is little defended. This silence is made even more striking in light of the fact that recent philosophers critical of theism have made important and widely known appeals to animal suffering as a way of pressing the argument for atheism that springs from evil. In the most commonly discussed argument for atheism from evil William Rowe presents, as his centerpiece example, the image of a deer, burned in a forest fire started by lightning, dying slowly and in great pain, alone in the woods. What kind of God, he asks, could possibly permit preventable suffering in an animal that lacks moral responsibility, if, as seems to be the case, that suffering exists and serves no purpose?[12]

This lack of attention might be excusable if the standard explanations for evil so often invoked by contemporary theists were easily adaptable to evils of

---

[11] R. Dawkins, *River out of Eden* (New York: HarperCollins, 1996), 132.
[12] W. Rowe, 'The Problem of Evil and Some Varieties of Atheism', *American Philosophical Quarterly*, 16 (1979), 335–41.

this sort. But there is the trouble. Far from being easily adaptable, the standard explanations seem largely impotent when it comes to explaining nonhuman-animal suffering, making the Darwinian problem of evil all the more intractable. Indeed, for Kitcher, theists' attempts to take on the Darwinian problem of evil 'frequently resemble the flailings of seventeenth-century Aristotelians or late-eighteenth-century phlogistonians'. Can the theist do any better than that? That is the question of this book.

In what follows I will develop a variety of explanations that theists might defend in attempting to come to grips with the Darwinian problem of evil. After a brief and undoubtedly less-than-complete discussion of the argument from evil, I consider four general explanatory approaches that theists can take to the problem. In my view, any successful explanation will have to fall into one or more of these four approaches. The first, and perhaps most notorious, way that theists might try (and have) to explain animal pain and suffering is to simply deny the phenomenon altogether. Descartes is typically identified as the most ardent advocate of this view, though others have extended and developed the Cartesian explanation in more sophisticated ways. If a Cartesian or neo-Cartesian explanation of animal pain and suffering is to succeed it will have to show that such suffering is either not real or not morally significant. In Chapter 2 I consider whether or not such explanations of either sort have any merit at all. Approaches which raise questions concerning the nature of animal thought and cognition involve numerous disciplines and require careful reflection on the nature of mentality, consciousness, and the phenomenon of pain itself. As a result, in additional to considering whether or not contemporary philosophy of mind might be marshaled in support of such an explanation, I will also bring to bear the importance of a range of evidence that has been adduced in animal behavior, neuroscience, and ethology.

In Chapters 3 through 6 I will turn to consider explanations which assume that animal suffering is both real and morally significant. In Chapter 3 I examine the explanation that has been most widely embraced in the history of western theistic reflection on the problem; namely, that animal pain and suffering can be accounted for and justified by appeal to the moral wrongdoing of certain free creatures, human or preternatural. It is obvious that at least some of the pain and suffering experienced by animals is, knowingly or not, brought about at the hands of free creatures through hunting, domestication, factory farming, and so on. However, the explanations discussed in this chapter aim to argue that the totality of animal pain and suffering can be traced to some primeval misdeed by human or angelic free creatures such as the Fall of Adam and Eve or of Satan and his cohorts. As noted earlier, explanations of this sort largely fell out of favor in the late nineteenth century precisely because they seemed to be undercut by Darwinian accounts of biological origins; in light of the fact that animal pain and suffering so clearly predated the advent of free creatures (or human beings at least), it is hard to see how the pain and suffering can be a consequence of their actions. In spite of this, explanations of animal suffering in such terms have continued to surface during the twentieth and twenty-first centuries. Some of these explanations solve the apparent problem of prehuman-animal pain and suffering by simply denying it. This solution is frequently defended by so called young-universe creationists, who claim that all major phyla came into existence roughly simultaneously somewhere between 6,000 and 10,000 years ago. However, others argue that explanations that appeal to the Fall can succeed even if we concede that animals, and their pain and suffering, predate free human creatures.

A number of philosophers and theologians over the last two millennia have argued that animal pain and suffering is permissible because it is a necessary condition for securing certain greater goods *for animals themselves*. For example, some have argued that mechanisms producing pain and suffering are the only way to insure that embodied organisms engaged in intentional action can protect themselves against serious threats to their physical integrity. Others have claimed that pain and suffering are essentially connected to the possibility of intrinsically good animal action, or to securing goods that animals will enjoy in states of postmortem existence. In Chapter 4 I examine explanations of this sort.

In Chapters 5 and 6 I explore an entirely different sort of explanation for nonhuman-animal pain and suffering. Philosophers and theologians commonly make a distinction between moral evil, evil that is culpably caused by free creatures, and natural evil, evil that results from natural causes for which no creature is culpable. Cast this way, it seems that the vast majority of animal pain and suffering falls into the latter category. Predation, disease, exposure, fire, famine, and so on are all natural causes of the natural evil of animal pain and suffering. Because of this, one might reasonably suspect that strategies often deployed by theists to explain natural evil could be pressed into service to explain this animal suffering. The most common explanation of natural evil, and the one that seems initially most likely to be of use in this context, is one that argues that there are overridingly good reasons for a created natural order to operate by regular and well-ordered laws of nature, a feature of the world I call 'nomic regularity'. One by-product of such law-likeness might be that organisms sometimes unintentionally blunder into lines of causation which cause them injury and, in turn, pain and suffering. If one could argue that the goodness of a nomically regular universe required the possibility of nonhuman-animal pain and suffering, and that the goodness secured in this way outweighed the evil of permitting such pain and suffering, one would be on the road to a successful theistic explanation of that pain and suffering. I will consider accounts developed along these lines in Chapter 5. Unfortunately, most attempts to defend theism in this way further argue that the outweighing goods that are secured by permitting natural evil are goods for human beings of one sort or another. Insofar as that is the case, such explanations will struggle to explain prehuman pain and suffering, in much the way that the explanations in Chapter 3 do.

I will argue that accounts of this sort cannot succeed unless they adopt the further claim that it is a good for the cosmos to come to contain significant (pockets of) order through a process that moves from chaos to such order via nomically regular means. I explore the defensibility of this claim in Chapter 6. Amended in this way, the 'nomic-regularity' explanation of natural evil can succeed as an explanation of nonhuman-animal pain and suffering because a universe that moves from chaos to order via nomic regularity will require two things. First, it will require a long prehuman history—since the accumulation of complex states (molecular, planetary, galactic, biological, etc.) will come to be via nomically regular means that move from the simpler to the more complex, and such processes naturally take enormous amounts of time. Second, it will require a long pedigree of prehuman animals capable of experiencing pain and suffering, since these animals will be necessary precursors to descendants capable of ever more complex forms of mental life and moral value. While such a view faces a number of challenges, the most immediate one is the apparent implausibility of the claim that a universe that proceeds from chaos to order over time is for that reason good. I thus explore various ways in which the goodness of this feature might be defended.

It should now be clear to the reader that the aim of this book is not to defend the adequacy of a single theistic 'solution' to the Darwinian problem of evil. The explanations offered in Chapters 2 through 6 do not add up to a unified and coherent account, if for no other reason than that some of the explanations they defend are mutually inconsistent. Yet while no critic of the Darwinian problem of evil could employ all of the attempted explanations outlined in the book, it is also true that the explanations in these chapters are not entirely mutually exclusive. In Chapter 7 I take account of this fact, describing which explanations might be harnessed together and the extent to which this would (or wouldn't) strengthen the critic's response to the Darwinian problem.

While there is little doubt that the readers of this book will be largely professional philosophers, I have tried to make most of the arguments accessible to a broader audience who might be interested in the Darwinian problem of animal pain and suffering. Although there are different points of entry that one might take into the topic, I will be approaching it as an instance of the general type of difficulty raised by the problem of evil. One need not be an expert in contemporary philosophy of religion to appreciate the problem of evil, of course. But casting the issue in those terms requires that the reader have some acquaintance with the contemporary state of the discussion in academic philosophy. The first chapter provides the reader with such an overview along with an explanation of how the project of this book fits in as a partial response to this more general problem. Since the aim of that initial chapter is to try to bring novices up to speed on the contemporary discussion, there will be some fine-grained facets of that discussion that will necessarily be set aside. These issues will not be relevant to my attempt to address the problem of animal pain and suffering specifically, though they would be relevant to a complete discussion of the ways in which evil might count as evidence against the existence of God. In cases where these omissions might be of further interest to readers I offer suggestions for additional reading in the notes.

1

Problems of and Explanations for Evil

The phrase 'the problem of evil' connotes different things to different people. For some it points to the existential problem we face when we confront evil directly—the way it is experienced when we or our loved ones are its victims. Understood this way, the problem of evil is the problem of how we can find hope or meaning when pain and suffering threaten to snatch them from us. In these cases, evil is a cause of *despair*. For others 'the problem of evil' constitutes evidence that the universe is not a place created and providentially tended by an omnipotent and morally perfect father. In these cases evil is a cause of *doubt*. Sometimes the doubts raised by reflecting on evil are doubts about the truth of theism itself. But for many theists the doubts raised by evil are doubts not about the existence of God as much as they are about some aspect of the divine nature (the goodness, power, or wisdom of God), or perhaps about how deep our grasp of divine creation and providence are when so much evil seems to make so little sense to us. Doubts of this sort are often reflected in the writings of religious authors who are themselves afflicted by evil. The most famous instance of this is found in the Hebrew Bible's book of Job, but it is not confined there. The Hebrew prophet Habakkuk provides a typical expression of such doubt when he reacts to the impending doom of the nation of Judah at the hands of the pagan Babylonians:

How long, O Lord, must I call for help, but you do not listen? Or cry out to you, 'Violence!' but you do not save? Why do you make me look at injustice? Why do you tolerate wrong? Destruction and violence are before me; there is strife, and conflict abounds. Therefore the law is paralyzed, and justice never prevails. The wicked hem in the righteous, so justice is perverted.

(Hab. 1: 1–4)[1]

Different problems and puzzles call for different solutions and explanations. In this chapter my aim is to describe the problem that I will be addressing in this book and to provide some criteria for what will count as a suitable resolution of that problem.

To do this I will begin with a brief and somewhat opinionated introduction to the recent discussion of the problem of evil in contemporary philosophy of religion. *That* problem of evil consists of various types of arguments aimed at

---

[1] All biblical citations are from the New International Version unless otherwise noted.

showing the truth or rational preferability of atheism over theism. Assessing these arguments will accomplish two things. First, it will provide newcomers with an overview of those recent arguments and of responses to them. Those arguments and responses can and will inform the explanations for animal pain and suffering I discuss in subsequent chapters. Second, it will afford an opportunity to consider the claim made by some theists that reflection on this problem of evil shows us that attempts to explain evil should be abandoned altogether. If these theists are right, the project of developing explanations of evil in the way I intend to here should be avoided. As a result it will be important to consider these arguments to see why the project of this book is still a needed and indeed an urgent one.

1.1 THE CONTEMPORARY 'PROBLEM OF EVIL'

Arguments for atheism from evil take a variety of forms. Some arguments intend to show that the existence of God is positively inconsistent with the existence of evil. Others aim to demonstrate the more modest claim that the existence of evil provides only some evidence against theism. And, of these latter, some take the evidence provided by evil to be strong enough to make belief in theism irrational, while others take it to provide merely one piece of an evidential case, the whole of which may or may not make belief in theism unreasonable.

Arguments for atheism from evil also have various starting points. Some argue that the existence of any evil provides sufficient grounds for constructing an argument for atheism. Others argue that it is only the vast *quantity* or *duration* of evil in the world that raises difficulties. Still others argue that it is one *type* of evil or another (animal pain and suffering, or horrendous evil, for example) that fits ill with the claims of theism. Others, finally, argue that some particular *token instance* of evil shows us that theism is untenable (the Holocaust, for example). In addition to different starting points, arguments for atheism from evil differ along two other dimensions: (i) the degree to which we are (or can be) certain about their factual premises and (ii) the sorts of logical relations that hold between the premises and the conclusion. Philosophers appeal to these two dimensions to describe two different types of argument from evil. The first type, standardly designated 'Logical Arguments', appeal to some fact about evil that is virtually *certain* and affirm that that fact is *incompatible* with the existence of God. The second type, often called 'Evidential Arguments', either (a) appeal to some fact about evil that is virtually certain and then affirm that this fact reduces the probability of the existence of God, or (b) appeal to some fact about evil that is not certain but only likely to some degree or another and affirm that this fact (if it indeed holds) is incompatible with the existence of God.[2] In what follows we will consider arguments of both sorts.

---

[2] I thank Dan Howard-Snyder for suggesting this characterization. This way of casting the division puts J. L. Mackie's version of the argument squarely on the logical side (see his 'Evil and

In the middle of the twentieth century the dominant version of the argument from evil could be stated in the following simple form:

(1) If there were a God, there would be no evil.
(2) There is evil.
(3) Thus, there is no God.

The success of this simple argument hinges on our assessment of premise (1). Is it true, and if so, why? If we are inclined to accept premise (1) it is probably because we think that if there were a God, that God would be all-good, all-powerful, and all-knowing. Any being that is all-good would, by definition, want to prevent evil. And of course, any being that is all-knowing and all-powerful would be aware of all evil and would be capable of preventing it. In light of all this, it seems reasonable to think that if there were a God, there would be no evil.

These considerations put us in a position to consider a more fully articulated version of the argument from evil, a version that counts as an instance of the Logical Argument:

(4) If there were a God, he would be omniscient, omnipotent, and wholly good.

(5) (a) A wholly good being would prevent the occurrence of every evil it is in his or her power to prevent; (b) an omniscient being would be aware of all possible and actual evils; and (c) an omnipotent being would be able to prevent all evils.

(6) Thus, if there were a God, there would be no evil.

(7) There is evil.

(8) Thus, there is no God.

If this argument is a good one, it shows us how the existence of evil and the existence of God are logically incompatible.

Since premises (6) and (8) merely draw conclusions from other premises, the critic of the argument can only object by rejecting premises (4), (5), or (7). Although some religious traditions deny premise (7) (that is, deny the reality of evil) this does not seem to be a very promising response. The reality of evil seems as clear and evident to us as the reality of anything. The mere fact that I can (and sometimes do) experience excruciating pain alone seems good enough reason to accept (7).[3]

Omnipotence', *Mind*, 64 (1955), 200–12), while the versions of the argument defended by William Rowe and Paul Draper are instances of the first and second type of evidential argument respectively (see, e.g., their 'The Problem of Evil and Some Varieties of Atheism', *American Philosophical Quarterly*, 16 (1979), 335–41, and 'Pain and Pleasure: An Evidential Problem for Theists', *Noûs*, 23 (June, 1989), 331–50, respectively).

[3] As one referee of the manuscript astutely noted, this sentence makes subtle mention of something that is of crucial, if not always widely noted, importance in discussions of the problem of evil. The crucially important fact is that it is not simply the actuality of evil (in this case, pain and suffering) that generates a problem of evil, rather it is the fact that God has permitted circumstances

Some philosophers have instead rejected premise (4). After all, why not simply account for the reality of evil by denying that God is all-powerful or all-knowing? Perhaps God is very, very powerful, but still not capable of preventing all evil. Or perhaps God is very, very knowledgeable, but still falls short of knowing every truth that could be known. One could accept these things and thus deny premise (4).

In rejecting premise (4) one undermines the Logical Argument in one sense. Still, rejecting the premise comes at the price of conceding the conclusion (i.e. that atheism is true)—hardly much comfort for the theist. Theism is the claim that there exists an all-good, all-knowing, all-powerful being who creates and providentially superintends the universe throughout its existence. If this is right, then to deny that there is an all-powerful or all-knowing being (as the one who rejects premise (4) does) is to deny the truth of theism. And to deny the truth of theism is, as a simple matter of logic, to affirm the truth of atheism. So while rejecting (4) undermines the argument, it does so only by providing a different route to the same conclusion.[4]

The theist's last remaining option, then, is to reject premise (5). And, indeed, this premise has been the primary focus of attention by critics. What should we think of it? The most serious problem for premise (5) is part (a). And the problem is that it is false. A simple example shows us what is wrong with the claim that a good being always prevents every evil it can. Imagine that I am a surgeon and that you come to me with a case of cancer. Your cancer will take your life if you don't have an operation to remove the tumor. Recovering from this operation, however, includes a good deal of post-operative pain and recovery time. Still, you want the life-saving surgery and so you ask me: 'Will you do the operation?'. 'Of course not!', I reply. 'I'm a good person; and by definition no good person would allow evil to occur. Pain and suffering are evils, and this operation involves *lots* of pain and suffering. Therefore, as a good person, I must

which make evil possible even when it is not actual. The fact that God has created human beings who have it in their power to freely cause horrendous evil in the world, or the fact that sentient beings have the capacity to experience pain and suffering of the sort that seems to defeat the possibility of a meaningful life—it is these possibilities themselves, not simply actual instances of them—which require some explanation on the theistic framework.

[4] In the Introduction I mentioned that my review of the contemporary state of the discussion of the argument would, in some places, pass over subtleties that are not directly relevant to my aims in this book. This is one such case. A number of philosophers think that (4) can be denied without simply endorsing atheism. For example, process theists argue that God increases both in power and knowledge over time and that these limitations preclude God's preventing all evil. For two representative examples see David Ray Griffin's *Evil Revisited: Responses and Reconsiderations* (Albany, NY: State University of New York Press, 1991) and Charles Hartshorne's *Omnipotence and Other Theological Mistakes* (Albany, NY: State University of New York Press, 1984). Likewise, open theists argue that it is impossible for God to know many truths about the future and that this impossibility entails that some evils will not be preventable by God after all (see, for example, John Sanders's *The God Who Risks: A Theology of Providence* (Downers Grove, HI: InterVarsity Press, 1998)).

refuse.' If I were to say such things, I would show only that I am confused. Of course no good person inflicts *needless* suffering on others. But sometimes the permission of pain and suffering are *required* to bring about some *greater good*, or to prevent some *greater evil*. If the surgeon refuses to allow this bit of pain and suffering, and thereby contributes to my death, he is surely a bad person, not a good one. Perhaps at most we can claim: 'A wholly good being would prevent the occurrence of every evil it is in its power to prevent *unless that being had some morally sufficient reason for not doing so*'.

What would it take to have a morally sufficient reason for permitting an evil? Three conditions must be met.

(A) The Necessity Condition: the good secured by the permission of the evil, E, could not have been secured without permitting either E or some other evils morally equivalent to or worse than E.[5]

(B) The Outweighing Condition: the good secured by the permission of the evil is sufficiently outweighing.[6]

(C) The Rights Condition: it is within the rights of the one permitting the evil to permit it.

The case of the confused surgeon shows us why the Necessity Condition is required. If the surgeon proceeds with the operation, and later informs you that you also could have been cured by taking a single pill which is just as effective

---

[5] This way of casting the standards of moral permissibility rules out the possibility that God permits 'gratuitous evil'. I think that gratuitous evils are not morally permissible by God. It would however be unfair to present this as settled territory, since a number of theists disagree. For defenses of the permissibility of gratuitous evils one should consider Peter van Inwagen's 'The Argument from Particular Horrendous Evils', *Proceedings of the American Catholic Philosophical Association*, 74 (2000), 65–80, and William Hasker's *Providence, Evil, and the Openness of God* (London: Routledge, 2004), chs. 4 and 5.

[6] One might object that the Outweighing Condition is questionable for the following reason. Consider two states of affairs: (1) P freely loves his neighbor, (2) P freely refrains from loving his neighbor. (1) is good, (2) is bad, and permitting (2) is a necessary condition for securing (1). Imagine that (2) obtains and (1) does not. That is an evil state of affairs and, according to (B), God only has a morally sufficient reason for permitting it to obtain if the good secured by the permission of the evil is sufficiently outweighing. But is the good sufficiently outweighing? One might think that the good God aimed at in this case was the good set forth in (1). But that good never came to pass. So is there some other outweighing good that suffices here? The standard reply would be that the outweighing good consists in the freedom to make morally significant choices between competing courses of action. I suspect that most theists would find this answer sufficient. However, I have, as one referee pointed out, elsewhere argued that the good of such freedom is only that of an instrumental good, and thus it is hard to see how it could rise to the level of a good sufficient to outweigh the obtaining of (2). I am now of two minds about this claim. Still, if one were to accept it, one should hold that whether or not permitted evil satisfies the Outweighing Condition can only be determined by considering the totality of the good obtained and the evil permitted by a particular *type* of evil. If God permits the good of free choice with the aim of bringing about love among neighbors, and the result is that the sum total of the goodness of the actual love of neighbors plus the goodness of the necessary conditions required to secure that goodness, i.e. morally significant freedom does not outweigh the evil of the free refraining from love of neighbors then God did not have a morally sufficient reason to allow that evil. I thank Dan Howard-Snyder for pressing this concern.

and which has no ill side effects, you would be rightly indignant. The surgeon is only justified in permitting you to experience the pain and suffering of surgery and recovery if such permission is *necessary* to secure your well-being. Likewise, a wholly good and omnipotent being can only permit evils in order to secure good which could not otherwise be secured without permitting the occurrence of evils equally bad or worse.

The Necessity Condition requires that certain goods could not have been obtained without allowing either the evil in question or some other evil which is as bad or worse. In some instances it may be the case that a particular good can only be secured by allowing a very specific sort of evil. Perhaps the only way to cure your cancer is through surgery that carries the risk of great pain and suffering. But it is likely that many outweighing goods can be secured by allowing a range of evils, none of which is singularly necessary for this purpose. If I want to buy a new car that is blue and has both leather seats and a Bose stereo system, I may arrive at the car dealer's lot only to find that no car has all of these options. Some are blue with leather seats, some have leather seats with sound system, but none has all three. I value all of the options equally, so I choose the blue car with leather seats. We might say that in order to get the car I had to live without the sound system. But that is not exactly right. In order to get the new car I had to live without the sound system *or some other feature that I value just as much.* The absence of the sound system was not a necessary condition for getting the car, but the absence of the sound system *or something equivalent* to it was. Similarly, when explaining evil one needs to show not why permitting some particular evil is itself necessary for some greater good, but why permitting that evil *or one just as bad* is necessary. This fact yields some important consequences to which I will return shortly below. However, in using the Necessity Condition I will not typically make reference to this additional complication.

The Outweighing Condition stipulates that the greater good in question is 'sufficiently outweighing'. Why not rather say that the greater good merely be 'outweighing'? What is the force of 'sufficiently' here? Note that there may be cases in which the evils that are necessary for bringing about certain greater goods are allowed, and in fact succeed in bringing about greater goods, but where the amount or severity of the evil that must be permitted is so great that the benefits of the greater good are simply too meager. We can imagine God considering, for example, the creation of a pair of worlds with the following features. World a has an overall balance of 100 units of goodness that are secured by bringing about those 100 units while permitting no evil (there is of course no metric for good and evil but we can pretend for the purposes of the example). World β has an overall balance of 101 units of goodness and thus seems to exceed a in overall goodness. However, this greater surplus of goodness in β is brought about by allowing 10^{10}-less-101 units of evil which are jointly necessary for securing 10^{10} units of goodness. Even if we assume that there was no other way to bring about a world with 101 or more units of goodness, the price of increasing the surplus of good is simply too high, since the additional unit of overall goodness comes at the price of 10^{10} additional units of evil. This is important, since those offering explanations for evil often provide plausible reasons for thinking that these evils are necessary conditions for certain goods, yet they just as often *refrain* from giving reasons for thinking that things are overall better with those evils and the goods they occasion than they would be without both.

The Rights Condition is necessary, since there may be circumstances in which one being can permit evils in the service of securing greater goods, but where the absence of a right to do so precludes such permission. If a stranger wants to take the life of my son in order to use his two kidneys to save the lives of her two children, we may conclude that saving two lives is better than saving one, and yet we still recognize that I have *no right* to permit the stranger to take my child and use him for such purposes.[7] Likewise, it may be the case that features of the moral situation (the intrinsic moral worth of persons for example) preclude God from having the right to allow some evils, even if they will lead to outweighing goods.[8]

What all of this shows us is that it is not the *reality of evil* that is incompatible with the existence of God, rather it is the reality of evils that are not or cannot be outweighed by some greater goods for which their permission is necessary. Evils of that sort would be *pointless* or *gratuitous* evils and are thus incompatible with the existence of the God of theism. In light of this, we can revise our Logical Argument one more time as follows:

(9) If there were a God, there would be no gratuitous evils (GEs).

(10) There is at least one GE.

(11) There is no God.

If there is a problem with this argument, it is with premise (10).[9] To defend this premise one needs to demonstrate that there is at least one GE; and showing this means showing that there is an evil the permission of which is either *not necessary* for bringing about an *outweighing* good or *not within the rights* of God to permit. Do some evils fall into one of these categories? Let's consider them in turn.

Initially it might appear quite difficult to show that permitting some evils is not really necessary for bringing about greater goods. How could we know such

---

[7] The example is a modification of one used by Swinburne in *Providence and the Problem of Evil* (Oxford: Oxford University Press, 1998), 11. Of course one might not agree that saving the lives of two persons through killing a third, innocent person is an outweighing good. But none of this matters for the general point that there are conditions where one is not morally permitted to allow the occurrence of preventable evils the permission of which is necessary to secure outweighing goods.

[8] We will consider one such proposed case in Chapter 6.

[9] Though a few theists have recently argued that we should reject (9). See, for example, Peter van Inwagen's 'The Magnitude, Duration, and Distribution of Evil', in his *God, Knowledge, and Mystery* (Ithaca, NY: Cornell University Press, 1995), 103–4, and William Hasker, 'The Necessity of Gratuitous Evil', *Faith and Philosophy*, 9 (1992), 23–44.

a thing? The first thing to note is that in order to have a clear sense of what events or states of affairs are necessary for other events or states of affairs often we would have to possess quite detailed and specialized knowledge—knowledge which we might or might not have. A simple example might help us here. I once watched a mechanic who was about to replace an air bag in the steering wheel of my car. I assumed that he would start the job by pulling off the steering wheel or doing some other work in the front seat. However, this mechanic began the job by opening the trunk of the car and fussing around there. I assumed that he was just wasting time, trying to pile up labor costs for the job. However, I later learned that changing the air bag requires disconnecting the battery, and that this car has the battery in the trunk, not under the hood. Who would have guessed that fiddling around in the trunk was necessary to replace the air bag? Not me—because I just didn't know how things were put together. It seems reasonable to assume that we are not much better positioned to know whether or not permitting some evil that in fact occurs is necessary for securing some greater good, now or perhaps in the very distant future. As a result, it seems best to avoid defenses of (10) that rely on showing that permitting a certain evil is not a necessary condition for some outweighing good.

Another way to defend premise (10) would be to produce an argument showing that *all* evils are gratuitous. One way we could know that all evils are gratuitous is by having good reason to think that it could *never* be necessary for God to bring about or allow some evil in order to secure a greater good. If God never had a good reason of this sort, then *all* evils would be gratuitous.

Arguments for this conclusion claim that if God were to exist, *all* evils would be gratuitous, since an omnipotent being would never have to rely on allowing evil in order to bring about some greater good. To say otherwise would be to say that God is sometimes at the mercy of having to allow certain evils to occur in order to get some outcome that he wants. But how could an omnipotent being be at the mercy of anything in this way? We can imagine such things in cases like that of the surgeon mentioned above. Surgeons sometimes must inflict or allow pain and suffering in their patients in order to cure them. But God? Surely not. An omnipotent being would never be subject to such limitations. If God wants to bring about a certain good, God, being omnipotent, could surely just actualize that good unconditionally.

While that line of reasoning initially *sounds* compelling, it is, for all we know, invalid. We can see this by considering one example. Theists and atheists alike largely agree that it is a good thing that God create a cosmos, and that it is a good thing when that cosmos contains creatures with morally significant free choice (i.e. the sort of freedom that allows creatures to choose between good and evil alternatives). Creatures with free choice can enjoy the good of making free and autonomous choices as well as of producing genuine moral good in the world, engaging in relationships of love and friendship, displaying genuine charity and courage, and so on. Yet creatures with morally significant free choice also necessarily have the ability to choose to do evil.[10] And if those creatures are genuinely free in making their choices, they cannot be determined to choose what they choose.

Now let's imagine that God is faced with the prospect of creating a universe. Wanting to maximize the varieties of good in the creation, and wanting to fill the creation with the greatest types of good, God decides to create a world containing a number of creatures with free choice. Can God create a world with such freely choosing creatures but in which those free creatures never choose to do wrong? Maybe or maybe not. We just don't know. When God considers all of the possible universes with free creatures in them, it just might turn out that in every one of them at least one of the creatures in them chooses to do wrong. And if that is indeed the case, God cannot create a world that contains the good of free choice, but which also has no evil in it. If that's the way things are in fact, a universe with evil is a necessary and unavoidable condition of getting a universe with the very great good of creatures with free choice.

The argument above is a descendant of the most widely cited response to the Logical Argument, a response known as the Free Will Defense which was first developed in detail by Alvin Plantinga.[11] However, it is worth noting that the argument here differs slightly from Plantinga's version. Plantinga argues that it is broadly logically possible that every free creature is such that it performs at least one evil act in every world in which it exists and which God can actualize. The epistemic version of the argument described above aims to show that there are, for all we know, some goods (like the good of free choice) which not even God can bring about without also allowing certain evils (specifically, morally evil choices) to occur. Since this is so, the atheist's general argument that God is never in such a position fails.[12]

Above we saw that trying to give arguments that particular evils are gratuitous is going to be difficult to defend. Now we have seen that the argument that all evils in general are gratuitous is also vexed. It is open to the critic of theism to offer other general arguments of this sort, though it is not easy to see how such other arguments would go.

Let's then turn to the second way of defending (10). In light of the Rights Condition (Condition (C) for the moral permissibility of allowing evils, listed

---

[10] Some contend that this is false. For example, perhaps robust morally significant freedom requires nothing more than an ability to choose between a variety of alternative goods. In addition, if we were free to choose between good and evil only when the choice would in fact be a free choice for good, we might be able to have morally significant freedom without in fact being able to choose evil. Some of these alternatives are considered by David Lewis in 'Evil for Freedom's Sake', *Philosophical Papers*, 22 (1993), 149–72.

[11] See his *God, Freedom, and Evil* (Grand Rapids, Mich. Eerdmans, 1974).

[12] This epistemic version of the argument seems to be suggested first in Daniel Howard-Snyder and John O'Leary-Hawthorne's 'Transworld Sanctity and Plantinga's Free Will Defense', *International Journal for the Philosophy of Religion*, 44 (August 1998), 1–21, at p. 21.

above) one might argue that there are some evils that it is not within God's rights to permit, even if that permission were a necessary condition for securing greater goods. If there are such evils, they would be gratuitous, since no greater good to which they might be connected could outweigh or justify them. Can the defender of the argument make the case that there are some evils of this sort? One might argue, for instance, that some evils are so horrendous that no one, God included, could be justified in allowing them even if they were necessary conditions for bringing about some outweighing good. For example, perhaps it would never be permissible to allow a child to die a painful, lingering death due to cancer, even if it is a necessary means to some great good. Unfortunately, arguments of this sort will all be grounded in moral principles that are highly contentious. As a result, it is hard to imagine that arguments of this sort will be of much value in supporting premise (10).[13]

For reasons of the sort we have been outlining above, the Logical Argument is not much defended these days. Instead most of the discussion of the problem of evil focuses on a second version, to which we now turn: the Evidential Argument.

1.2 THE EVIDENTIAL ARGUMENT

The problem with the Logical Argument is that we can (reasonably easily) conjure up possible explanations for God's permission of evil which, if they were true, would show that the existence of evil and the existence of God are compatible after all. Still, the average nonphilosopher who takes evil to be problematic for theism is often not impressed by the fact that there are *some possible goods* which *for all we know* can only be secured by way of permitting evils. One reason for this is that even if we can come up with an explanation that shows us that the existence of God and the existence of evil are compatible, it is still possible that the existence of evil makes the existence of God very *unlikely*. And if evil in fact makes the existence of God unlikely, theists still have a substantial problem on their hands. A simple example makes clear why this is so. Last year my son and I went to watch an NCAA college basketball game. With three minutes left in the game my favorite team was behind by thirty points and I decided to head for the parking lot for a quick exit. When I got home my wife asked me who won the game. I told her that the other team had won. When she asked for the final score I told her I didn't know it because I left with three minutes to go. She could have pressed me at this point on my belief that the other team won. After all, it is *possible* for a team to score thirty points in three minutes. But the circumstances required to make that happen are so improbable and belief that they occurred so incredible that there is no way that any reasonable person would believe anything

[13] We will, however, examine one version of this sort of argument at the end of Chapter 6.

other than what I believed: that my team lost. The mere *possibility* that my team could have overcome the gap and won the game did nothing to dislodge my belief that they lost.

Similarly, when considering the existence, magnitude, duration, and types of evil, some atheists are inclined to argue that although it is *possible* that God and evil of the sort permitted in our world both exist, it still seems very unlikely. What might support a judgment like this? In the case of the basketball game, I judged that it was unlikely that my team would win because I know all of the ways in which a team can score thirty points and it seemed to me highly unlikely that they could avail themselves of those means in under three minutes of playing time. Does the one who accepts the argument for atheism from evil know something that allows her to judge that the explanations showing the existence of God and evil to be jointly possible are unlikely? Above we saw that some argue for this compatibility by claiming that there are, perhaps, no worlds that God can create with free creatures that in fact always refrain from evil. Perhaps the defender of the argument can claim that it just seems very unlikely that among the infinity of worlds that God can create, none contains significant quantities of good, free creatures and no moral wrongdoing. Alternatively, one might not claim to believe anything as specific as that, but instead might simply claim that when he or she considers the vast amount of evil or some particular case of evil, it is simply unbelievable that its permission is necessary for securing outweighing goods. Arguments of this sort fall into the category of 'Evidential Arguments from evil' because they support the notion that evil gives us good evidence, even if not positive proof, that God does not in fact exist.

There is more than one way of formulating the Evidential Argument. In what follows we will consider two versions.

1.2.1 The 'direct' argument

The most common Evidential Argument claims that, all things considered, we have good reason to believe that some of the evil in our world is gratuitous. The argument can be framed most simply as a variant of the Logical Argument, as follows:

(12) If there were a God, there would be no gratuitous evils (GEs).
(13) It is probable that at least one of the evils in our world is a GE.
(14) Probably, there is no God.

In discussing the Logical Argument we saw that the defender of the argument is going to have a difficult time giving us a demonstration or proof of premise (10), the claim that there is gratuitous evil. The problem is that, for all we know, God has good reasons for allowing the evil we see around us to occur. What the defender of this Evidential Argument insists on is that even though, for all we know, there might be such reasons, it is not *very likely* that there are.

This way of putting the argument resonates with our ordinary way of thinking of the connection between the existence of God and the existence of evil. For some reason, citing certain possible, for-all-we-know reasons for the reality of seemingly gratuitous evil does not remove the persuasive force those evils have; and this leads us to doubt the existence of God. One reason for this is likely that the average person who is inclined to accept premise (13) is inclined to accept it on grounds other than those supposed in the Logical Argument. Defenders of the Logical Argument often accept that evils are gratuitous because of a more general argument that God's omnipotence renders all evils gratuitous. Defenders of the Evidential Argument accept (13) because they find themselves powerfully struck by the idea that some of the evil they see around them is just pointless.[14] Of course, advocates of this version of the argument would not go so far as to claim that they are *certain* that some evils are pointless. They would insist instead that the gratuitousness of some evil just seems to them vastly more probable than not. And because of this, they conclude that (13) is true and thus that atheism is also vastly more probable than not.

There are only three ways for the critic to respond to the argument cast this way. The first two aim to show that we have good reason to *reject* (13). One way to show this is to embrace (12) and show that we have very good reason to believe in the existence of God. This would entail that (13) is false. The second is to show that we do, after all, know all, many, or some of the reasons that God permits the evils in the world, and that this knowledge either shows us that (13) is false or at least drastically lowers our confidence in it. The third way is to argue that the atheist simply has *no good reason to accept* that (13) is true. Let's examine these responses briefly.

The first response takes the tack William Rowe has dubbed the 'G. E. Moore shift'.[15] The response is named after the twentieth-century philosopher G. E. Moore, who argued that we should reject many of the well-worn arguments for general skepticism because of the implausibility of their conclusion. Moore thought that arguments to the effect that we might always be dreaming or that we might be under the deceptive spell of an evil genius should not move us to accept skepticism at all. Such arguments have the general form:

(a) If the skeptic's premises are correct, then I do not know that there is a computer in front of me.

(b) The skeptic's premises are correct.

(c) I do not know that there is a computer in front of me.

---

[14] While it is true that many who find the Evidential Argument plausible do so because they take it to be merely obvious that there are some pointless evils, professional philosophers defending this position have offered positive arguments for this claim. See, for instance, Michael Almeida and Graham Oppy, 'Skeptical Theism and Evidential Arguments from Evil', *Australasian Journal of Philosophy*, 81/3 (2003), 496–516, and Nick Trakakis, *The God Beyond Belief: In Defence of William Rowe's Evidential Argument from Evil* (Netherlands: Springer, 2007).

[15] See his 'Problem of Evil and Some Varieties of Atheism'.

However, arguments of this sort invite us to accept a conclusion that is very implausible, by appealing to premises that are even *less* plausible. This naturally invites us to consider the following argument:

(a) If the skeptic's premises are correct then I do not know that there is a computer in front of me.

not-(c) I know there is a computer in front of me.

not-(b) The skeptic's premises are not correct.

The arguments share premise (a). They differ in that the skeptic adopts (b) and moves to the highly unbelievable (c), while the other adopts not-(c) and concludes the highly plausible not-(b). When confronted with arguments like this we must ask ourselves which of the two arguments is more believable. The only way to decide in this case is to ask ourselves whether premise (b) or premise not-(c) seems more plausible to us. Moore claims that not-(c) is patently more reasonable.

Likewise, one confronted with the Evidential Argument must compare that argument to the following one:

(12) If there were a God, there would be no gratuitous evils (GEs).
(15) There is a God.
(16) There are no GEs.

Since the Direct Evidential Argument and the above argument share premise (12), the only question is whether it is more reasonable to accept (13) (that there are GEs) or (15) (that God exists). One confronted with the problem of evil might well conclude that (15) is more reasonable and thus that the Direct Evidential Argument should be rejected.

What might convince us that it is more reasonable to accept (15) than (13)? Perhaps it is the evidence arising from consideration of one or more of the arguments that philosophers offer for theism. This sort of evidence is communicable and thus can be shared with the evidential critic who can subject it to direct critical scrutiny. Perhaps the various arguments that have been offered for the existence of God would suffice to convince the critic as well, perhaps not. Both parties in the dispute ought to be aware, however, that even if the critic of theism remains unconvinced that the (communicable) evidence favoring (15) outweighs the grounds the critic has for affirming (13), the theist might still reasonably conclude the opposite. One reason for this is that the theist might believe that the critic has simply misunderstood the weight of the evidence presented in favor of theism. In addition, or instead, the theist might be in possession of incommunicable evidence which the critic lacks and which accounts for the strength of his belief in (15).

We can illustrate this point as follows. Perhaps one day you and I meet. After some conversation, I mention that I am married. A skeptical look comes across your face. How, you wonder, could he have fooled someone into marrying *him?* You express your doubts, and I undertake to convince you that I am, in fact, married. I show you my wedding ring, some pictures of my wife and children in my wallet, etc. You survey the evidence, but none of it convinces you. Anyone, you tell yourself, can purchase a gold band, and anyone can download pictures and pretend they are pictures of family members. Having exhausted all of the evidence at my disposal, I surrender; I acknowledge that I am not going to convince you. But in surrender I only concede that you are entitled to maintain your belief that I am not married. I certainly do *not* concede that since the evidence I showed you was insufficiently convincing I should give up *my* belief that I am married. And the reason for this is simple: *my* evidence is not the evidence I shared with you. What I shared was the *communicable* evidence. What convinces me of this belief are my own memories of past experiences—memories that cannot be (directly) shared. In similar fashion, the theist is fully entitled to reject (13) on the basis of the fact that she is in possession of incommunicable grounds or evidence for her theistic belief that outweigh any likelihood she attaches to (13). The most obvious sort of incommunicable evidence that might be relevant here is religious experiences on the part of the theist.[16] In any case, unless the theist thinks that the communicable evidence is likely to be sufficiently weighty, something that seems doubtful to many theists in light of the recent doubts about the evidential value of theistic arguments, she will need to pursue one of the other objections to the Direct Argument, at least if her aim is to help the atheist see why she should not endorse atheism on the grounds of the argument found in premises (12), (13), and (14).

The second way that one might respond to the Direct Evidential Argument is to offer what appear to be good reasons for God to allow the evils that there are. If there are such reasons, it will make us far less confident that other evils (which we cannot explain) really don't have any explanation. Notice that one can respond successfully to the argument in this way even if one does not have an explanation for every evil or every type of evil permitted that someone might take to be gratuitous. What one will need is at least a few plausible explanations. An analogy will help us see why.

Last fall I was flying from Shanghai to Philadelphia and had to change planes in Tokyo. A couple sat next to me who did not stop complaining from the moment they sat down. And they had a number of complaints: the flight did

---

[16] Whether or not religious experiences can have the evidential value supposed in this discussion is controversial. Those interested in pursuing this topic further should consult the following. For introductory readings on the topic: Douglas Geivett and Brendan Sweetman, *Contemporary Perspectives on Religious Epistemology* (Oxford: Oxford University Press, 1992), sect. 4. For a more detailed examination of the issues: William P. Alston, *Perceiving God: The Epistemology of Religious Experience* (Ithaca, NY: Cornell University Press, 1991); Keith Yandell, *The Epistemology of Religious Experience* (Cambridge: Cambridge University Press, 1993); and B. Clark and W. Power (eds.), *International Journal for Philosophy of Religion*, 31, 2–3 (1992), special issue: 'The Epistemic Status of Religious Belief'.

not board quickly enough, the seats were uncomfortable, there was not enough room for their carry-on luggage, and so on and so on. In addition, they told me over and over again that everything the airline did was 'stupid'. They just could not believe that everything the employees did was so stupid. It was so 'stupid' that the people in the back of the airplane boarded first and took up all 'their' luggage space. And it was really stupid that they had to get off the plane in Tokyo with their carry-on bags since they were reboarding the same plane to the USA. It was even more stupid that the plane was taking off late and might cause passengers to miss connecting flights. What a stupid airline! You get the idea. Now I have seen airline employees do lots of things—things that were inscrutable to me. But my neighbors were being too harsh. Everyone knows that flights board from the rear to speed up the boarding time, and it is reasonable to suppose that all the passengers had to get off the plane and reboard because the security screening in Japan is more careful and thorough than the security screening in China. As for the flight leaving late, well, I had no idea what the cause of that might be. Nonetheless, I wasn't (yet) ready to chalk it up to stupidity.

Notice that my fellow passengers thought that three things were stupid: the boarding pattern, the fact that they had to get off the plane, and the late departure. I knew the explanation for the first, had a reasonable guess as to the explanation of the second, and had no idea what the explanation was for the third. But the known and reasonable explanations in the first two cases made me reluctant to think there was no explanation for the third. I was agnostic about that. In the same way, if a critic of the Evidential Argument can construct explanations that she knows or reasonably believes to be true, this should lead us to lower our confidence in (13) correspondingly.

However, such explanations are not necessary to turn back the force of the Direct Argument, for reasons we will see next.[17] If we can turn back the Direct

---

[17] Daniel Howard-Snyder has suggested that such reasons are unlikely to be sufficient either. The worry is this: Even if the critic of the Evidential Argument can come up with very plausible explanations for God permitting some evil (or even a lot of evil), what typically grips defenders of the Evidential Argument is the existence, duration, and magnitude of *horrendous evils* (mutilations, drawing and quartering, the wracking pain of cancer consuming guts and bones, the crushing hopelessness and despair of severe clinical depression, etc.). Whatever explanations the theist might offer for evil (that it is a necessary condition for morally significant freedom, that it is necessary for 'soul-making', etc.) could, perhaps, lower our confidence in (13) if we are thinking about non-horrendous evils. But, one might reasonably suppose, none of those explanations has the least bit of plausibility (or relevance) when it comes to explaining horrendous evils. Thus, even if the reasons I offer in attempting to explain why God might permit evil could serve to lower my confidence in claims like:

(13*) It is very unlikely that there is some justifying reason for people experiencing the evils of sore muscles, broken relationships, lost wallets, etc.

none of this will have any relevance at all to the confidence I have in claims like:

(13**) It is very unlikely that there is some justifying reason for people being exterminated through mass genocide, for the ravages of AIDS, etc.

Argument without offering such explanations then is there any reason to offer them at all? Some have argued that there is not, their denial arising directly out of the third way of responding to the Direct Argument.

1.3 THE INSCRUTABILITY RESPONSE

The third response to the Direct Argument claims that the defender of the argument is mistaken in thinking that we have good reason to affirm (13). There are more and less skeptical ways of defending this position. The more skeptical approach, taken by so-called skeptical theists, argues that we are in no position to judge whether or not (13) is true. To reasonably think otherwise, we would have to have some reason (indeed *good* reason) to think that we are well-positioned to judge that there are no goods (a) that God aims to bring about and (b) of which we are unaware, that might justify the permission of an evil. But, it seems, there is no good reason to think that we are well-positioned to make that sort of judgment. Furthermore, even if we were aware of all of the goods that God aims to bring about, we would further have to have some reason (indeed *good* reason) to think that we are well-positioned to understand how the permitted evils might serve as necessary conditions for outweighing goods. But, again, there seems no good reason to think we are well-positioned to understand such things. To think that, we would have to think that we are likely to know how various permitted evils might be necessary to secure goods in distant times and places. But what could make us think we are likely to know such things? After all, none of us thinks that we are in a position to describe *all* of the, say, *causal* consequences of the occurrence of any event. Particular events might be necessary conditions (causally or otherwise) for bringing about consequences hundreds or thousands of years hence. Absent omniscience, it is hard to know how we could grasp which

---

The reason for this is simply that any explanation I might have that is relevant to (13*) won't have any relevance to (13**).

Assessing this criticism of the second way would require a much longer discussion of theodicies of horrendous evil than I can undertake here. However, let's note a few things about it. First, this criticism of the second way is correct only if it is true that the explanations that serve to undermine our confidence in (13*) are not in fact relevant to our confidence in (13**). But it is not at all clear that this is right. For all I know the reasons that explain God's permission of broken relationships are quite relevant to the explanation of God's permission of mass genocide. Perhaps the good of morally significant freedom, or creaturely interdependence, or . . . do in fact serve to explain both. I don't think we are entitled to much confidence that this is the case . . . or that it isn't the case. Second, it is not clear that even if the explanations relevant to (13*) are not directly relevant to (13**), the explanations for the first should not still undermine our confidence in the second. This is what the 'stupid airline' example was supposed to illustrate. If a number of practices of the airline are unreasonable to me, and I then come into possession of a number of good reasons for some of these practices, this will, under suitable conditions, undermine my confidence that the other practices that seem unreasonable really are. Of course, the trick here is specifying what the 'suitable conditions' are.

events are necessary conditions for other particular events which are distant in time and space.[18]

We can, however, take a less skeptical approach in these matters. A less skeptical theist might argue, for example, that given the immensity of divine goodness and the finitude of our human cognitive and moral faculties, it seems likely that there are some, perhaps many, types of good that God aims to bring about in creation with which we are not in any way acquainted. And if we do not even know what the relevant goods are for which evils might be necessary conditions, our attempts to make judgments about whether or not evils are gratuitous will be futile. On this view, we should conclude not (as the skeptical theist does) that we are in no position to make judgments about whether or not there are unknown goods for which some permitted evils are necessary, rather we should conclude that we are (likely) *not well-positioned* to make such judgments.[19] The less skeptical theist might argue, second, that even if we believed ourselves to be acquainted with the goods God aims to bring about in creation, there is good reason to think that we would be unable to grasp whether or not permitting particular types or token instances of evil plays a role in bringing those goods about. Here the reasoning will be similar to that set out above. Since we are so poor at discerning the consequences of present events for the future, and so ill-equipped to understand which conditions might be necessary for states of affairs that are spatially or temporally distant, we would

---

[18] This more skeptical stance is defended in, for example, Michael Bergmann, 'Skeptical Theism and Rowe's New Evidential Argument from Evil', *Noûs*, 35/2 (2001), 279; Daniel Howard-Snyder, 'The Argument from Inscrutable Evil'; and William Alston, 'Some (Temporarily) Final Thoughts on Evidential Arguments from Evil', these latter both in Howard-Snyder (ed.), *The Evidential Argument from Evil* (Bloomington, Ind.: Indiana University Press, 1996), at pp. 292–3 and 321 respectively.

[19] Daniel Howard-Snyder has (in correspondence) challenged this first less skeptical claim as follows. Let S stand for the claim that 'God's cognitive and moral attributes swamp those of human creatures'. Let U stand for the claim that 'there are some, perhaps many, types of good that God knows of but with which we are unacquainted'. The less skeptical theist is committed to the claim that $P(U/S)>!0.5$. But why should we think this when a number of analogous conditional probabilities are low or zero. Consider U1: 'There are some, perhaps many, simple mathematical truths which God knows but with which we are unacquainted', or U2: 'There are some, perhaps many, ways in which chess pieces can move that God knows but with which we are unacquainted', or U3: 'There are some, perhaps many, types of salmon of which God is aware, but with which we are unacquainted', etc. The value of these conditional probabilities is, it is reasonable to think, zero. Why conclude any differently with respect to U? The answer is that U is not properly analogous to the other claims. What is true of U, and false of these alternatives, is that goodness is simply not a concept for which we have a transparent grasp of its intrinsic nature. Defending this claim in any detail would require, first, setting out an account of what goodness consists in. That is a task that outstrips a footnote (not to mention a page, section, or chapter). However, the view I find most plausible in this regard is a Platonic account defended along the lines recently proposed by Robert Adams (see his *Finite and Infinite Goods* (Oxford: Oxford University Press, 1999)). On this account goodness consists in a particular species of resemblance to the divine. Not surprisingly, there are many ways in which resemblance to the divine can occur and, given S, it is reasonable to think that those ways vastly outstrip our ability to grasp them.

be similarly poor at discerning which permitted evils are necessary conditions for purported outweighing goods.

Our less skeptical theist can add a third reason to be doubtful that we have good grounds for affirming (13). In considering the Necessity Condition we noted that an evil is permissible when it or some equally bad or worse evil must be permitted in order to secure an outweighing good (and the other two conditions for morally permitting an evil are met as well). To have the good of the new car I had to choose to live without the sound system or the blue color. Anyone who knew my preferences and saw the car that I actually picked would initially be surprised that it lacked the sound system and would be at a loss to explain it unless they were aware of the limited choices I confronted at the dealer. Even if one might surmise that the explanation for this fact was a limited range of available options, there would be no way of guessing that the two best options were a car that lacked only a sound system or a car that lacked only the blue color. This is relevant here since it shows us that unless we are aware of what the relevant options are when it comes to divine creation, it will be hard for us to know what evils are avoidable and which are not. If God had only two creative options that were identical except that one contained a murder in 1928 in Moscow and the other contained a murder in 2003 in Berlin, God might be ambivalent about the choice between them. If he actualizes the one with the murder in Moscow, philosophers in that world might puzzle over why God would permit such an evil to occur. They would likely be quite surprised and puzzled to learn that the only alternative that is as good or better would be a world with a murder in Berlin in 2003. How could these two evils be connected so that eliminating one would result in the other? The answer is that the creative options were limited. But there is no way one could know or guess such things without detailed (and unavailable) information about the options available to God. Considerations of this sort should provide us with a healthy dose of skepticism about our ability to make judgments about whether any evil is gratuitous or not, since evils not only might be necessary conditions for greater goods within a world, but might be necessary conditions for having a world that is greater on balance than alternative creation options.

Finally, our less skeptical theist can further plausibly claim that if theism is true we should expect that evil will sometimes be inexplicable for the simple reason that knowing the explanation for an evil can, in some instances, preclude the outweighing benefit that the evil was supposed to secure. In cases like that, God would have to obscure the reasons for permitting an evil from us in order to bring about the good or goods that explain the permission of the evil in the first place. To see how this might be so, let's consider another analogy. I have a friend whose teenage son likes to fix cars. But, like many teenagers, he is notorious about not returning his tools to their place. Despite my friend's repeated attempts to get him to change his ways, the bad habit continued. One day he learned that his son had invited some friends to help tune up an old car, and he decided to teach him a lesson. He found his timing light and hid it in a little used drawer in the garage.[20] As the son began working he discovered that the light was missing and spent two frantic hours tracking it down. When he finally discovered it, he believed it was just another instance of his own bumbling carelessness and resolved to change his ways.

While the son learned his lesson because his father hid the tool, he did so only in virtue of his mistaken belief that he had lost it *himself*. If, after he discovered the light, the father had instead told him that *he* had hidden the light in the drawer, the son might have continued in his old pattern, either out of resentment toward his father or from the mistaken belief that his own bad habits were not responsible for any of his troubles. It is easy to see how analogous principles may well apply in typical instances of evil. The point here is simply this: even if God *could* make us aware of the reason for our suffering, doing so might sometimes thwart some role the evil is intended to serve. As a result, in these cases, we can imagine that God would prevent our discovering the explanation for his permitting evil. This provides us with still further reason for thinking that our inability to see or understand the explanation for evils is not surprising or unexpected given theism.

As mentioned earlier, the most common way of objecting to the Evidential Argument by this third route is the way of 'skeptical theism'. However, the reasons set out above provide good grounds for thinking that 'less skeptical theism' has significant merit. Both views share in common a central thesis—a thesis I will refer to as *inscrutabilism*—according to which we have no good reason to think we are in a position to endorse (13) or claims of its ilk. When it makes a difference in what remains in the chapter, I will speak in the voice of the less skeptical theist.[21]

What the observations make plain is that the atheist's confidence in (13) arises not because *she can see that there are no* morally sufficient reasons for some evils, but because *she cannot see that there are any* such reasons. That is, the atheist considers actual types or token instances of evil, fails to see any point to them, and thus concludes that they're pointless. This general style of argument, moving from a failure to perceive something to a conclusion that the thing is absent, has been labeled a 'noseeum' inference.[22]

---

[20] For younger readers, a timing light is a device used to tune up a car in the days before electronic ignition.

[21] This is, of course, to defend a stronger claim when the weaker (mere 'skeptical-theism') claim would suffice. Still, the arguments provided here seem to me to warrant the stronger claim. For those who find defense of the stronger position implausible, they are invited to reinterpret the arguments in the remainder in the voice of the skeptical theist.

[22] See, for example, S. J. Wykstra's 'Rowe's Noseeum Arguments from Evil', in Howard-Snyder (ed.), *The Evidential Argument from Evil*, pp. 126–50. It is worth noting here that while the literature casts the arguments in terms of 'not seeing' reasons for the permission of evil, what is really at stake is the inability of those defending the Evidential Argument to *conceive* of such reasons. So, to return to my basketball-game analogy earlier, when I left the game with three minutes to go and

Are *noseeum arguments* good arguments? Sometimes they are. If my wife asks me to get her the milk from the refrigerator and I open the door, look carefully, and don't see any milk there, it is reasonable for me to conclude that there is no milk in the refrigerator because 'I don't see it'. That is a good noseeum argument. But not all noseeum arguments are good. Imagine that you go to the doctor to get your immunizations. The doctor removes the protective sleeve from the needle and is about to inject you with it when he accidentally drops it on the floor. He picks it up and appears ready to inject you when you object: 'Doctor, I think that needle might be dirty; there might be germs on it!'. The doctor holds the needle up to the light, closes one eye, and stares at it intently. After a few seconds he says, 'I have looked very closely and I don't see any germs on it; there's nothing to worry about'. This doctor has made a noseeum inference—and it is a *bad one*.

What separates good noseeum inferences from bad ones? For a noseeum inference to be good two conditions must be met. First, it must be the case that I have good reason to think that I am looking for the thing in question in the right place. If my wife asks me if we have any milk and I look in the oven, I am looking in the wrong place. My failing to see it *there* would not be good evidence that we don't have any milk. Second, it must be the case that I have good reason to think that I would see the thing in question if it really were there. If my wife asks me if we have ants in our lawn and I look out the window and say 'Nope. I don't see any', I have made a bad noseeum inference. I am looking in the right place, but ants are too small to be seen by me even if they are there.

With this we can return to the question of whether or not the atheist is in a good position to make a noseeum inference to the claim that there are gratuitous evils. Are defenders of the Direct Evidential Argument more like me when I conclude that there is no milk in the refrigerator, or more like the doctor who deems the needle clean? For the reasons described above, inscrutabilists argue that they are like the doctor. Even if they are looking in the right place (and how would we know that they are?), there is no reason to think that they would find what they are looking for if it were there.

Two things might be thought to follow from the reply of the inscrutabilist if it is indeed correct. First, this reply would succeed in undercutting the support for (13) and thereby defanging the Direct Evidential Argument. Since the reasons for evil would be inscrutable if present, we can show the atheist that the appearances are no more trustworthy here than they are in the doctor case. Let's call this the 'inscrutability reply' to the Evidential Argument.[23] Second, and just as relevant

my favorite team was behind by 30 points, I concluded that they lost because, given what I know about the rules of basketball, I could not conceive of a plausible scenario in which they went on to win. The defender of the Evidential Argument is making a parallel *no-conceivum* inference.

[23] There has been a great deal of discussion of what I am calling the 'inscrutability reply' in recent years. Defenders of the evidential argument from evil have argued against this reply. Those interested in pursuing this argument are encouraged to look carefully at the article by Michael Bergmann,

for our purposes, considerations of inscrutabilism might serve more generally to undercut one's enthusiasm for engaging in the task of trying to 'explain' evil at all. There are a number of reasons for this. If our capacities for explaining apparently pointless evil are as meager as this reply suggests they might be, and since, on inscrutabilism, there is no way to know whether or not this is the case, there is not much incentive to look for connections between evils and outweighing goods. Further, since inscrutabilism shortcuts the need to seek out explanations for evil to defeat the Evidential Argument, and since we have reason to think that our attempts to explain evil would fail miserably even if we tried, perhaps the task of explaining evil is best ignored altogether. Such theorizing, we might conclude, is simply beyond our ken. Let's label this stance 'noumenalism'. The label is apt in this case since, like Kant, the inscrutabilist is here arguing that given what we know about our own cognitive capacities, we have good reason to think that we will always be stuck at the 'level of appearances' when it comes to evil—never able to know very much in the way of the truth about evil 'as it is in itself'. If inscrutabilism and noumenalism are right, then we have a powerful response to the Direct Argument, and also good reason to desist from looking for explanations for evil.

Before going further, let's take stock. In the preceding sections we have considered three ways in which one might respond to the Evidential Argument under consideration. The first way is to argue that the evidence in favor of theism (that is, in favor of (15)) is sufficiently strong to outweigh the plausibility of the claim that there are some gratuitous evils (premise (13)). This approach does not seek to undermine any reasons we might have for endorsing (13) directly, but rather appeals to evidence in favor of (15), a claim which is (as far as these arguments are concerned) incompatible with (13). The second way is to argue that there are good reasons that would justify God in permitting some (or much or all) of the evil that is permitted in the world. These reasons, if plausible, serve either to undermine or significantly lower our confidence in (13). Of course, these good reasons only defeat the Evidential Argument if they lower our confidence in (13) enough to make us think that it is false (or at least less likely than the denial of the conclusion of the Evidential Argument; that is, less likely than the denial of (14)). The third way aims to show that any initial confidence we had in (13) is misplaced, since we are not in a proper epistemic position to affirm its truth. This is the way afforded by inscrutabilism and noumenalism. As we will see shortly below, however, there is at least one other way to argue that we are not in a proper position to affirm the truth of (13) that does not involve appeal to inscrutabilism or noumenalism, and it is this approach that will be followed in the remaining chapters of the book.

cited earlier, as well as the article by Daniel Howard-Snyder and M. Bergmann, 'Grounds for Belief in God Aside, Does Evil Make Atheism more Reasonable than Theism?', in M. Peterson and R. van Arragon (eds.), *Contemporary Debates in Philosophy of Religion* (Malden, Mass.: Blackwell, 2003), 13–25.

1.4 THE ARGUMENT FROM DISTRIBUTION

As mentioned earlier there is more than one way of formulating the Evidential Argument from evil. The Direct Evidential Argument took as its evidence the existence of particular instances of evil which, as far as we can make out, occur for morally permissible reasons. A second and more recent form of the Evidential Argument takes as its starting point the general pattern or distribution of evil. In other words, the inspiration for this argument comes not from considering a case of apparently pointless evil and concluding that there is likely no God. Rather, it comes from consideration of phenomena like those pointed to in the writings of the Hebrew prophet Jeremiah, who puzzled over the apparently indifferent distribution of evil:

You are always righteous, O LORD, when I bring a case before you. Yet I would speak with you about your justice: Why does the way of the wicked prosper? Why do all the faithless live at ease?

(Jer. 12: 3)

Evil befalls the virtuous and the wicked in at least equal measure, and pain and pleasure do not seem to be distributed in ways that accord with merit or desert. It seems that things would be otherwise if there were indeed a God.

The Argument from Distribution has been developed in detail by the philosopher Paul Draper.[24] Draper asks us to consider two rival hypotheses which might be cited to explain the observed pattern or distribution of pleasures and pains that we find among human and nonhuman animals. Draper designates the observed pattern '*O*.' The two explanatory hypotheses in this instance are *Theism* (*T*) and the *Hypothesis of Indifference* (*HI*), where the Hypothesis of Indifference is the claim that 'neither the nature nor the condition of sentient beings of earth is the result of benevolent or malevolent actions performed by nonhuman persons'.

When we try to assess the credibility of two competing explanations, we do it by considering the relevant evidence and then asking ourselves: Are things more likely to be this way if Hypothesis 1 is correct or if Hypothesis 2 is correct? If we think that things are more likely to be as they are if Hypothesis 1 is correct than they are if Hypothesis 2 is correct then, all other things being equal, it is more reasonable to believe Hypothesis 1 over Hypothesis 2. The last time I was in Boston I happened to be outside of Fenway Park at the end of a Red Sox game. Throngs of fans poured out, many of them with Red Sox shirts and caps on. In addition, there was a small handful of fans wearing Yankees caps and shirts. Fans with Red Sox caps on looked depressed and dejected. Fans with Yankees caps on were smiling from ear to ear, giving each other high-fives while whistling and

---

[24] See, for example, his 'Pain and Pleasure', 331–50.

whooping as they walked down the street. There are two hypotheses that one might have for this behavior. Hypothesis 1: The Red Sox won and the Yankees lost. Hypothesis 2: The Yankees won and the Red Sox lost. Would the evidence here be more likely if Hypothesis 1 were true or Hypothesis 2 were true? Of course, the answer is: if Hypothesis 2 were true. And so we should conclude (again, all other things being equal) that the Yankees won.

Draper then asks us to consider the question: Would we expect things to be the way O describes them to be if T were the case or if HI were the case? He thinks it is fairly obvious that the answer is that it is more likely that things would be as O describes them if HI were the case, for two reasons. First, when we set aside pleasure and pain that seem to have biological value for organisms, there is no connection between the remaining types of pleasure and pain and moral goods that are taken to be central in theism (like justice and virtue). If theism were true we would expect this nonbiologically-relevant pleasure and pain to have some connection with bringing about such goods. They don't. Second, if HI were true we would expect that nonbiologically-relevant pleasure and pain would rather be a mere by-product of the systems that produce biologically relevant pleasure and pain, and indeed this is exactly what we find. As a result, given the relevant evidence, it seems that HI is much more probable than T. And thus it is more reasonable (all other things being equal) to accept atheism than theism.[25]

There are a number of important distinctions between the Direct and the Distribution Arguments. In the Direct Argument, if we have reason to think that some evil is gratuitous, then we have reason to think atheism is true. In the Distribution Argument, we are led to focus our attention on a certain range of phenomena (the distribution of pleasure and pain, to take Draper's specific example) and ask what explanations seem more likely if we concentrate on those phenomena alone. What the argument does not tell us is whether or not those phenomena are the only or the most relevant phenomena in deciding between the competitors. To see why this matters, let's return to my story about the Red Sox and Yankees fans. Yankees fans don't like the Red Sox and most of them don't like Red Sox *fans* either. Let's imagine that immediately after a game that the Red Sox won (and the Yankees lost), the fans cleared out of the stadium when, suddenly, an earthquake struck. As a result of the quake, the Red Sox's beloved Fenway Park crumbles to the ground. Perverse as it might be, many Yankees fans would be happy about that. In fact, the destruction of Fenway might even outweigh any disappointment they might have felt from having lost the game. So now imagine that as my evidence I see the distraught Red Sox

---

[25] Above I noted that this procedure can be used to decide between competing hypotheses only when 'all other things are equal'. In this case that would mean that we take the prior probability of each hypothesis to be roughly the same, and that we regard other evidence available to us as not tipping the scales in competing directions. Are all other things equal when it comes to the competing hypotheses of theism and the hypothesis of indifference? The answer is no. As a result, this argument will only become a plausible argument for atheism if these other factors can be 'controlled for'.

fans, the cheery Yankees fans, and the stadium behind them lying in ruins. What should I think about who won the game given the totality of my evidence? Well, nothing really. There is another perfectly reasonable explanation for the evidence of the happy Yankees fans and the distraught Red Sox fans—an explanation which has nothing to do with who won or lost. Those distraught looks might be caused by the collapse of the stadium instead.

Similarly, if we focus our attention simply on the distribution of pleasure and pain, we may conclude that *HI* is more reasonable that *T*. But perhaps other evidence is more relevant. And here the problems raised for the Direct Argument seem to be equally problematic for the Distribution Argument. As in the case of the Direct Argument, perhaps the more relevant data when it comes to assessing the likelihoods of *T* and *HI* comes from arguments for the existence of God. If one judges those arguments to be sound, the balance will tilt against *HI*. Or perhaps the various explanations that might be offered for God's permission of evil will be judged to be plausible and sufficient for us to conclude that evil provides no evidence favoring *HI* over *T*. Finally, the Distribution Argument faces a problem similar to the one faced by the noseeum inferences in the Direct Argument. In that case we had to acknowledge that we are not well positioned to know what goods God might want to secure in creation nor how present evils might be necessarily connected to outweighing goods. In the case of the Distribution Argument we must concede, for reasons cited by the inscrutabilists, that we do not know whether or not other facts beyond the distribution of pleasure and pain—facts known or unknown—can or should tip the balance of probabilities in such a way that *HI* is more or less probable than *T*. Once again there are relevant facts that are inscrutable.

As a result, inscrutabilists raise an objection that seems to undercut the two most prominently discussed versions of the argument from evil. What is more, the claims of the inscrutabilist might be thought to encourage noumenalism. It is important then that we give some consideration to inscrutabilism and noumenalism, since one might reasonably think that accepting these claims obviates the need for a book that attempts to give any explanation for apparent evils—as this book aims to do. In light of these two positions, we can imagine a theist arguing as follows: 'There is no need for theists to give an explanation for animal suffering, since they already know how to respond to evidential challenges to theism based on apparently gratuitous evil or the distribution of evil, and that is simply to admit that they have no probative value, and that we have no business aiming to figure them out'. Is the noumenalist right? Is it time to stop reading?

1.5 INSCRUTABILISM AND EXPLAINING EVIL

There are at least two ways that one might resist the claims of the inscrutabilist-noumenalist. The first is to argue that, contrary to appearances, the inscrutabilist cannot turn away the evidentialist challenge by appealing to inscrutability alone. If the defender of the evidential argument can give us reason to think that she is warranted in accepting (13) in the face of the inscrutability reply, the theist will need to look for explanations of God's permission of evil that serve to undercut that warrant. The second is to argue that even if the inscrutabilist reply to the evidential argument succeeds, there are other reasons, not related to turning back the Evidential Argument, which make it worthwhile to continue to propose explanations for evil.

I am not going to have anything to say about the first way here, except that I think that the inscrutabilist response to the Evidential Arguments succeeds. The reason I will not say anything further is straightforward enough: if it turns out that I am wrong and that the inscrutabilist response to these arguments fails, the theist will need to offer either considerations that explain (at least some of) the evil in our world or considerations that raise the probability of theism in comparison to its competitors. That is the very thing this book aims to do. As a result, if inscrutabilism fails, explanations of the sort I consider here are crucial for turning back the Evidential Argument.

What if the inscrutabilist challenge succeeds? In this case the explanations I offer here will not play any crucial role in responding to the Evidential Arguments. There are nonetheless good reasons to continue to pursue explanations for evil. One such reason is that theists in the major theistic traditions already believe that God has revealed some explanations for evil or at least some clues that are starting points for explanations in texts taken as divinely authoritative in their tradition. For example, Christians, Muslims, and Jews all claim that at least some evils experienced by human beings are punishments for wrongdoing. Theists have good reason to consider these purported explanations in order to assess their defensibility. Furthermore, while it is likely that there are some goods that God aims to bring about in creation of which we are unaware, this is not true for all goods. Theists typically take themselves to be aware both of what some of these goods are (the glory of God, bliss in the beatific vision, love and friendship between persons, etc.), and of the ways in which suffering and evil are instrumental in securing those goods. In fact, the authoritative texts of the major theistic traditions often give some quite specific examples of such explanations. For Christians, to take just one example, the pain and suffering involved in the Passion and Crucifixion of Christ are genuine evils that serve greater goods. As a result, I suspect many theists would be willing to admit that explanations for evil are not *entirely outside our ken*, as the most extreme inscrutabilist might hold.

This shows us at least one good reason why noumenalism should be rejected, and why the task of attempting to construct explanations for evil should be pursued. However, were one to reject this line of argument, it is still useful for the theist to construct explanations for evil, where possible, in an attempt to help the critic see how it could be that evils of the sort permitted in the actual world are necessary for securing outweighing goods. We might see the usefulness of such explanations by reconsidering our analogy of the doctor and the dirty needle above. Perhaps the patient can help the doctor see the unreasonableness of his belief by pointing out that his judgments about the cleanliness of the needle are based on an errant noseeum inference. But it wouldn't hurt to also hand him a magnifying glass or a microscope. Insofar as we can demonstrate to him the error of his reasoning *and* the falsity of his conclusion, so much stronger will the case against him be. If the theist wants to blunt the force of the reality of evil for the critic, the same is true in this case. How much better if the theist could go beyond arguing that our ignorance makes it unreasonable to accept the claim that there are gratuitous evils, to supplying suitable reasons that might explain God's permission of actual evils.

1.6 DISTASTEFULNESS, PRIDE, AND ARROGANCE

Considerations arising from inscrutabilism and noumenalism provide one reason why enthusiasm sometimes runs low when it comes to generating explanations for evil. Others lack enthusiasm for such a project because they think it to be distasteful, prideful, or arrogant.

Those who find this sort of endeavor distasteful argue that attempting to explain evil somehow serves to blind us to the genuine horror of evil, to console us into complacency, or perhaps to induce a stoic resolve with respect to evil and its consequences. Such blindness, consolation, and resolve often have the direct and unfortunate further effect of deflating our enthusiasm for opposing it.[26] Unfortunately, critics of the project of explaining evil are in some measure right. Explanations for evil are sometimes used to lull the theist into a form of complacency concerning evil. One sees this, for example, in some of the works of the seventeenth-century German philosopher Gottfried Leibniz. In his much discussed, and often lampooned, work the *Theodicy* Leibniz cites the work of another philosopher approvingly when he affirms that

> vices and crimes do not detract from the beauty of the universe, but rather enhance it, just as certain dissonant notes would offend the ear by their harshness if they were heard quite alone, and yet in combination they render the harmony more pleasant. [There are also] various goods involved in evils, for instance, the usefulness of prodigality in the rich and avarice in the poor; indeed it serves to make the arts flourish.[27]

While Leibniz takes the gravity of evil more seriously in other places, passages like this underplay the severity of evil and our need to be concerned about it.

---

[26] See, for example, Terrence Tilley, *The Evils of Theodicy* (Washington, DC: Georgetown University Press, 1991).

[27] G. W. Leibniz, *Theodicy*, ed. Austin Farrar, trans. E. M. Huggard (LaSalle, Ill.: Open Court, 1988), 440.

Who could object to vices that enhance the beauty of the cosmos and contribute towards the flourishing of the arts!?

However, such inadequate explanations of evil are not reason enough to abandon our task altogether. There is, on the contrary, reason to be emphatic about the (obvious) fact that attempts to explain evil, even if they succeed, do not make it any less real, serious, and horrible. The patient whose hand is amputated due to an incurable gangrenous infection might understand that the loss was required in order to save his life. But explaining why this evil was unavoidable does not serve to diminish his suffering and loss. The loss is real and the suffering painful. No explanation of the necessity of the loss and suffering suffices to 'explain it away'. In the same way, by attempting to explain evil the theist is not, and ought not think herself to be, attempting to 'explain it away'.

Those inclined to lay the charges of pride and arrogance on those attempting to construct explanations for evil typically do so because they overestimate the explainers' ambitions. Some theists offer explanations of evil with the aim of showing in no uncertain terms exactly why God allows (at least some of the) evils that there are. We are all too familiar with the proclamations of televangelists who write off natural disasters to the sins of those who are afflicted. These confident condemnations are unsettling, in part, because of the self-righteous tones in which they are uttered. On the other hand theists who shy away from *any* attempt to explain evil are themselves forced to confront the fact that sacred writings in the major theistic traditions often provide such explanations in spite of them. Texts such as the Hebrew book of Job sometimes adopt a more skeptical stance towards the human endeavor to understand evil. But this stands in stark contrast to the fact that in some cases the explanations are plain. As noted earlier, Christians regard the Passion and death of Christ as genuine evils—but they are clear about the fact that they are evils which serve to bring about the great good of salvation for humanity. There is nothing intrinsically prideful or arrogant about claiming to know the explanations for such evils. Rather, in cases like this Christians are simply telling things as they must be told if they are to be faithful to their own narrative tradition. Such explanations are, or ought to be, rather a humble submission to one's own tradition.

In what follows we will be considering explanations of evil that for the most part stretch far beyond anything that comes straight out of purported revealed texts or theistic theological tradition. What of these? Explanations of this sort can be arrogant or prideful when they are confidently offered as the whole and sober truth concerning God's permission of evil. But this sort of thing is, and ought to be, rare. More common are attempts to show how certain goods we highly value in our world might be unavoidably caught up with the possibility of evil—perhaps even some quite severe evil. The theist offering such explanations has to be open to the possibility that he or she will be shown ways in which the goods in question might arise without any evil at all, or will be shown that the goods in question can't possibly be reasonably taken to be outweighing. Offered in that spirit, such explanations need not smack of pride or arrogance. Such a theist is not aiming to offer the whole or sober truth about evil. These explanations are merely attempts to figure out ways to piece together parts of the theist's paradigm that may seem anomalous to her or to those who view her commitments from the outside.

Indeed, one might think there to be something more prideful or arrogant in the stance of the theist who can comfortably ignore the challenges raised by sincere critics like Rowe or Draper. Is there nothing that theists can say to them, or at least to their audience, to help them see how by their lights the pieces of the apparently disparate puzzle of creation fit together? Or is there something theists can say and yet care not to? Can theists rest content merely throwing up their skeptical hands and sending the critics on their way? It seems rather that the theist ought, as best he or she can, engage the critic by offering some sort of explanation as to how one might make sense of the apparent chaos. This book is an attempt to see how this might go when it comes to the pervasive and palpable reality of suffering among nonhuman animals.

1.7 WHAT ARE THE STANDARDS?

Before we proceed it is worth asking what an 'explanation' for evil looks like in this context. What is the critic of the argument from evil up to when trying to 'explain' the existence of evil, undercutting the suspicion that some evils are gratuitous? One thing that would not be useful here is the sort of explanations used to turn back the Logical Argument: explanations that show the mere logical compatibility of the existence of God and evil. Contemporary philosophers of religion call such explanations 'defenses'. Defenses will be of little use in our context because, as we have already seen, they do not aim to provide explanations that undercut the *evidential* value of evil.

Alternatively, the theist might aim to provide the known truth about why God permits evil. Such explanations, typically called 'theodicies', carry their own liabilities. First, even if one were capable of delivering on the promise of theodicy, it would be hard to know that one had succeeded. The theist's insight into the explanations for God's permission of evil is, by all accounts, simply too weak or impaired to give us any confidence that we have found a true explanation for evil, even when we have. Thus, as David Lewis claimed, constructing theodicy is just 'too hard'.[28] Second, it is not clear that such a true explanation, were we to find one, would move the critic who endorses (13). Perhaps such true explanations would involve claims which the critic is nonetheless in doubt about (or even believes false).

---

[28] Lewis, 'Evil for Freedom's Sake', 152.

Those who have tried to find a middle way between defense and theodicy are not in complete agreement about what is necessary. Lewis claims that we need to develop 'hypotheses that are at least somewhat plausible, at least to the Christian [or other theist presumably]',[29] which show how evil provides a permissible and necessary means for certain goods. Yet this standard also seems too high. It would be nice if the theist could devise such hypotheses. But the theist's task in this context is to preserve the reasonableness of theistic belief in the face of the apparent evidential challenge raised by evil. In that context the theist may freely admit that she is not aware of any *plausible* hypotheses which turn back the evidential challenge. Still, there might be a variety of reasons which are, for example, *true for all she knows* and which are such that if they were true they would constitute good explanations for evil (that is they would be consistent with theism and would explain why permitting the types of evil would be necessary for securing outweighing goods). Reasons like these would not fairly count as *plausible* (nor *implausible*) but rather as *as plausible as not, overall.*

Peter van Inwagen argues that what is required is rather 'a story according to which God and suffering of the sort contained in the actual world both exist, and which is such that . . . there is no reason to think that it is false, a story that is not surprising on the hypothesis that God exists'.[30] However, this standard turns out to be too high still. To see why, consider the following variation on an analogy van Inwagen employs in discussing this issue. Suppose that Jane wishes to defend the character of Richard III in the face of evidence that Richard murdered two princes in the Tower. What evidence might she have? Perhaps the following: Richard's hold on the throne was tenuous and the princes were regarded as the primary alternate claimants; a loyal servant of Richard confessed to having carried out the murders on his behalf; Richard never produced the two claimants alive to quell rumors of their murder. All of these provide Jane with 'some reason' to think that Richard had the princes murdered and thus to think that Richard is morally contemptible.

Still, what if Jane also accepts the following claims as, at least, epistemically possible: while Richard's claim to the throne was tenuous, the two princes had already been ruled ineligible to assume the throne by Parliament; the loyal servant's confession was coerced; and a claimant to one of the interred princes' duchies had been given charge of the Tower the very night they were rumored to have disappeared.[31] In light of these additional possibilities, Jane considers the possible hypothesis that the claimant murdered the princes, believing that Richard would ultimately be framed for the crime. Jane does not *know* this hypothesis to be true, it is not *rendered plausible by what she knows*, and she

---

[29] Lewis, 'Evil for Freedom's Sake', 152.

[30] Peter van Inwagen, 'The Problem of Evil, the Problem of Air, and the Problem of Silence', in *God, Knowledge, Mystery* (Ithaca, NY: Cornell University Press), 156.

[31] As John Howard, later first Duke of Norfolk, was in fact.

has *some reason to believe it false*. Still, the hypothesis allows her to maintain the reasonableness of her belief in Richard's good character, since she is not justified or warranted in *rejecting* this epistemic possibility in light of the *totality* of the claims she justifiably accepts.

This, in fact, is the sort of reasoning we engage in all the time when we encounter evidential challenges to beliefs we hold with some confidence. When someone tells me that a trusted colleague was seen entering my office after hours, my first inclination is to assume that he was looking to borrow some books, not to steal them. Do I know that to be the case? Of course not. Is it rendered plausible by what I know? Surely not—he could have just as easily been borrowing a pen or an Ethernet cable. Instead, it is a hypothesis which, if true, would explain the observed evidence by invoking hypotheses which are consistent with my standing belief that he is morally upright, and which I have no good overall reason to reject. Similarly, to deflect the evidential worries raised by evil, one need only be able to construct hypotheses (a) which show how certain permitted evils meet conditions (A) through (C) described above, and (b) which she is not justified or warranted in rejecting in light of the claims she justifiably accepts.

Put this way, the task of deflecting the evidential worries raised by evil can look quite different depending on one's starting point, varying as we vary which claims one reasonably accepts and which claims the reasonable acceptances warrant one in rejecting. In what follows I will be offering a variety of potential explanations that might meet this standard, though the success of these explanations will depend largely on the extent to which one thinks the explanations (and what those explanations presume) warrant rejection in light of one's justified acceptances. In offering these explanations I will seek to show that the explanations do not stand in tension with most of what I will take to be a common set of justified acceptances endorsed by individuals who are reasonably well-educated in matters of contemporary philosophy and science.

Still, there will undoubtedly be cases in which differences in justified acceptances will fall along the very lines that divide theists and nontheists. In such cases, the explanation of evil in question will function differently for each group. For example, if the justified acceptances of theists give them insufficient reason to reject a purported explanation of evil, that explanation can serve to maintain the reasonableness of the theists' belief in the face of evidential weight of the evil in question. However, the same explanation may not deflect the evidential force of the same evil for a nontheist whose justified acceptances are quite different. If we encounter cases like this (and perhaps we will when considering explanations of the sort we will consider in, for example, Chapter 3) the task of explaining evil might divide into two different tasks: preserving reasonable belief in God in the face of evil (for theists), on the one hand, and showing that evil does not provide evidence sufficient to make it reasonable to deny theism (for the nontheist), on the other. Some explanations might be successful at one task, some at the other, and some at both.

Since the uses of the terms 'theodicy' and 'defense' are now firmly entrenched in the literature, I will avoid using them to describe the quite distinct sorts of explanations that are relevant for these purposes. Although I share the common aversion to neologisms, in this case the new category deserves a new name. Since Leibniz was accorded the courtesy of naming one of these two entrenched methods of explaining the reality of evil ('theodicy'—the title of the only book-length work he published), perhaps we could grant him the favor one more time. In the final (Latin) section of the *Theodicy* (unfortunately not contained in the only published English-language edition of the work) Leibniz offers a masterful and insightful summary of his views on evil, cast in the terms of traditional scholastic Latin. The title of the section is 'De Causa Dei', a phrase adapted from juridical contexts referring to the case offered at trial on behalf of a defendant's innocence. Such a case is offered *de causa X* or 'on behalf of X's innocence in light of the evidence'. The phrase provides an apt description of the sort of explanation I aim to develop here. For this reason, I will designate any explanation of evil of the sort I am seeking a *causa dei* (or 'CD' for short).

2

Neo-Cartesianism

What a book a devil's chaplain might write On the clumsy wasteful, blundering, low, and Horribly cruel works of nature!

(Charles Darwin)

In Chapter 1 we established standards that must be met for an explanation of evil to be successful. Among the standards is the requirement that the evils permitted are outweighed by the goods at which permission of those evils aims. However, when we are clear-headed about the evils permitted (and the evils that in fact obtain) in the realm of nonhuman-animal pain and suffering, the prospect of providing any sort of explanation in terms of outweighing goods might seem especially and distinctively bleak. A critic of this enterprise might sensibly worry here that while we might be able to come up with a laundry list of goods which require the permission of nonhuman-animal pain and suffering, such goods, as good as they might be, just cannot possibly outweigh the immeasurably vast quantity of animal pain and suffering contained in actual terrestrial history. Animal pain and suffering is indeed very bad, and no good we know of could be sufficient to outweigh *millions* of years of suffering on the part of *trillions* of organisms.[1] This is a natural reaction for one to have towards CDs which present some good as sufficient to outweigh the millions of years of pain and suffering of trillions of organisms. But there is an assumption standing behind such reactions. The assumption is that animal pain and suffering is in fact a bad thing, and that it is a bad thing the badness of which we understand sufficiently well that we further know how to weigh it against some of the potential goods that might be cited by theists as outweighing it. So, how bad is animal pain and suffering?

Anyone can see that the question admits of no easy answer. It would be hopelessly naive simply to assume that the nonhuman-animal experiences of pleasure and pain will be qualitatively or morally equivalent to those experiences in human beings. Is it equally naive to assume that the difference between human- and nonhuman-animal experiences of pain and suffering is so radical

---

[1] This is the reaction, for example, of David Ray Griffin in *God, Power, and Evil* (Philadelphia, Pa.: Westminster, 1976), 191–2.

that the evil of nonhuman pain and suffering can be easily outweighed? Surely this would not be equally naive. After all, it is obvious that many animals are neuroanatomically and neurophysiologically quite different from us. It is possible that these differences make a qualitative difference when it comes to the case of animal pain and suffering.

We will have opportunity to consider the 'How bad is animal pain and suffering?' question on more than one occasion. In this chapter we will begin thinking about the question by considering the plausibility of the most extreme answer; namely, that animal pain and suffering has such a radically different character that it has no moral significance whatsoever. This view is perhaps most famously attributed to Descartes, who is reputed to have held that animals do not experience pain and suffering, or indeed any sentient state. Thus, Descartes and the Cartesians are reputed to have been seen torturing animals and marveling at how well their behavior mimicked the behavior of organisms, like ourselves, who *really do* experience pain and suffering.

Such a position would not amount to a CD, since if there is no such thing as animal pain and suffering, there is no such thing as an argument *from it* to atheism. If instead there is such a thing as animal pain and suffering, but it turns out to be something that is not at all bad, then there is *no need* to explain God's permission of it. In fact, to the extent to which the information available to us leads us to be in doubt about the reality or moral significance of animal pain and suffering, to that extent we should withhold judgment about whether or not animal pain and suffering (if any there be) constitute any problem for theism at all. Because of this, it will prove worthwhile, as we get started, to look carefully into this matter. Although such explanations do not count as CDs, since they deny the existence of the apparent evil, they do still count as explanations of a phenomenon that is apparently troublesome by the theist's lights. Because of this, these neo-Cartesian explanations, if they are to blunt the force of the apparent evil of animal pain and suffering, will still have to meet the same epistemic standards that genuine CDs do; that is, they must still be such that we are not warranted or justified in rejecting them given our reasonable acceptances.

I will begin this chapter with a look at two recent 'neo-Cartesian' attempts to explain animal pain and suffering and why these attempts fail. However, I will argue that a closer look at Descartes's own views may point us in the direction of a more defensible position. I will in turn argue that there are many theories of phenomenal consciousness in contemporary philosophy of mind that are congenial to this Cartesian view and that, if we take them seriously, have substantial implications for our assessment of the badness of animal pain and suffering. Finally, I will look at a variety of objections which aim to show that these variants of neo-Cartesianism fail to clear the hurdle set for a successful CD; namely, that it must be such that we are not warranted in rejecting it given our acceptances.

2.1 TWO RECENT DEFENSES OF NEO-CARTESIANISM

Central to neo-Cartesian explanations is the idea that nonhuman creatures, even if sentient, lack some human characteristic essential to conscious suffering. The two most prominent defenses of neo-Cartesian explanations, developed by C. S. Lewis and Peter Harrison, attempt to isolate such characteristics.

Lewis sets out his position as a series of 'speculations' which lean heavily on a proposed distinction between sentience and consciousness. What follows is the core of Lewis's explanation of his own view:

Suppose that three sensations follow one another—first A, then B, then C. When this happens to you, you have the experience of passing through the process ABC. But note what this implies. It implies that something in you which stands sufficiently outside A to notice A passing away, and sufficiently outside B to notice B now beginning and coming to fill the place which A vacated; and something which recognizes itself as the same through the transition from A to B and B to C, so it can say 'I have had the experience ABC.' Now this is something which I call Consciousness or Soul . . . The simplest experience of ABC as a succession demands a soul which is not itself a mere succession of states, but rather a permanent bed along which these different portions of the stream of sensation roll, and which recognizes itself as the same beneath them all. Now it is almost certain that the nervous system of one of the higher animals presents it with successive sensations. It does not follow that it has any 'soul,' anything which recognizes itself as having had A, and now having B, and now marking how B glides away to make room for C. If it had no such 'soul,' what we call the experience ABC would never occur. There would, in philosophic language, be 'a succession of perceptions'; that is, the sensations would in fact occur in that order, and God would know that they were so occurring, but the animal would not know. There would not be 'a perception of succession.' This would mean that if you give such a creature two blows with a whip, there are, indeed two pains: but there is no co-ordinating self, which can recognize that 'I have had two pains.' Even in the single pain, there is no self to say 'I am in pain'—for if it could distinguish itself from the sensation—the bed from the stream—sufficiently to say 'I am in pain,' it would also be able to connect the two sensations as *its* experience. The correct description would be, 'Pain is taking place in this animal'; not, as we commonly say, 'This animal feels pain,' for the words 'this' and 'feels' really smuggle in the assumption that it is a 'self' or 'soul' or 'consciousness' standing above the sensations and organizing them into an 'experience' as we do.[2]

There are a number of confusions in Lewis's discussion—confusions which make it hard to know exactly how to unpack the view he wants to defend. The central line of argument is that while animals are sentient creatures, and as such can be in states that can be fairly described as pain states, these animals cannot suffer because they lack something else which is a necessary condition for such pain to

---

[2] C. S. Lewis, *The Problem of Pain: How Human Suffering Raises Almost Intolerable Intellectual Problems* (New York: Collier, 1962), 132–3.

carry moral significance. It is in this sense that the view Lewis defends counts as neo-Cartesian. In the course of the discussion above he seems to suggest all of the following points:

1. In order to be conscious (in a way that allows for morally relevant suffering), one must have the experience of 'passing through' distinct sensations.
2. The experience of passing through distinct sensations requires a continuity of perception: the ability to remember past experiences, distinguish them from present experiences, and (perhaps) anticipate future experiences.
3. In order to have the experience of passing through distinct sensations, one must be conscious of oneself, i.e. conscious of something over and above the succession of distinct sensations.
4. To be conscious of oneself, one must have the ability to recognize oneself as being a permanent and enduring thing.
5. To be conscious of one's experiences, one must have the ability to recognize the succession of experience as one's *own*.

If animals had sentience but lacked 'consciousness',[3] Lewis claims, they would have momentary sentient states, but would be unable to be genuine *subjects of experience*, since they could not unify the succession of sentient states to form a single, coherent diachronic experience. Thus, we might truly say of an animal exhibiting pain behaviors that, as Lewis later puts the point, 'Their nervous system delivers all the *letters* A, P, N, I, but since they cannot read they never build it up into the word PAIN'.[4]

Many commentators on Lewis focus on the first two of the five claims above, and take him to be suggesting that what animals lack is a *continuity of consciousness*. Without such continuity, animals cannot reflect on past experienced pain, nor consciously anticipate future pain. If one lacks these conscious retrospective and prospective capacities, one can only experience pain as an item of instantaneous awareness, and pain of that sort is not morally significant, since it is not bad even by the animal's lights.

It is not clear why Lewis thinks we should accept that merely instantaneous awareness of pain is neither morally significant nor bad. (Perhaps he was never the victim of the schoolboy prank of having a thumbtack placed on his seat.) Were that true, that might suffice to give the neo-Cartesian all he needs. However, Lewis argues for this conclusion by claiming that the experience of animals does not contain the sort of *unity* that generates a self, ego, or subject of conscious awareness. When a mouse exhibits pain behaviors, it is undoubtedly true that the neural tissue which gives rise to these behaviors is *in the mouse*. Still, there is a

---

[3] It should be clear at this point that 'consciousness' as it is used by Lewis here is more accurately characterized as 'self-consciousness' in contemporary philosophical terms. However, I will stick with Lewis's taxonomy for the remainder of the discussion of his view.

[4] Ibid. 138.

sense in which the experience is not *owned* by the mouse, for the mouse does not take itself to be the *subject* of these experiences. As a result, though the mouse has some of the ingredients necessary for being conscious of pain in the momentary fragmentary sensations occurring within its body, it lacks the recognition of itself as having those sensations and thus is not conscious (or conscious of them) in a manner that makes suffering possible.

Let's separate out two aspects of Lewis's suggested distinction between consciousness and mere sentience. On the one hand we have a presence or absence of a continuity of experience. Call this condition in the merely sentient animal 'No-Continuity'. Further, Lewis suggests that the merely sentient animal lacks the requisite ownership of its own experiences. Let us call this condition 'No-Subject'. Subsequent defenders and critics of Lewis focus primarily on No-Continuity. We turn to some of their criticisms below. But first, what should be said of No-Subject?

No-Subject is committed to the claim that the mental state, of nonhuman animals exist as isolated states of conscious awareness that lack any subjective 'owner'. As Lewis himself suggests, it is hard to know exactly how to conceive of such isolated states. Perhaps an animal in the condition of No-Subject is like a genuinely Humean bundle, a creature whose mentality consists of a mere aggregation of distinct conscious experiences. Animal minds, on this view, would lack the requisite complexity to constitute a conscious (or self-conscious) self. Unfortunately, Lewis does not develop this idea to give us an understanding of what it is for a subject to *own* its own experience in the requisite sense.[5]

What about No-Continuity? Critics of Lewis such as C. E. M. Joad have argued that attributing to animals a condition of No-Continuity fails to provide a satisfying explanation of animal suffering. Indeed, Joad sets out what many take to be the two primary objections raised by Lewis's critics. The first of these objections contends that animal behavior shows us that animals do have the continuous consciousness Lewis claims they lack. The fact that animals cower in the face of impending pain shows that they can learn from past experiences of pain, implying animal memory, and that they can anticipate pain, implying conscious anticipation.[6]

Others have taken this to be a serious objection to Lewis's position as well. But the objection seems easily deflected. Lewis does not deny that animals behave *as if* they had such continuity of consciousness. But he does claim that such 'as-if' behavior does not require actual retrospective and prospective consciousness. An animal that behaves as if it learned from a past situation of similar circumstances

---

[5] Perhaps a proposal developed below—that suffering requires higher-order awareness of other mental states—can serve to explain the difference between being a genuine subject rather than a mere aggregate of conscious states.

[6] C. E. M. Joad and C. S. Lewis, 'The Pains of Animals', *Month*, 189 (1950), 95–104, repr. in Andrew Linzey and Tom Regan (eds.), *Animals and Christianity: A Book of Readings* (New York: Crossroad, 1989), 39–71, 101–6.

need not *consciously* recall the past in order to behave differently in the present (though memory may direct present behavior nonetheless). The same can be said for behaviors of apparent anticipation of pain. Peter Harrison claims, for example, that *protozoa* are able to 'remember' things (that is, they act now in accordance with environmental conditions of the past through habituation). Yet there is little temptation to think protozoa have a continuity of consciousness, even though they behave in ways that might be described as 'learned'. Protozoa can learn because the 'memory' required for such learning does not require actual conscious awareness.[7]

The fact that we, as humans, can use conscious episodic memory in learning erroneously tempts us to believe they are necessarily linked. But they are not *necessarily* linked. Why do dogs cower when the master scolds and threatens with a rolled-up newspaper? It could be that the dog remembers a past encounter with the newspaper and recoils out of fearful expectation of punishment. But there need not be any conscious link between the present misbehavior and the recollection of a previous episode of punishment. Cowering or 'cringing' has been claimed by some to be an innate characteristic of canine behavior that is derived from a larger repertoire of wolf social behavior. The cowering reaction has the effect of making the dog look smaller and thus less threatening to the more dominant creature in the dog's social hierarchy. No conscious intention is required, for the behavior might well be merely an adaptive, reflexive reaction to aggression.[8] So we can separate the question of whether dogs and other creatures can learn—which they surely can—from the question of whether that learning requires episodic memory. Creatures who lack the capacity to form an internal representation of a past experience could not have conscious episodic memory. Yet even such creatures could learn to adapt their behavior appropriately in light of prior experiences.[9]

Joad's second objection appears to be directed toward the adequacy of explanations of both the No-Continuity and No-Subject varieties. It is less easily

---

[7] Peter Harrison, 'Theodicy and Animal Pain', *Philosophy*, 64 (1989), 79–92.

[8] Stephen Budiansky, *The Truth About Dogs* (New York: Penguin, 2001), 81–5.

[9] Of course as Dan Howard-Snyder has pointed out it can be the case that behavior that we take to be pain-signaling is *contingently* connected with internal conscious awareness of pain and suffering even if it is not necessarily so connected. One can imagine a critic of Lewis on this score arguing as follows: 'Now, suppose that the evolutionary facts are these. Animals that developed a pain-causes-avoidance-behavior mechanism tended to survive whereas those that did not did not. To be sure, evolutionary theory does not *require* that pain itself is adaptive, but it does require some mechanism to account for avoidance behavior, and suppose this is the one that was naturally selected. Then, as a matter of contingent fact, pain is a part of the mechanism that causes avoidance behavior. Animals that didn't develop it tended not to survive because they didn't get the only thing that was on offer as the cause of avoidance behavior. So the capacity to feel pain is adaptive, after all—not in itself, of course, but because it is part of the only mechanism evolution has to offer for what is adaptive in itself, namely avoidance behavior. You don't feel pain, you die. That is an evolutionary fact.' There is no doubt that this account might be correct. The CDs in the remaining chapters will assume that it is in fact correct.

deflected. Joad notes that on Lewis's view animals still experience real pain, even if the experience is only instantaneous. He writes: 'Pain is felt even if there is no continuing *ego* to feel it and to relate it to past and future pain. It is the fact that pain is felt, no matter who or what feels it . . . that demands explanation'.[10]

In a reply to Joad, Lewis remarks that there is an important difference between single instances (even iterated 'single' instances) of pain and having the capacity to be miserable from repeated instances arising from the capacity to link consciously each instance of pain by recalling past instances. So, while we should have sympathy for all animals that suffer, Lewis suggests that 'the more coherently conscious [an animal is], the more pity and indignation its pains deserve'.[11] No doubt Lewis is right on this last point. But his reply to Joad only succeeds if Lewis can convince us that it is continuous consciousness of pain, rather than pain *simpliciter*, that carries moral significance. Lewis does little to make that case, aside from expressing the hope that a truly instantaneous pain might have an 'unvalue' indistinguishable from zero.

Peter Harrison takes up No-Continuity as a condition distinguishing animals from humans, and attempts a more robust defense. Contrary to Joad's claim that animal behavior implies prospective awareness, Harrison argues that animal behavior need not indicate any conscious awareness at all. Harrison then develops his No-Continuity view of animal sentience to explain why, by his lights, their experience lacks any moral significance.

Harrison begins with a critique of those assumptions that lead many of us to think that animals do in fact experience pain. First, evolutionary theory reinforces the evident continuity between human beings and the rest of the animals, bolstering the argument by analogy for animal suffering. Second, there is a tendency to assume that evolutionary continuity implies continuity of mental function: that any differences between humans and other creatures are only of degree and not of a fundamental kind. Finally, the evolutionary paradigm naturally leads to the assumption that pain is adaptive. Animals that experience pain under situations that are likely to kill or harm them are likely to flee such situations and avoid them in the future. The capacity to feel pain thus carries an evolutionary payoff. It is thus concluded that this adaptive capacity to feel pain must be real.

Harrison rightly notes, however, that it is not the capacity to experience pain itself that is adaptive but rather the behavior associated with this supposed capacity; that is, the fleeing and future avoidance. The fact that we take such behavior to indicate that animals experience pain can be dismissed as a product of an unjustified association we make between the pain and the behaviors. 'We should speak of animal responses, not as reactions to pain, or expressions of pain, but rather as adaptive behaviors and physiological reactions to potentially

---

[10] Joad and Lewis, 'The Pains of Animals', 61.   [11] Ibid.

damaging stimuli. Their function is not primarily, or even at all, to express some internal state, but to adapt the organism behaviorally to a harmful aspect of its environment.'[12]

In addition, Harrison appeals to empirical data to defend the claim that, at least in the human case, many adaptively relevant pain behaviors occur before the conscious experience of pain. As a result, adaptive pain behaviors do not require the attending experience. He cites the behavior of retracting one's hand from a hot surface as an example of a reflexive act that occurs before information from the nervous system registers in the human brain as pain. That we (humans) suffer from burning our fingertips on hot objects has nothing to do with our pulling our hands away from them to prevent severe or permanent damage. 'The point is that an appropriate response can be elicited without the necessity of a feeling of pain, or a conscious decision. . . . [R]esponses to damaging stimuli do not require the experience of pain.'[13] As a result, Harrison thinks the case in favor of the reality of animal suffering is weak.

However, even if animal pain is real, Harrison, like Lewis, argues for a No-Continuity condition: nonhuman creatures lack the continuity of consciousness necessary for suffering. Harrison tries to improve on Lewis's neo-Cartesianism by developing a view that successfully bypasses the troublesome objection raised by Joad and noted above, namely, that instantaneous experience of pain is nonetheless evil. To do so, he invites the reader to consider the following thought experiment. Jones has been having nightmares every night. However, suppose Jones sleeps right through the nightmares and wakes up each morning refreshed with no memory of his nocturnal 'terrorization'. Should we regard Jones as worse off for having such nightmares? Harrison claims that Jones would not be, and would not regard himself as, worse off. Indeed, it is not until Jones wakes up in the middle of one of these nightmares and finds himself consciously aware of the memory of the nightmare that he finds himself troubled by them. Only when there is continuity between the nightmare and the waking state can Jones regard his nightmares as troublesome.

Harrison's second example involves a drug he takes to be fictional—an 'amnesiaesthetic',[14] which paralyzes a patient during surgical procedures, without anesthetizing, and erases the patient's memory of the procedure once it is complete. Are there any moral implications of choosing to use amnesiaesthetics rather than anesthesia when pain-inducing procedures are performed? Harrison argues that there are not. Given that our continuity of consciousness is broken

---

[12] Joad and Lewis, 84.   [13] Ibid. 84–5.

[14] Harrison regards these drugs as utterly fictional, apparently unaware of amnestics such as scopolamine which act in roughly the way he describes, absent the paralytic features, which can be obtained by administering a purified form of curare, d-tubcurarine. (See Daniel Dennett, 'Why You Can't Make a Computer that Feels Pain', in *Brainstorms: Philosophical Essays on Mind and Psychology* (Cambridge, Mass.: MIT Press/Bradford, 1981), 209–10.)

by the drug, whether or not we feel pain during the operation is irrelevant, since we 'would not be inclined to say: *[We] experienced pain*'.[15]

Harrison's final example involves consideration of the experiences of infants. He points out that while we all experienced instances of pain as a baby, none of us 'owns' these experiences; we have no sense that they happened to *us*, precisely because of the lack of continuity of consciousness between these earlier states and our current state.

All three of these examples aim to show that if animal experience were characterized by Lewis's No-Continuity, then even if animals were to have instantaneous conscious awareness of pain, the lack of continuing consciousness would render that pain morally insignificant. In this way Harrison's account provides an answer to Joad's second objection.

There is, however, a further problem with this view, one that challenges the claim that instantaneous experiences of pain *simpliciter* are not morally salient.[16] The point can be illustrated using a prospective version of Harrison's second thought experiment. If one is about to undergo horribly painful surgery and is presented with the option of taking either an amnesiaesthetic or a traditional anesthetic, is there reason to prefer one to the other? Or if one were to discover after surgery that the doctor had used an amnesiaesthetic rather than an available anesthetic might one not also be reasonably indignant? There is no consensus on how to view past pains that are not remembered. Yet there is widespread agreement on how we should regard the prospect of future pain even when we know it will not subsequently be remembered. Nearly all of us anticipate that *we* would undergo the intensely unpleasant experiences of surgery and would not want the amnesiaesthetic to be administered. If these intuitions are correct, then it would seem that it is not merely the absence of anticipation or recollection in a sentient being that makes the important moral difference required for an explanation of evil. As a result, Harrison fails to make the case that the absence of a continuity of consciousness is sufficient to deprive the experience of animals of any moral significance.

2.2 DESCARTES TO THE RESCUE?

Earlier we looked at the standard Cartesian view, according to which animals are mere unconscious automata. The numerous critics of this view have rejected it for a variety of reasons. Some see it as inviting moral atrocities against animals. Some see it as inconsistent with what we know about our own evolutionary origins and our neuroanatomical similarity to other species. Still others find it an affront to common sense.

[15] Harrison, 'Theodicy and Animal Pain', 89.
[16] This point has been raised by Robert Wennberg in 'Animal Suffering and the Problem of Evil', *Christian Scholar's Review*, 21 (1991), 122–4.

While the unconscious-automata view strikes many as implausible, there are hints that this was not the only view of animals' mentality endorsed even by Descartes himself. There is no doubt that in some texts Descartes likens animals to mere machines. For example, in a letter to Mersenne of 1640 he writes: 'For in my view, pain exists only in the understanding. What I do is explain all the external movements which accompany feeling in us; in animals it is these movements alone which occur, and not pain in a strict sense'.[17] The view presented here was widely adopted by later Cartesians including Arnauld and Malebranche and used for specifically theodicean purposes. These later Cartesians argued that divine goodness would not permit animals to feel the pain that their behaviors appear to signal, and the Cartesian position supplied an easy route to that conclusion.

A closer examination of some of the texts of Descartes's later career, however, indicates that he may have held, or may have come to hold, a more subtle position than the one attributed to him by his successors. In these later texts Descartes allows for the reality of animal sensation, while denying that animals have 'thought'. On this view 'sensation' can be regarded as a function of the corporeal mental capacities, while thought is accomplished through the powers of the immaterial mind alone.

This fits in well with the account we find in Meditation 6, where Descartes provides an argument for the reality of the external world that essentially relies on a broadly Aristotelian psychology. For Aristotelians, the mental capacities were parceled out among the sensitive, imaginative, and intellectual powers of the soul. Sensitive and imaginative powers confer awareness of and facility with particulars, whereas intellectual powers confer, among other things, awareness of universals, apperception, and the ability to deliberate.[18] Aristotelians attributed all three sorts of powers to human beings, while admitting only sensitive and imaginative powers for animals. Further, they argued that sensitive and imaginative faculties were 'corporeal powers', meaning that the activities of these souls were carried out via the operation of corporeal organs, in this case through the sensory faculties and the brain. Thus, while animals had sensitive and imaginative powers, these powers were exercised wholly through the activity of the relevant corporeal organ.[19] The intellectual powers, on the other hand, do not operate by way of the activity of a corporeal organ. Although the soul of a human being might be embodied, some of the functions of the human mind could be carried on

[17] René Descartes, *The Philosophical Writings of Descartes*, iii. *The Correspondence*, ed. John Cottingham, Robert Stoothoff, Dugald Murdoch, and Anthony Kenny (Cambridge: Cambridge University Press, 1991), 148.

[18] For a representative Aristotelian defense of these claims one can consult St Thomas Aquinas. Concerning the claim that sensitive and imaginative powers are directed towards awareness of particulars alone see *Summa Contra Gentiles* (*SCG*) *ii* chs. 66–7. Concerning the claim that the intellectual soul confers powers of awareness of universals, apperception, and free choice see *SCG ii* chs. 51, 49 (§8), and 47–8 respectively.

[19] See *SCG ii*, ed. V. Bourke (Notre Dame, Ind.: Notre Dame Press, 1995), chs. 80–2.

without the direct involvement of the material component of the substance.[20] Thus, Aquinas could say: 'If the intellect were a body, the intelligible forms of things would not be received into it except as individuated. But the intellect understands things by those forms of theirs which it has in its possession. So if it were a body, it would not be cognizant of universals but only of particulars. And this is patently false. Thus, no intellect is bodily'.[21]

In the sixth Meditation Descartes similarly argues that the powers of sensation and imagination are not part of my essence, since they do not presuppose thought, and thus concludes that these powers inhere in some corporeal substance to which my soul is intimately connected.[22] On this view sensation and imagination are carried out through a corporeal organ (i.e. the brain alone or in conjunction with certain sensory neural pathways) and thus sensation and memory can be present even in beings lacking immaterial souls. This view seems to allow that animals have both sensation and memory, while lacking the suite of mental capacities grounded in the intellect (i.e. awareness of universals, apperception, and freedom). As a result, Descartes's views appear to permit animals to have the same first-order sensitive and imaginative states that humans have, including pain.

To attribute this view to Descartes on the evidence of the argument from Meditation 6 would be a stretch. But, in fact, some of his late correspondence gives further reason to believe that Descartes held just such a view. In a letter to the Marquis of Newcastle in 1646 Descartes writes: 'All the things which dogs, horses, and monkeys are taught to perform are only expressions of their fear, their hope, their joy; and consequently they can be performed without *thought*'.[23] Here Descartes attributes fear, hope, and joy to animals while denying that they are capable of thought, i.e. the activity characteristic of the immaterial soul alone. Likewise, in a 1649 letter to More, Descartes goes so far as to insist that his view only denies *thought* to animals, and not life or sensation: 'For brevity's sake I here omit the other reasons for denying thought to animals. Please note that I am speaking of thought, and not of life or sensation. I do not deny life to animals since I regard it as simply in the heat of the heart; and I do not deny sensation, in so far as it depends on bodily organ'.[24]

Putting the pieces together, we might understand Descartes's view in the following way. What animals lack is only those capacities conferred by the intellectual soul, such as the ability to think about universals, to reflect on one's own mental states, to deliberate. On this view, while it might be true that animals see, hear, and smell, they are not capable of reflecting on those first-order mental states, and thus of regarding them as pleasurable or not. So while they may hear a symphony, they never say to themselves 'That

---

[20] Ibid. chs. 50–1, 55.   [21] Ibid. ch. 49 §4.
[22] Descartes, *Writings*, ii. 54–5.
[23] Descartes, *Writings*, iii. 303.   [24] Ibid. 366.

was wonderful!', since they lack any reflective awareness of their own sensory
states.

We might use this view to construct a continuum of neo-Cartesian explanations
of animal pain quite different from those of Lewis and Harrison.

2.3 FOUR NEO-CARTESIAN ALTERNATIVES

On the more subtle interpretation of Descartes, higher-order cognitive capacities,
not first-order sensory ones, form the basis for morally significant distinctions
between our conscious lives and the lives of other creatures. We have seen
Descartes ground these cognitive differences in ontology. As a substance dualist,
who saw mind and matter as distinct substances, he could conceive of thought as
a power of the immaterial mind alone, leaving the powers of sensation to inhere
in corporeal substance. Yet we need not presuppose a *Cartesian ontology* in order
to fashion a *neo-Cartesian explanation*. Indeed, contemporary non-Cartesian
theories of consciousness provide the resources for fashioning several alternative
neo-Cartesian explanations for the problem of animal suffering.

Classical Cartesian theodicy founders on the implausibility of the thesis that
animals are unconscious automata. Yet contemporary philosophical discussions
of consciousness agree on at least this: there are many different notions of
consciousness. So it is open to the neo-Cartesian to affirm that animals are
conscious, in an ordinary sense of 'conscious', while denying they are conscious
in yet another ordinary sense of the term.

Obviously, animals are alive and often awake. They are not unconscious in
the way rocks are. Animals can have occurrent mental states that play a role in
the control of their bodily movements and behavior. These are features of any
organism that is *sentient*, and, clearly, some animals are sometimes conscious in
this sense. Let us call this sort of consciousness *creature consciousness*.[25] In addition
to attributing consciousness to the organism as a whole, individual mental states
of sentient creatures can also be called *conscious* when they are states of awareness
of something. Let us call this relational notion of the consciousness of a mental
state *access consciousness*.[26] Insofar as a housefly can accurately represent a state of
affairs external to itself, it has access to its surroundings and is consciously aware
of what is nearby.

[25] The label comes from William Lycan (*Consciousness and Experience* (Cambridge, Mass.: MIT
Press, 1996)), who compares it also to Ned Block's 'access consciousness' and Roger Shepard's
'objective consciousness'.

[26] The term comes from Ned Block ('On a Confusion about a Function of Consciousness',
Behavioral and Brain Sciences, 18 (1995), 227–87), though the account developed here will not
presuppose everything Block claims for his notion of *access consciousness*. For example, Block thinks
it is a fallacy to analyze phenomenal consciousness in terms of access consciousness. I disagree in
what follows.

Most philosophical discussions of consciousness, however, have focused on a third, more mysterious conception of consciousness. This sort of consciousness involves the peculiarly subjective or phenomenal character of experience, the particular way it is like to have certain sorts of experiences, or the qualitative aspect of sensory awareness (*qualia*). Let us call this sort of consciousness *phenomenal consciousness* and ascribe such consciousness both to particular mental states and to the subjects of such mental states.

Plainly, a creature can be in a state of access consciousness without being in a state of phenomenal consciousness. A familiar example is the common experience of driving on psychological 'autopilot', when one is not aware (phenomenally) that one is driving, even though one is plainly aware (in the creature and access senses) of the road ahead (as evidenced by the fact that one would appropriately respond to any unanticipated or unusual interruptions). The phenomena of 'blindsight' and 'deafhearing' provide other more commonly cited examples of the distinction between these two types of consciousness. Patients who have sustained damage to their primary visual cortex may retain the ability to detect, discriminate, and localize visual stimuli presented in the areas of their visual field in which they report that they are subjectively blind. Such 'blindsighted' patients report that they are no longer able to see, and yet they are capable of giving correct motor responses to changes in their environment that could only be detected through the visual modalities. In a natural sense, they are conscious of what they think they do not see (they have some access to the external information), while in another sense they are blissfully unaware, for they are not phenomenally conscious of this access.[27]

Patients with corresponding damage to the auditory cortex similarly report being unable to hear, while nonetheless showing a capacity to detect, localize, and exhibit appropriate autonomic reactions to sound. As with blindsighted patients, it is natural to regard these patients as deaf when we consider phenomenal consciousness, while acknowledging that they have mental states which manifest auditory access consciousness.[28]

Using these distinctions we are now in a position to formulate four proposals for a distinction between human and nonhuman consciousness. Each of the four proposals, if true, would have the moral significance necessary to sustain a neo-Cartesian explanation with respect to animal pain.

The first proposal exploits the distinction between access consciousness and phenomenal consciousness:

1. Many nonhuman creatures are conscious inasmuch as they are alive, awake, and have sensations. These creatures have mental states that give them

---

[27] For a discussion of this phenomenon and its potential implications for animal consciousness see Peter Carruthers, 'Brute Experience', *Journal of Philosophy*, 86/5 (1989), 258–69.

[28] See Monica Meijsing, 'Awareness, Self-awareness and Perception: An Essay on Animal Consciousness', in Marcel Dol, Soemini Kasanmoentalib, Susanne Lijmbach, Esteban Rivas, and Ruud van den Bos (eds.), *Animal Consciousness and Animal Ethics: Perspectives from the Netherlands* (Assen: Van Gorcum, 1997), 130.

perceptual access to features of their environment in a way that allows them to make the requisite discriminations necessary for psychological control over their behavior. Yet, unlike the sensory states possessed by humans, the mechanisms whereby these organisms have access to the world lack any phenomenal character whatsoever. There is an intrinsic difference between the sensory states of nonhumans and humans in this phenomenal respect.

On this proposal the pain of animals is *blind pain*, inasmuch as the creature has no phenomenal sense of the pain, even though it can have informational access to a harmful situation.

Critics of classical Cartesian theodicies are not likely to be impressed. Though the proposal does not characterize animals as *unconscious automata in the creature or access senses*, it does seem to make them *unconscious automata in the phenomenal sense*. If deer pain is intrinsically different from human pain in this proposed way, then deer and other creatures turn out to be phenomenally unconscious *zombies*. To speak of pain in such creatures would be to speak of mental states that are merely similar in function but intrinsically different in a respect that critics might well regard as the most fundamentally important sense of being conscious.

Neo-Cartesianism of this first sort sees nonhuman sensory states as lacking phenomenal character and regards this as an *intrinsic difference* between sensory states in humans and those in other creatures. A second neo-Cartesian explanation could detach the second part of that claim. Those pressing this second explanation could persist in maintaining that the pain sensations of other creatures lack phenomenal properties, but maintain that this does not mark an intrinsic difference between pain states in humans and pain states in other creatures. The key to this proposal is to deny that phenomenal consciousness is an intrinsic feature of mental states. Just such a claim is a consequence of a contemporary theory of consciousness with considerable currency.

On strictly functionalist theories of the mind, all psychological properties are representational or functional properties. It is thus natural for functionalists to regard the difference between a state's being phenomenally conscious or not to turn upon relational facts about the state, and not upon intrinsic, qualitative features of the state itself. For example, according to Higher Order Thought (HOT) theories, a mental state's being conscious consists in having an accompanying conceptual mental state that represents the first state as its intentional object.[29] This general theory of state consciousness can then be employed to generate a theory of phenomenal consciousness on which a

[29] See, for example, David Rosenthal, *Consciousness and the Mind* (Oxford: Oxford University Press, 2002). To avoid obvious counterexamples, Rosenthal requires that this representation of the first-order sensory state must be immediate, and not the result of perception or inference.

phenomenally conscious mental state is a state with non-conceptual content which is the object of a higher-order intentional state and which causes that state non-inferentially.[30]

Our neo-Cartesian theodicist, buoyed up by the prospect of being fashionably up to date in the philosophy of mind (generally a rather unfamiliar feeling for Cartesians), is now in a position to formulate a second proposal:

2. For a mental state to be a conscious state (phenomenally) requires an accompanying higher-order mental state (a HOT) that has that state as its intentional object. This HOT must be a thought that one is, oneself, in that first-order state. Only humans have the cognitive faculties required to form the conception of themselves being in a first-order state that one must have in order to have a HOT.

On this second proposal no intrinsic difference in states of pain or other sensory states grounds the phenomenal difference. Instead the phenomenal properties turn on the extrinsic features of the state, in other words, whether the creature is aware of itself as being in that first-order state. There is nothing it is like for such a creature to be in pain, not because the state of pain in that creature is intrinsically different, but because the creature lacks the relevant access to itself and to that state of pain.

Is a neo-Cartesian explanation available only to those who accept functionalist theories of phenomenal consciousness? Indeed not. Those who think phenomenal consciousness is an intrinsic qualitative feature of first-order states can concede that this is a further similarity between humans and other creatures while persisting in the belief that only humans have higher-order access to these first-order states. Thus, we have a third neo-Cartesian proposal:

3. Some nonhuman creatures have states that have intrinsic phenomenal qualities analogous to those possessed by humans when they are in states of pain. These creatures lack, however, any higher-order states of being aware of themselves as being in first-order states. They have no access to the fact that they are having a particular feeling, though they are indeed having it. Since phenomenal properties of states of pain and other sensory states are intrinsic to the states

---

[30] This view has been defended most thoroughly by David Rosenthal (see, e.g., Rosenthal, *Consciousness*, 2002). Other higher-order views of phenomenal consciousness are defended as well, but may not be as suitable for the purposes of a neo-Cartesian CD. For example, Higher Order Perception or 'Inner Sense' views hold that the higher-order mental state be a state which, like the first-order state, has analog content and which has as its intentional object the first-order state. This sort of view is defended most recently by Lycan (see his *Consciousness and Experience*). One might think it more likely that animals have such higher-order analog states. But, as we will see below, the evidence that animals have any such higher-order states, analog or conceptual, is very thin. Dispositional Higher Order Thought theories, according to which the first-order state must have the disposition to cause such higher-order states (see, e.g., Peter Carruthers, *Phenomenal Consciousness: A Naturalistic Theory* (Cambridge: Cambridge University Press, 2000)), may be useful in constructing neo-Cartesian CDs as well.

themselves, there is no difference on this score between humans and other creatures.[31]

One might object to an explanation of this sort by arguing that it does not, after all, show that animal pain and suffering is not real or not morally relevant. The reason for this, the objector continues, is that mental states which have the phenomenal features characteristic of painful sensations are intrinsically evil and thus bad, whether the animal knows it has these states or not. Access to the states, the critic might contend, is irrelevant to whether it is bad to be in the state itself. Clearly, if a state is intrinsically bad, it is not made better merely in virtue of the fact that the creature does not know about it.

The objection misses the mark. For, defenders of this third proposal, no less than those defending the second, can plausibly respond that so long as an animal lacks the higher-order access, so long as it cannot represent itself as being in a state of pain, there is nothing about its situation that is of intrinsic moral disvalue. For, lacking any such access, there is simply no victim or subject for whom it can be said that there is a way it is like for it to be in such a state of pain.[32]

Does a neo-Cartesian explanation require that other creatures lack any higher-order access to states of pain? Not at all. For even if an animal has higher-order access to a first-order state of pain, it would lack any moral disvalue if the animal did not find the state to be undesirable. Such a mental state might bear some similarity to the conscious experience of persons with a damaged or absent prefrontal cortex. Individuals who have undergone a prefrontal lobotomy, for example, sometimes report an awareness of familiar pains but paradoxically insist that they no longer find the pain to be undesirable or unpleasant. They claim

[31] Here it should be noted that dispositional higher-order-thought theories might provide another variant on this theme as hinted at in the previous note. In the dispositional view, first-order mental states must have the disposition to cause higher-order conceptual mental states having the first state as their target in order to be phenomenally conscious. One might argue that human and nonhuman animals have first-order mental states that are intrinsically equivalent, but since animals, in fact, lack the resources for having higher-order conceptual states, those intrinsically identical states never yield phenomenal consciousness in them.

[32] This is not to deny that the state possesses a phenomenal quality. This third neo-Cartesian CD treats such phenomenal properties as simple, irreducible, intrinsic features of the first-order state. Thus, phenomenal properties cannot literally be 'what it is like for a subject to be in a state', since that is a complex and relational property. Those who find *what it is like-ness* to be a necessary feature of the phenomenal are invited to return to the second neo-Cartesian proposal. Let me note also a second reason to be suspicious of this objection. On this view mental states can be intrinsically evil whether or not the person in whom they are occurring is aware of them. But if such a view is right, presumably the same thing will be true for intrinsically good mental states of which one is unaware. For example, being in possession of mental states which represent things that are aesthetically beautiful would, I suppose, turn out to be good even if one lacks an awareness of having such mental states. If correct, such a conclusion would encourage the view that it is good to take those with blindsight to the art museum, since it would allow the blindsighted person to have mental states which represent beautiful things, even though he or she would not be aware of having such states. The incredibility of this conclusion further casts doubt on the argument of the critic of this third neo-Cartesian CD.

the pain 'feels' the same, even though it no longer bothers them.[33] As a result, creatures of this sort have first-order pain states, and second-order awareness of them. But because they lack the capacity to regard those states as undesirable, such creatures do not *suffer* because of their pain.

We then have available a fourth neo-Cartesian proposal:

4. Most nonhuman animals lack the cognitive faculties required to be in a higher-order state of recognizing themselves to be in a first-order state of pain. Those that can on occasion achieve a second-order access to their first-order states of pain nonetheless do not have the capacity to regard that second-order state as undesirable.[34]

This fourth view faces at least one immediately obvious objection: if animal pain were understood on this model, then such animals would be incapable of properly motivating the sorts of avoidance behaviors pain typically elicits. After all, if the prey did not find the pain of being eaten by a predator undesirable, there would be no way of explaining the fact that it struggles to get free.

This objection rests on the assumption that animal behavior is motivated, at least sometimes, by the actual or anticipated pleasantness or unpleasantness of the animal's mental states. But there is no evident reason to think this is true. On evolutionary grounds, it is reasonable to suppose that if animals exhibit certain behaviors when they are exposed to potentially injurious (noxious) stimuli, they do so because reacting this way has proven to be adaptive. The adaptiveness of the behavior is utterly detachable from any feelings of pleasantness or unpleasantness that may attend the mental state that generates the behavior. Thus, if the prey seeks to escape the predator, to cower, to whimper, etc., it does so because such behaviors have, for whatever reason, proven to be adaptive, or to be related to adaptive capacities the organism possesses. But this is true whether or not the mediating mental states are regarded as pleasant or not. As we will see in the next section, even humans often exhibit pain-avoidance behaviors in the presence of noxious stimuli without (or prior to) feeling the unpleasantness attending the noxious stimulus. This is so even in some cases where the person, in retrospect, takes the unpleasantness of the stimulus to be the explanation for his action. For example, we know that when we withdraw our hand from a hot object the behavior is initiated before the painful sensation

---

[33] See a discussion of this and related phenomena in Roger Trigg, *Pain and Emotion* (Oxford: Clarendon, 1970), 125–42, and Antonio Damasio, Daniel Tranel, and Hanna Damasio, 'Individuals with Sociopathic Behavior Caused by Frontal Damage Fail to Respond Autonomically to Social Stimuli', *Behavioural Brain Research*, 41 (1990), 81–94.

[34] This is not the 'mad pain' described by David Lewis ('Mad Pain and Martian Pain', in Ned Block (ed.), *Readings in Philosophy of Psychology*, i (Cambridge, Mass.: Harvard University Press, 1980). Since animals display pain behaviors, they do not act like Lewis's madman or indeed like prefrontal-lobotomized patients. Thus, it is essential here to insist that finding a state to be undesirable is not to be understood behavioristically, but rather in terms of the presence of a distinct higher-order affective state.

is felt, even though most would claim that they moved their hand away because 'it hurt'.[35]

Common to all of these neo-Cartesian proposals is the thesis that nonhuman creatures lack some psychological capacity that grounds a morally significant distinction adequate for an explanation. The successful neo-Cartesian explanation must steer around a rock of Scylla and not exaggerate the psychological difference between humans and nonhumans. Yet it must also avoid a whirlpool of Charybdis by not leaving unexplained states in animals that are simply not good.

Constructing a successful explanation requires that the components be such that we are not justified or warranted in rejecting them in light of what we accept. However, some might argue that the neo-Cartesian positions set out above fail to get over even this low hurdle, since some things we justifiably accept, or ought to accept, do warrant their rejection. First, many will find the views on mind presupposed on the various neo-Cartesian explanations implausible. For example, those who think that HOT theories of consciousness are false will have good reason to reject the second explanation, while those who think they are true will find the third untenable. And so on. I do not aim to defend or reject any of the underlying views presupposed there. As one's commitments in the philosophy of mind go, so will go one's stance with respect to the possibility of the explanations. However, another thing many accept, or might accept, is that the evidence of ethology, neuroscience, and evolution renders these descriptions of animal mentality untenable or doubtful. A further thing we accept, or ought to accept, is that animals deserve moral consideration. However, the neo-Cartesian explanations described above preclude such consideration. Can the neo-Cartesian respond to these two concerns?

2.4 EMPIRICAL OBJECTIONS TO THE NEO-CARTESIAN EXPLANATIONS

In the last section I argued that there are a variety of positions defended in contemporary philosophy of mind which would deliver the distinctions required to sustain a neo-Cartesian explanation. But one might wonder if evidence from outside of philosophy might serve to undercut such a view. If the known facts of science, for example, were inconsistent with these neo-Cartesian views, this would make them inconsistent with our justified acceptances and thus mandate their rejection. And one might suppose that there would be strong evidence from cognitive ethology, neuroscience, and evolution to rule out the neo-Cartesian position. What should the neo-Cartesian say about such evidence?

Ethology is the study of animal behavior in light of evolutionary considerations. Cognitive ethology looks specifically at the extent to which animal behavior

---

[35] This and similar issues are discussed in detail in Section 2.4.

might best be explained in terms that attribute cognitive mental states to animals. Fundamental to the standpoint of the cognitive ethologist are the claims that animal behavior is profitably explained by postulating these inner mental states, and that, like us, the behavior of organisms is often best understood in terms of their information-processing capacities.

Those who are attracted to cognitive ethology as a tool for understanding animal behavior are attracted because of its apparent success in explaining the seemingly thoughtful behavior of animals. But it is worth noting at the outset that it is an open question whether the success of these explanations requires that we actually attribute the cognitive states to the animal. There are two distinct species of cognitive ethology: strong and weak.[36] Weak Cognitive Ethology (WCE) recognizes the utility of explaining and predicting animal behavior in cognitive terms, but does not go so far as to actually attribute the mental states to the animals. On WCE we can consider animals and their behavior to be analogous to chess-playing computers and their behavior. We can readily see the utility of explaining the behavior of the computer by saying things like 'It is trying to fend off the challenge of the queen' or 'It is trying to lure the queen side rook', without going all the way to actually attributing beliefs, desires, and intentions to the computer. The friend of WCE adopts this same antirealist stance towards explaining animal behavior. Strong Cognitive Ethology (SCE), on the other hand, uses the same explanatory strategies, but goes further in actually attributing the cognitive states to the organism. Of course, simply assuming the truth of SCE would beg the question against, say, advocates of our first neo-Cartesian explanation. Defenders of SCE will thus need independent arguments in support of their views.

Some have tried to argue that there is something fundamentally amiss with SCE. On this line of argument, the behavior of animals is always subject to a 'deeper' explanation than that given by the friend of SCE; specifically, an explanation in terms of neurophysiology. However, because of the complexity of such explanations, we are typically unable to provide them. In cases like that it might be useful to us to make appeal to these cognitive explanations. This might seem to show that SCE offers explanations of deep and abiding value. On a closer look, however, it seems that explanations in terms of SCE should be advanced only apologetically and with some embarrassment, since their utility merely serves to highlight our inability to explain them via their 'real' causes.[37] These considerations seem to show us that, in the end, cognitive explanations of animal behavior are superfluous, redundant, or merely 'folksy'.

In spite of its initial appeal, this argument is a bit too quick. One might imagine any physicalist deploying the same argument against attempts to explain

---

[36] D. DeGrazia, *Taking Animals Seriously: Mental Life and Moral Status* (Cambridge: Cambridge University Press, 1996), 87.

[37] I am indebted to Jonathan Bennett for laying out this argument with some care, along with the response I discuss below. See 'How is Cognitive Ethology Possible', in Carolyn Ristau (ed.), *Cognitive Ethology: The Minds of Other Animals* (Hillsdale, NJ: Erbaum, 1991), 39–41.

human behavior in cognitive terms. Since human behaviors are subject to explanations at the level of physiology, should we thus offer explanations of human behavior in intentional terms only apologetically or with embarrassment? Only the eliminativist could be happy with such a result. Furthermore, it is clear that there are times when cognitive or intentional explanations of the behaviors of complex nonhuman living organisms and sometimes of inanimate entities are useful. The example of chess-playing computers mentioned above makes this plain. Adopting the 'intentional stance' towards behavior in nonhumans is useful because it focuses our attention on explanatorily useful groupings of events and/or properties that would be overlooked in neurophysiological explanations. Jonathan Bennett, considering this sort of argument against cognitive ethology, invites this critic of SCE to consider a case in which a cognitive ethologist and a neurophysiologist are faced with explaining the behavior of an animal which is threatened by a predator. Bennett continues:

If our cognitive account of the animal is good enough, we may be able to predict that it will climb the nearest tree, say; but if we are less well-informed, we may be in a position to predict only that the animal will behave in some way that increases its chances of escaping the predator. . . . Now the superhuman physiologist may be able to predict that the animal will move just exactly thus and so. . . . But if the physiologist isn't quite that good and can only approximate to a perfect prediction, he won't be able to predict that the animal will improve its chances of escaping the predator. He will be able to predict that the animal will make approximately such-and-such movements, which means that it will go towards the tree and make climbing-like movements; but for all he can tell, the animal might not quite get to the tree or . . . The physiologist's inability to predict whether the animal will do anything to improve its chances of escaping matches our inability to say even approximately what kinds of movements the animal will make (e.g. climb, swim, or lie still). Neither basis for prediction is better than the other. They merely cater to different legitimate interests.[38]

Not every sort of activity which is subject to an explanation of this sort is best or even usefully explained in this way. We might describe the behavior of the Venus flytrap or the phototropism of a tomato plant in terms of beliefs and desires. But this would be wrongheaded. For the cognitive explanatory picture to be of value, it must be the case that we take the organism to be capable of appropriating information from the environment in such a way that mental states are formed which figure centrally in behaviors aimed at satisfying the organism's desires. Thus, cognitive explanations of the Venus flytrap's behavior would be a dead end.

From this we might conclude that cognitive ethology does have a legitimate and important role in explaining animal behavior. What implications does this have for the plausibility of neo-Cartesian explanations? In the first three explanations what matters is the presence or absence of phenomenal consciousness

---

[38] Bennett, 'How is Cognitive Ethology Possible', 40.

(or awareness thereof) arising from second-order mental states. In the fourth explanation what matters is the capacity of the organism to form reflective pro or con attitudes towards such second-order mental states. Do the explanations invoked by SCE require or suggest that animals have these sorts of mental states or mental capacities as well? It is not immediately obvious that they would, since these explanations typically invoke only beliefs and desires, and it is not at all clear that beliefs and desires depend on such second-order mental states.

If, however, we had some understanding of the exact mental capacities involved in either phenomenal states arising from second-order awareness or in the capacity to form reflective pro and con attitudes, and we had some (behavioral or anatomical) reason for attributing those mental capacities to animals, then neo-Cartesianism would be in serious trouble indeed. At least some advocates of SCE think that there is little reason to attribute such states to animals. The prominent primatologist and advocate of SCE Gordon Gallup, Jr., argues that we have no reason to attribute second-order mental states to anything other than humans and other humanoid primates.[39] Gallup defends the claim that the only sure sign that animals have any awareness of their own mental states is the presence of self-concepts. If the animal has the capacity to conceive of itself, it can thus think of itself and thereby have an awareness of itself. On Gallup's view: 'Either you are aware of being aware or you are unaware of being aware, and the latter is tantamount to being unconscious. The sleepwalker is sufficiently aware to navigate and avoid colliding with obstacles, but unaware of being aware. . . . If a species fails to behave in ways that suggest it is aware of its own existence, then why should we assume it is aware of what it is doing?'[40]

Through a series of widely known studies Gallup argued for the presence of such self-awareness in certain primates using evidence from experiments which involved placing a red dot on the foreheads of mirror-trained primates and noting that, when viewing their images in the mirrors, the primates would immediately touch the spot on their forehead, signaling that the primate recognized the mirror image as an image of itself. Gallup takes this behavior as evidence that the primate recognizes that it is seeing 'itself' in the mirror, and thus that the primate has 'self-awareness'. It is worth considering, however, whether such experiments show that even primates exhibiting these types of behaviors have self-awareness of the sort relevant for neo-Cartesian CDs. It seems not. In these experiments Gallup shows at most merely that some animals have the capacity to recognize *certain bodies as their own*. This is a form of self-awareness, but it is surely different from having second order awareness *of one's own mental states*.

---

[39] Gordon G. Gallup, Jr., 'Do Minds Exist in Species Other than Our Own?', *Neuroscience and Biobehavioral Reviews*, 9 (1985), 631–41.

[40] Ibid. 638.

Are there other less stingy ways of reading the behavioral evidence which license attributing the needed type(s) of second-order states to animals? As a first attempt, one might simply argue that pain-related behaviors themselves suffice for such an attribution. But, as we saw earlier, the empirical evidence from phenomena such as blindsight makes it clear that one cannot generally infer the existence of second-order awareness from behavior in this simple fashion. In addition, since we know that pain-related behaviors are sometimes correctly explained without any appeal to second-order awareness of pain states, there is no straightforward way to infer one from the other. For example, numerous simple organisms exhibit behaviors typically associated with pain, such as recoiling from potentially injurious (noxious) stimuli, without any pain quale. This is true of microorganisms, snails, jellyfish, etc. What is more, there is strong evidence that in many cases pain-related behaviors *in human beings* are not intrinsically connected with the conscious awareness of pain states. First, there are well-documented cases of human beings displaying both physiological and behavioral evidence indicative of experiencing pain, while the patients report not actually feeling pain. These cases are indeed human cases of the *blind pain* that the neo-Cartesian hypothesizes as the typical case in animals.[41] Second, we know that in some cases pain behaviors are not mediated by the qualitative mental states that accompany the noxious stimulus. In cases of simple pain avoidance, such as withdrawing a hand from a hot surface, it has been demonstrated that the pain-related behavior is initiated before the conscious awareness of pain.[42] In cases like this, the feeling of pain is an epiphenomenon.

Evidence of this sort shows us that when we see animals exhibiting types of behavior that are typically associated with feelings of pain in the case of human beings, we cannot make any confident inferences about the mental states of those animals. Still, one might argue, we know that even if jellyfish and other organisms lack second-order awareness of pain which mediates behavior, *we* do not. As a result, the capacity for such awareness appears at *some point* in evolutionary history. If we can discover the physical basis for such awareness, then we can perhaps discern which organisms actually experience pain in the way that we do. We will return to this below when we consider the neurological objection.

Before we turn there, let's consider a second way one might try to appeal to *behavioral* evidence as a way of undercutting the neo-Cartesian position. The first three neo-Cartesian views depend essentially on the fact that animals lack a second-order awareness of their own mental states. Depending on the view, this lack entails either that the animals have no phenomenal mental states at all or that they lack access to the phenomenal character of their mental states. Perhaps

---

[41] See Bob Bermond, 'The Myth of Animal Suffering', in Dol et al. (eds.), *Animal Consciousness and Animal Ethics*.

[42] See B. Libet, 'The Neural Time Factor in Conscious and Unconscious Events', in G. Block and J. Marsh (eds.), *Experimental and Theoretical Studies of Consciousness* (CIBA Foundation Symposium 174) (New York: John Wiley and Sons, 1993).

we might be able to make an empirical case for the implausibility of these views by showing that at least some organisms exhibit behaviors that seem to require a capacity specifically for second-order awareness of their own mental states. While showing this would not conclusively demonstrate that they have the sort of *phenomenal consciousness* which figures centrally in these explanations, it would at least show that they have the one necessary ingredient, namely second-order awareness of their own first-order states, that the first three views suppose them to lack. So, is there any evidence that animals have this second-order awareness? What sorts of behaviors might animals exhibit that signal such mental states?

It is worth noting to start that very few behaviors seem to require such conscious awareness. In this regard Dutch neuroscientist Bob Bermond remarks, 'almost no human capacity *requires* consciousness, e.g. conditioning, acquisition of complex procedural knowledge, learning of natural and artificial grammars, breakthroughs in physics and mathematics, solving equations, and learning processes and decisions which steer our behavior in daily situations'.[43] However, there are two sorts of behaviors which seem especially suggestive of such conscious awareness. First, apparently *deceptive behaviors* seem to indicate that animals are aware of the mental states of others, perhaps implying a general capacity for 'awareness of mental states'. Jane Goodall among others has described behavior in which chimpanzees go to great lengths to avoid looking at—sometimes even obscuring—otherwise unnoticed fruit while dominant males are present, and then go on to eat it after the others leave.[44] What does such evidence show? Some have argued that such attempts at deception require that the deceiver have a sense for the mental states that other organisms would form were they to see the unnoticed fruit. In order to realize that the dominant male will come to see the fruit if it is not obscured, the nondominant chimp must be able to represent to itself the actual and potential states of mind of other chimps. But having a capacity to represent first-order states of perceptual awareness is just what the neo-Cartesian denies of animals. In addition, animals sometimes seem to show a more direct awareness of the first-order mental states of others. For example, some experimental results describe chimpanzees removing the blindfold from a trainer's face in order to lead him to a box filled with food which only the trainer could open.[45] These chimps, recognizing that the trainer had covered eyes, inferred that he was unable to represent the nearby environment visually, and thus would be unable to know about both the box and what to do with it. To form such mental states the chimps would, so the argument goes, have to be able to know that the trainer lacks something, and that 'something' is first-order visual states concerning his environment. Being able to think about or direct

[43] Bob Bermond, 'A Neuropsychological and Evolutionary Approach to Animal Consciousness and Animal Suffering', *Animal Welfare*, 10 (2001), 54.

[44] Cited in Gallup, 'Do Minds Exist', 635.

[45] See D. Premack and A. J. Premack, 'Does the Chimpanzee Have a Theory of Mind?', *Behavioral Brain Science*, 4 (1978), 515–26.

one's attention to those first-order states shows that the chimps have *second-order awareness*.

Yet while such evidence is suggestive, it is not decisive. Behavior of the first sort can be explained by simple conditioning. Past instances in which the chimp looked at or failed to obscure the fruit would have led to loss of reward. The second case is a bit more interesting, but still not decisive. It might simply be the case that the chimp recognizes that eyes are necessary for proper navigation without having any further thoughts about the states of mind that using the eyes might lead to. Consider what we would infer if, instead of the case described above, we saw a chimp pick up a trainer who had both legs amputated, and carry him to the locked box. Would we infer that the chimp knew what state of mind the trainer without legs would be in, or would we infer simply that the chimp recognized that the trainer lacked equipment necessary for navigating? Nothing more than the latter would be necessary here. Similarly, in the described experiment chimps may be doing nothing more than coming to an awareness that the key-toting experimenter lacks the necessary navigational equipment. No stronger conclusion is warranted here.[46]

If considerations of animal behavior are not decisive, perhaps neuroscience and evolution will raise more trouble for the neo-Cartesian. Unfortunately, the evidence against the neo-Cartesian explanations from these quarters is thin. Neuroscience is of limited use, since we simply do not know what explains phenomenal or second-order consciousness at the neural level. While a number of interesting experiments have been done on this front, none has delivered any decisive positive information. We do know that there is no consciousness 'lobe'. The neural capacities which underlie consciousness are distributed across various perceptual systems and seem to depend on specific forms of neural, structural, and dynamic complexity, rather than the presence of a distinct structure. As a result, losing the capacity for phenomenal consciousness in one perceptual modality might leave the others fully intact.[47]

But even if we limit our focus to a single (and most widely studied) sensory modality, there is no neurological story to tell about how to explain the sort of conscious awareness relevant here. To see this it is instructive to consider one widely studied visual phenomenon, known as binocular rivalry. The phenomenon is particularly important here, since it is thought to provide a case where real progress might be made in securing neuroscientific data on

---

[46] Detailed studies on chimp 'gaze-following' behavior have been undertaken in an attempt to determine whether or not second-order awareness is required or indeed is the best explanation of consequent chimp behavior. The most extensive studies were performed by Daniel Povinelli and are reported and discussed in his *Folk Physics for Apes* (Oxford: Oxford University Press, 2003). Povinelli argues that the behavior evidence supports the view that chimp behavior deriving from 'gaze following' is not best explained by appeal to the formation of second-order mental states concerning the mental states of other chimps. Povinelli infers that chimp behavior is best explained by appeal to 'low-level' or first-order cognition (see esp. pp. 22–34).

[47] L. Weiskrantz, *Consciousness Lost and Found* (Oxford: Oxford University Press, 1997).

the nature of phenomenal consciousness. This phenomenon emerges when a subject is simultaneously shown distinct and difficult-to-blend images, one image in one eye and the other in the other eye. One might think that under such circumstances what the subject would perceive is a combination of the two images, much like what one would see if two transparencies were laid on top of one another. But instead subjects report states of conscious awareness that toggle back and forth between the two images. If there was some way of tracing the pathways of the inputs from one eye during that period when the subject is consciously aware of the image presented to that eye, perhaps we could see evidence of some pattern of neural activity that toggled on and off in a way that correlates with reported conscious awareness of that image.

In one experiment researchers presented subjects with images that are typically processed in distinct regions of the visual cortex. The researchers chose images of a face, which are typically processed in the fusiform face area (FFA), and an image of a house, typically processed in the parahippocampal place area (PPA). When the two images were presented to different eyes at the same time, the pattern of toggling states of awareness was accompanied by corresponding patterns of activation in the FFA and PPA. Some have taken such research to show that phenomenal conscious awareness or second-order awareness of faces and houses is (token) identical with patterns of activation in the FFA and PPA respectively. Are they right? Perhaps they are—but the evidence of these experiments is insufficient to show it. The reason for this is that the pattern of neural activation during rivalry is the same pattern of activity that we find when subjects are shown the two images in alternating fashion to both eyes simultaneously. This shows that during rivalry the visual processing pathways alternately suppress one another so that it is as if the subject has only one functioning eye. Thus, what such experiments show is that when we see a house, certain neural states are activated, and when we see a face, other neural states are activated, but none of this tells us which part of those patterns of activation (if any!) constitutes the phenomenal conscious awareness of the image presented.[48]

Consideration of evidence of this sort shows us that the neuroscientific critique of neo-Cartesian explanations is going to be difficult to mount, but it also shows us why the evolutionary critique will have a hard time succeeding. We can press as hard as we like on the fact that there is continuity and similarity between the peripheral and central nervous systems of humans and their evolutionary neighbors. But since we don't know what sorts of similarities and continuities

---

[48] There is a vast literature on binocular rivalry. For those interested in further discussion of the phenomenon, a slightly outdated summary of some recent work can be found in Patricia Churchland's *Brain-wise* (Cambridge, Mass.: MIT Press, 2002), 134–48. Other recent work of interest includes David Alais and Randolph Blake (eds.), *Binocular Rivalry* (Cambridge, Mass.: MIT Press, 2005) as well as Frank Tong, 'Competing Theories of Binocular Rivalry: A Possible Resolution', *Brain and Mind*, 2/1 (2001), 55–83.

are relevant to phenomenal or second-order awareness, these observations can do no work for the critic.

One might think that even though we do not know enough about phenomenal consciousness in general, we surely know enough about the neural basis of pain to be able to say that the experience of some animals in pain must closely resemble normal human nociception. But, once again, this is simply not the case. What we do know is that many organisms are capable of perceiving noxious stimuli, and are capable of producing adaptive behaviors in response to those pains. But we further know that in many cases pain behaviors are not caused by the qualia associated with nociception. In one notable series of studies on rats with severed spinal columns, for example, James Grant and his colleagues showed that a number of pain-related behaviors seemingly explained by conscious awareness and memory of pain were explained entirely by complex neural processing in the spinal column. These complex pain-related behaviors could be carried out not only without conscious awareness, but without the brain at all.[49] Thus, nociception and pain-related behavior do not require second-order phenomenal consciousness of pain. What we do know about nociception therefore leaves ample room for the possibility of the first three explanations.

What is more, we know enough about *human* pain perception to know that there is also room for the fourth explanation. The fourth explanation held out the possibility that nonhuman animals might have a sort of phenomenal conscious awareness of pain which sufficed to inform the organism that a noxious stimulus had been applied, but in which the conscious state lacked the undesirable qualitative character we typically associate with pain. Such a nociceptive mechanism might seem quite exotic. But, in fact, the possibility of organisms whose nociceptive capacities work in this way is not exotic at all. For such a thing to be possible, we would have to think of human nociception as involving two distinct pathways. First, it must involve a pathway that allows the subject to detect that a noxious stimulus has been applied. Second, it must involve a pathway that allows the subject to attach a certain measure of importance or

----

[49] James Grant, 'Learning and Memory without a Brain', in Marc Bekoff, Colin Allen, and Gordon M. Burghardt (eds.), *The Cognitive Animal: Empirical and Theoretical Perspectives on Animal Cognition* (Cambridge, Mass.: MIT Press, 2002), 77–88. Studies of this sort have led those in the neuroscience and animal-behavior community to attempt to formulate criteria for distinguishing between animals that are capable of phenomenally conscious awareness of pain and those that are not. The criteria offered by Gary Varner are typical. Varner presents a table of six conditions which he describes as 'relevant to consciousness in the animal kingdom'. The conditions are: the presence of nociceptors, the presence of a central nervous system (CNS), connections between nociceptors and the CNS, the presence of endogenous opioids, whether pain killers affect responses, and the similarity of human- and nonhuman-animal pain behaviors. Varner concludes that all six conditions are only met by mammals. I mention Varner's work not because his criteria strike me as determinative, but rather because it shows that attempts by mainstream scientists to provide criteria for phenomenal awareness of pain by no means indicate that the neo-Cartesian position is unsustainable. See Gary Varner, *In Nature's Interests? Interests, Animal Rights, and Environmental Ethics* (Oxford: Oxford University Press, 1998), 53.

significance or affective weight to the stimulus—this is the component which gives pain its undesirable qualitative character. Indeed, in the human case at least, perception seems to involve just such a pair of pathways. In nociception in particular there is at least one pathway which appears to detect the 'cognitive significance' of the noxious situation, and a second that detects the 'emotional' or affective importance of the situation. The latter of these two centrally involves the right neocortex and the prefrontal cortex, the part of the mammalian brain structure which appears last in evolutionary history. The distinctness of these two pathways is important and warrants some brief reflection.

There are three types of cases which display the nature of these distinct perceptual pathways. The first two concern nociception specifically, while the third relates to perception more generally. First, as we have already seen in the discussion of the fourth explanation, there are cases in which lobotomized patients report that they continue to sense or experience pain, but without *disliking* or *being displeased by* the pain. These patients report that they understand that the pain sensation signals a noxious stimulus, but they simply are not motivated to do anything to rid themselves of the sensations. For example, such patients uniformly refuse analgesics which would eliminate or alleviate the sensations.[50] Second, patients with induced loss of function in the prefrontal cortex often display a generalized indifference to the threat of pain and other potentially negative consequences of their behavior. As a result, these patients not only engage in practices which knowingly involve noxious stimulation, but they will act in ways that harm their own long-term interests (spending money recklessly, engaging in wanton patterns of social behavior). In all of these cases the patients report that they understand the negative consequences of their behavior, but they are not motivated to do anything to stop those consequences from occurring.[51]

What both types of case show is that detection of noxious stimuli takes place via two quite distinct neural pathways.[52] On the one hand there is a 'discriminative' pathway, which discerns the 'cognitive features' of the stimulus (location, intensity, duration, etc.). On the other hand there is an 'affective' pathway, which accounts for the unpleasant feeling or 'painful' part of nociception. The two types of case noted above yield dramatic effects when the first pathway is deactivated and the second is not; namely, that the subject is aware of the fact that something harmful is going on, but is not motivated to act accordingly. This is obviously problematic in the human case, since the fitness advantage of a nociceptive mechanism would be lost if it detected dangers in the environment but failed to motivate behaviors. But there is no reason to think that nonhuman animals must have both components to produce adaptive behavior. If nonhuman

---

[50] See a discussion of this and related phenomena in Trigg, *Pain and Emotion*, 125–42.

[51] Damasio et al., 'Individuals with Sociopathic Behavior'.

[52] This is no novel discovery on my part. Indeed, Colin Allen reports that 'it is practically a piece of philosophical dogma that the affective aspects of pain can be completely dissociated from the sensory aspects' ('Animal Pain', *Noûs*, 38 (2004), 620).

animals simply had the first pathway coupled with mechanisms that produced appropriate avoidance behaviors, these animals would appear to exhibit the normal suite of pain-related behaviors, without having phenomenal experiences of pain which have the undesirable qualitative character we typically associate with pain.[53] Furthermore, these cases confirm that in human beings the 'affective' pathway terminates in the prefrontal cortex, a region of the mammalian brain which was the last to evolve (and so occurs only in humanoid primates). Thus, the evidence available to us would tend to indicate that the affective side of pain is not experienced by organisms other than humans and other humanoid primates.

Finally, there is evidence that such dual-processing pathways are not unique to nociception. Of course, we are all familiar with a number of instances of multiple-processing pathways, such as the distinct visual perceptual pathways that process light and dark, on the one hand, and color on the other. However, the parallel between nociception and non-nociceptive perceptual pathways is even closer than that. As in nociception, there is evidence that other sensory modalities also have distinct 'sensory' and 'affective' dimensions. In the case of visual perception, a certain pair of disorders, prosopagnosia and Capgras syndrome, reveal two such pathways quite clearly. Prosopagnosiacs lack the capacity for facial recognition. What is remarkable, however, is that these individuals show clear affect-related autonomic and other physiological signs typical in cases where people see things that are familiar. The result is that while they lack the relevant cognitive capacity, their ability to generate the appropriate affect is undiminished.[54] Those with Capgras syndrome, on the other hand, are able to recognize ordinary objects and faces as being identical from one encounter to the next. But, unlike the prosopagnosiac, they lack appropriate affect-related autonomic responses to these objects. Typically, when one sees one's parents, children, spouse, etc. the stimulus induces a cascade of physiological responses characteristic of recognition of something familiar. Those suffering from Capgras syndrome seem unable to process the affective importance of the situation in this way. The result, interestingly, is that those suffering from the disorder mistakenly infer that a familiar-looking object or person is in fact a substitute. This results in strange reports from such patients. For example, they might report to the police that some imposters looking and sounding just like their own parents have taken up residence in the parents' house. Or they report that someone has been stealing their shoes at night and replacing them with exactly identical shoes.[55]

---

[53] A brief discussion of the distinct pathways can be found in section II of Virginia Hardcastle's 'When a Pain is Not', *Journal of Philosophy*, 94 (1997), 381–409.

[54] Bob Bermond, 'Consciousness or the Art of Foul Play', *Journal of Agricultural and Environmental Ethics*, 10/3 (1998), 230.

[55] See, for example, William Hirstein and V. S. Ramachandran, 'Capgras Syndrome: A Novel Probe for Understanding the Neural Representation of the Identity and Familiarity of Persons', *Proceedings of the Royal Society B: Biological Sciences*, 264 (22 March 1997), 437–44.

Evidence of this sort opens up the possibility that organisms might have one set of pathways and not another. Specifically, nonhuman animals might have the cognitive pathway while lacking the affective one. Such differences would, of course, require other differences. For example, it would have to be the case that animal behavior, unlike human behavior, is never mediated by the affective states that accompany noxious stimuli. But these additional differences are also undetectable and thus irrelevant to the acceptability of this explanation.

2.5 THE ETHICAL TREATMENT OF ANIMALS

Are there disturbing ethical consequences for neo-Cartesian explanations? Must those who deny the reality of animal suffering agree that there is nothing objectionable in any possible treatment of nonhuman creatures? Apparently many Cartesians accepted this implication with glee. Some report of Cartesians that 'They kicked about their dogs and dissected their cats without mercy, laughing at any compassion for them, and calling their screams the noise of breaking machinery'.[56]

Robert Wennberg alleges that, in the final analysis, neo-Cartesianism is stuck with such consequences, and presents a stark choice for us:

Indeed if we cannot join those particular followers of Descartes who 'kicked about their dogs and dissected their cats without mercy' [. . .] then we must part company with those who would seek to construct a theodicy based on a denial of animal pain.[57]

Do such claims pose a serious problem for the neo-Cartesians? There are at least three issues that need addressing. First, does the endorsement of a neo-Cartesian explanation imply that one should regard any treatment of nonhuman creatures as morally permissible? Second, if animals cannot, in fact, suffer, does our treatment of them turn out to be morally inconsequential? Finally, do the hypotheses of neo-Cartesian explanations imply that nonhuman creatures have only instrumental value and lack any inherent worth?

In addressing the first question, we would do well to recall what is required to endorse an explanation. One must provide an answer to a question of the form 'Why would the God of traditional theism permit X?' (where X is a type of event that appears to be gratuitously evil)—an answer that one is not warranted in rejecting given the claims one justifiably accepts. As neo-Cartesians, one need not claim to know, or even accept, the hypothesis that nonhuman creatures never experience states that are intrinsically evil. We need only leave open the

---

[56] J. P. Mahaffy, *Descartes* (London: Blackwood, 1901), 181, cited in A. R. Kingston, 'Theodicy and Animal Welfare', *Theology*, 70/569 (1967), 485.

[57] Richard Wennberg, *God, Humans, and Animals* (Grand Rapids, Mich.: Eerdmans, 2002), 313–14.

possibility that this is so, for all we accept. Inasmuch as we do not know that animals never suffer, it would be morally reckless to act as if we did. Normally, one ought not shoot at what is moving in the brush, unless one knows it is not an unintended target. Similarly, one should not treat animals as if they do not suffer, unless one knows this is so; we have no such knowledge.

Yet one might press further. Suppose some version of the neo-Cartesian explanation turns out to be true. Would it follow that our treatment of animals is morally inconsequential? It does not. Kant famously denies that animals have intrinsic worth, while insisting that there can still be wrongful acts of cruelty to animals. He deems our duties to animals as indirect duties toward humanity:

> If a man shoots his dog because the animal is no longer capable of service, he does not fail in his duty to the dog, for the dog cannot judge, but his act is inhuman and damages in himself that humanity which it is his duty to show towards mankind. If he is not to stifle his human feelings, he must practice kindness towards animals, for he who is cruel to animals becomes hard also in his dealings with men.[58]

On Kant's account, then, cruelty to animals is wrong because it is damaging to one's humanity and because it disposes one to harm other persons. Plainly, Kant has provided a morally relevant reason why we should not join those who wantonly beat dogs and dissect cats, and moreover a reason that is compatible with neo-Cartesianism.

Nonetheless, some have argued that the Kantian response is insufficient since by denying animals intrinsic value or worth apart from their role in serving human ends, it does not accord them the sort of worth our moral judgments concerning them require. Surely, causing animals needless injury is wrong for reasons beyond the fact that it might lead one to treat one's neighbors with indifference or hostility. The moral judgments we make about cases of apparent cruelty to animals seem to require that we take such mistreatment to be intrinsically wrong.

Wennberg puts the objection to the Kantian response this way:

> [With the Kantian line] we end up with a radically truncated moral belief. For one thing, the action of beating a dog with a baseball bat is no longer appalling in-and-of-itself . . . [Thus,] whenever we are reasonably convinced that the beating of the pet (or non-pet) will not have negative secondary effects we can beat without restraint.[59]

Can neo-Cartesian theodicies support the claim that animals inherently merit moral respect even if they cannot suffer?

Given that we are engaged in the project of theodicy, our central task is to consider whether or not a theistic or fully Christian worldview coheres with the existence of evil. As a result, Christians at least can help themselves to distinctively Christian claims when arguing for such coherence. In light of that, defenders

---

[58] Immanuel Kant, *Lectures on Ethics*, ed. Peter Heath and J. B. Schneewind (Cambridge: Cambridge University Press, 2001), 240.

[59] Wennberg, *God, Humans, and Animals*, 314 n. 3.

of neo-Cartesianism can appeal to the fact that the Christian Scriptures portray the natural world as possessing intrinsic worth in virtue of its status as a divine creation. Christian environmentalists have long appealed to the fact that God creates, owns, and redeems the natural order as evidence of its inherent moral worth. In creating the world God declares it good even before human beings come on the scene to use it as an instrument or to exercise dominion over it (Gen. 1: 28). Scripture contains repeated affirmations of God's ownership of creation (e.g. Ps. 24: 1). Finally, God is described both as entering into covenantal relationships with the natural world and as engaged in the project of redeeming it (Gen. 9: 8–17; Rom. 8: 18–22).

As a result, Christians are obliged to regard nature as having worth apart from its role in serving human ends. What sort of claim does the worth of the natural world make on human creatures? Critics of Christianity have often argued that the Judeo-Christian Scriptures accord human beings a dominion over nature (in Genesis 1: 28) which has encouraged wanton environmental destruction. But claims of dominion are balanced by claims that human creatures are stewards of the created order. As a result, Christians are obliged to acknowledge a prima facie duty to safeguard the integrity of nature. Such a duty would undoubtedly preclude pointless destruction of the environment as well as wanton disregard for the integrity of animals.

Grounding the moral worth of animals in the general worth of nature and its integrity would require a great deal more work. For example, one might wonder exactly what 'preserving the integrity of the natural order' amounts to. Am I destroying the integrity of nature if I disrupt the smooth sandy surface of the beach with my foot, or if I swat a mosquito? Answers to these questions will have to be filled out by way of a developed account of the proper functioning of nature and its components. On such an account, interventions in nature will only count as violations of natural integrity if they serve to thwart the proper functioning of nature or its components. This will explain why walking on the beach is not morally objectionable (though perhaps destroying erosion-protecting sand dunes would be). It will also explain why predation, a natural feature of the animal food chain, is not an evil (though perhaps trophy hunting would be).

2.6 CONCLUSION

Neo-Cartesian explanations of animal pain and suffering differ from the other explanations I will defend in the book, since they deny rather than explain their reality. I suspect that few will find the neo-Cartesian position to be compelling or even believable. This itself is interesting in light of the fact that the evidence against the neo-Cartesian position is quite weak.

One explanation for its lack of convincing power might be that human beings are so strongly inclined to attribute mindedness to nonhuman entities. When we see apes grooming one another or wolves hunting in a pack, our natural tendency is to describe their behaviors in terms of conscious mental states. This tendency exhibits itself most strongly in explanations of the actions of domesticated animals and animals that are most closely related to humans phylogenetically.[60] We are more likely, that is, to attribute intentional states to chimps and house cats, for example, than we are to make such attributions when explaining the behavior of eels or lobsters. But research has shown that the tendency is indeed more pervasive than that. We are also strongly inclined to attribute intentional states to inanimate entities when those entities are portrayed as engaging in a drama or competition. Stewart Guthrie characterizes this tendency as follows:

anthropomorphism is not limited to our views of other animals but is broad and deep everywhere in our thoughts and actions. It colors perception and responses to perception throughout life, as when we speak to our plants, cars, or computers, see a natural disaster as punishment for human misdeeds, or feel that nature shows design. Indeed, the impulse to find faces in the clouds, knotty wood, and other nonhuman forms and to hear a human presence in unidentified sounds in the night appears universal. Literary critics and art historians find it throughout the arts, where they usually call it personification, and ethnographers and folklorists report it in every culture. It arises spontaneously and is no respecter of training or rationality.[61]

While there is a wide variety of explanations for this anthropomorphizing tendency, the fact that we are inclined to make such attributions makes perfectly good evolutionary sense. Insofar as we regard things that look like us as having inner mental states like our own we are far more likely to generate and sustain sentiments of moral sympathy for our fellow human beings. This tendency will, of course, lead us to falsely attribute intentional states to things which look like us but in fact lack them. However, such false attributions would be a relatively harmless evolutionary by-product. In any case, our tendency to find the neo-Cartesian explanation unbelievable may well have inescapable evolutionary roots of its own.

Still, we must remain mindful of the fact that one need not believe the neo-Cartesian views to be true in order to think that they add up to a successful explanation. One need only believe that our acceptances do not warrant rejection of the view. Neo-Cartesian explanations at least live up to this minimal challenge.

---

[60] See, for example, Harold A. Herzog and Shelley Galvin, 'Common Sense and the Mental Lives of Animals: An Empirical Approach', in Robert W. Mitchell, Nicholas S. Thompson, and H. Lyn Miles (eds.), *Anthropomorphism, Anecdotes, and Animals* (Albany NY: State University of New York Press, 1997).

[61] S. Guthrie, 'Anthropomorphism: A Definition and a Theory', in Mitchell et al. (eds.), *Anthropomorphism*, 53. See also Guthrie's landmark account of anthropomorphism in *Faces in the Clouds* (Oxford: Oxford University Press, 1995).

3

Animal Suffering and the Fall

The earth dries up and withers,
the world languishes and withers,
the exalted of the earth languish.
The earth is defiled by its people;
they have disobeyed the laws,
violated the statutes,
and broken the everlasting covenant.
Therefore a curse consumes the earth;
its people must bear their guilt.

(Isaiah 24: 4–6)

Evolution is also the most inefficient and cruel method for creating man that
could be conceived. If God is a God of love and wisdom and power (as the
Bible teaches), then how could He ever be guilty of devising such a scheme as
evolution? . . . If one wishes to believe in evolution, he is free to make that choice,
but he certainly should not associate a wise, powerful, loving God with such a
monstrous system.

(Henry Morris)

3.1 BIBLICAL AND HISTORICAL BACKGROUND

In formulating attempts to explain evil in the world, theists have typically
distinguished that evil into two broad categories. On the one hand there is moral
evil, that is, evil which is partially caused by creatures exercising their freedom
in a way that renders those creatures blameworthy. On the other hand there
is natural evil. Natural evils are those evils that either do not have creaturely
free acts as part of their causal history or, if they do have such events in their
history, there is no sense in which the creature whose free act is involved
is blameworthy. There is no doubt that some instances of animal pain and
suffering count as moral evils. But it also seems, at least initially, that most
instances of animal pain and suffering fall rather into the category of natural
evil. The vast majority of cases of injury, predation, disease, etc. in the animal

world appear to involve no creaturely free action. In fact, most animal pain and suffering seems to have occurred before any free creatures appeared on the scene at all.

It is interesting to note, then, that most western theists in the last two millennia reflecting on the reality of evil have argued that the cause—at least the remote cause—of all evil in our universe is that most momentous of all moral evils: the Fall of Adam. For many theists, and for almost every major Christian thinker reflecting on evil, the Fall has played a central role in explaining both the origin and persistence of evil in the universe. Although the Fall narrative in Genesis has been interpreted in a variety of ways, all appeals to the Fall which aim to provide an explanation for evil contend that our once innocent world was stricken with a pervasive corruption as a result of the evildoing of creatures with morally significant freedom. Exactly how the Fall leads to that pervasive corruption, how pervasive that resultant corruption became, and why the corruption persists is a matter of substantial disagreement. For some, the primary corrupting effect is experienced by free creatures now beset by struggles against forces (internal and external) that make a life of virtue without divine intervention an impossibility. For others, the tentacles of corruption stretch past the moral arena, reaching into the very fiber of the natural world itself. Tornadoes, hurricanes, disease, blight, drought, and deformity all reflect the corrupting effects of moral wrongdoing.

While some in the western theistic traditions are motivated to adopt this view of evil because they take it to be a divinely revealed truth, others, struck by the pervasive reality of evil generally and human sinfulness specifically, think that the depths of corruption found in the world around us demand an explanation that cannot be captured by simple appeal to the collective wrongdoing of individuals. Something about our world seems more deeply and radically askew—something that can only be explained by a corruption which has eroded the integrity and thwarted the flourishing of the natural order on a cosmic scale.

In this chapter we will look at a variety of attempts to argue that natural evil in general, and animal pain and suffering in particular, can be explained by appeal to forms of creaturely moral evil that yield just such cosmic corruption and degradation. We will examine this CD first not because explanations of this sort are obviously the most plausible or potent available. Rather, we begin here because explanations of evil which accord the Fall a central explanatory role have had such an enduring place in theistic reflection.

While most of the commentary on the Fall and its consequences has focused on its legacy of human guilt and the human proclivity for sin, there is little doubt that the Hebrew and Christian Scriptures provide encouragement to accord even greater explanatory scope to the Fall. In the Fall narrative itself it appears that the author of Genesis intends to signal that the wrongdoing of the initial human pair carried in its wake consequences not only for them and their progeny, but also for their *environment*. In fact, when God issues the curse as it pertains to Adam, the very first line describes the curse in terms of its effect on the natural world;

> Cursed is the ground because of you;
> Through painful toil you will eat of it
> All the days of your life.

(Gen. 3: 17)[1]

Many take this text to speak primarily to the way in which human work is transformed in the wake of the Fall. Prior to the Fall work is, among other things, portrayed as intrinsic to the exercise of the dominion over creation commanded of Adam by God in the opening chapter of Genesis. Tending the garden provides a means for human creatures to express the divine image by becoming, in essence, co-creators with God. And through work human beings were to take joy in this manifestation of divine goodness through human flourishing. After the Fall work still functions in such a way that it permits human beings to participate in the unfolding of creation by exercising their causal powers in creative ways, but this work now becomes *painful* and *toilsome*. Participating in this divine gift would now come at the price of sweat, suffering, and exhaustion.

While the passage undoubtedly has these implications, it is also clear that the curse is directed not simply towards human beings and their activity, but towards the ground *itself*. It is the cursing of the ground that *explains* the fact that work will now be toilsome. The notion that the Fall brings with it a curse which affects the nonmoral natural order is, in fact, found even earlier in the narrative, where the curse is directed toward the deceiving Serpent:

> Cursed are you above all livestock,
> and all the wild animals!
> You will crawl on your belly,
> and you will eat dust,
> all the days of your life.

(Gen. 3: 14)

While this aspect of the curse is directed primarily at the Serpent, the text further indicates that livestock and wild animals are affected as well. The implication of the passage is that the effects of the curse on the Serpent are simply more profound than the curse directed at the rest of the organisms in nature.

Similar references to the 'cursed ground' are found in other texts from the Hebrew Scriptures. Genesis 5: 29 makes direct reference to the effects of the curse on the order of nature:

He named him Noah and said, 'He will comfort us in the labor and painful toil of our hands caused by the ground the LORD has cursed'.

---

[1] All biblical citations are from the New International Version unless otherwise stated.

Furthermore, Isaiah 24: 6, quoted in the epigraph to this chapter, affirms that the cursing of the ground and the corruption of nature is a direct result of moral wrongdoing.

In the Christian Scriptures the fallout from Adam's sin is also claimed to have a direct effect upon the natural world. In the epistle to the Romans Paul extends the scope of the effects of the Fall from the cursed ground and livestock to the entirety of creation. There he writes:

> For the anxious longing of creation waits eagerly for the revealing of the sons of God. For the creation was subjected to futility, not willingly, but because of him who subjected it, in hope that the creation itself also will be set free from its slavery to corruption into the freedom of the glory of the children of God. For we know that the whole creation groans and suffers the pains of childbirth together until now.
>
> (Rom. 8: 19–22)

As we will see below, earlier pseudepigraphical texts claim that the curse is the cause of a wide variety of natural evils, including inclement weather, earthquakes, destructive natural phenomena, the ferocity of animals, and so on. All of these conditions of nature were seen as evil and were attributed to the Fall. Most of these texts appeal to the Fall as an explanation of these evils only to the extent that human creatures are its victims.[2] As a result, premodern theists were not much inclined to apply this reasoning to explain pain and suffering in the nonhuman-animal world. However, in the text from Romans above St Paul focuses on the fact that the Fall has wrought a brokenness or 'futility' in the very structure and function of the natural order as a whole. On this picture, one is led to assume that even if humans were removed from the scene altogether, there would be something about the rest of the natural order that would stand in need of repair and redemption.

Furthermore, Paul builds on a claim, hinted at in Genesis 3, that death itself is the result of the Fall. In that earlier text God tells Adam 'for dust you are, and to dust you will return' (Gen. 3:19), a clause widely understood as providing the explanation for death in humans and in all other organisms as well.[3] While Genesis 3 hints at the notion, the text most often cited in support of the view comes from Romans 5:

> Therefore, just as sin entered the world through one man, and death through sin, and in this way death came to all men, because all sinned—for before the law was given, sin was in the world. But sin is not taken into account when there is no law. Nevertheless, death reigned from the time of Adam to the time of Moses, even over those who did not sin by breaking a command, as did Adam, who was the pattern of the one to come.
>
> (Rom. 5: 13–14)

---

[2] See Norman P. Williams, *The Idea of the Fall and of Original Sin* (London: Longmans, Green, 1927), 157–8.

[3] For more on the history of the doctrine see J. N. D. Kelly, *Early Christian Doctrines* (San Francisco, Calif.: HarperCollins, 1978), chs. 7 and 13.

One could read both the text of Genesis and the text of Romans as implying that human death is an evil and that this evil is the result of the Fall. Such a reading would leave open the question of whether or not the biblical text views nonhuman-animal death as an evil at all. But the texts were not traditionally interpreted in such a way that human- and nonhuman-animal death were regarded differently, and for obvious reasons. Death seems intrinsically evil, since it is contrary to the natural good of the creature which undergoes it. As a result, death, even in the case of nonhuman organisms, is an evil and so could not be part of the originally intended design plan. This theme is echoed in Christian theology through the medieval period. St Thomas Aquinas, for example, argues that all death must be a result of the Fall, since death is the privation of being and as such is contrary to the very nature of a living substance:

But according to this condition it [the body] does not have an aptitude for the form but rather opposition to the form. And indeed any corruption of any natural thing whatsoever is not consistent with the form. For since form is the principle of being, corruption which is the way to non-being, is opposed to it . . . and all defects are contrary to the particular nature of this thing determined by the form[4]

In addition to texts that directly describe the Fall and its consequences, there are numerous prophetic texts in the Hebrew and Christian Scriptures which describe a time of future redemption in the New Heaven and the New Earth when, it seems, death, suffering, and predation are no longer part of the order of nature. In that time,

> The wolf will live with the lamb,
> The leopard will lie down with the goat,
> The calf and the lion and the yearling together;
> And a little child will lead them.
> The cow will feed with the bear,
> Their young will lie down together,
> And the lion will eat straw like the ox.
> The infant will play near the hole of the cobra,
> And the young child put his hand into the viper's nest.
> They will neither harm nor destroy
> On all my holy mountain,
> For the earth will be full of the knowledge of the Lord,
> As the waters cover the sea.

> (Isa. 11: 6–9)

In Revelation the description of the Holy City makes it clear that death and pain have no part of the eternal order,

---

[4] *De Malo*, q. 5 a. 5, from *St Thomas on Evil*, trans. Jean Oesterle (Notre Dame, Ind.: University of Notre Dame Press, 1993).

I saw the Holy City, the new Jerusalem, coming down out of heaven from God, prepared as a bride beautifully dressed for her husband. And I heard a loud voice from the throne saying, 'Now the dwelling of God is with men, and he will live with them. They will be his people, and God himself will be with them and be their God. He will wipe every tear from their eyes. There will be no more death or mourning or crying or pain, for the old order of things has passed away'.

(Rev. 21: 2–4)

These prophetic texts were quite reasonably taken to provide grounds for affirming that pain, suffering, and death were not part of the original design plan either. Since the present reality of pain, suffering, and death requires some further explanation, it seemed quite natural to appeal to the scattered clues offered elsewhere in the text to conclude that these and other natural evils are defects to be explained as manifestations of moral evil, and specifically the moral evil of the Fall.

In addition to these biblical texts, there are sundry pseudepigraphical texts which draw connections between the Fall and animal pain and suffering in striking fashion. The most illuminating of these is found in *The Life of Adam and Eve*. The text, held to be of Jewish origin, was composed between the first century BC and the destruction of the Second Temple in AD 70. Although there are numerous manuscript variants of the text, most of them share in common a narrative account that bears directly on the connection between the Fall and the reality of the subsequent pain, suffering, and death, both in human and nonhuman animals. In the story Adam and Eve have been expelled from the garden and have had their first child, Seth. As a result of the expulsion, they are all now subject to natural decay and disease. At one point Adam, who has become mortally ill, implores Eve and Seth to return to the garden and to plead with God to allow them to take some of the oil from one of the trees of the garden so that Adam might be anointed with it. They agree.

Along the way Seth is attacked by a ferocious beast. The text continues as follows:

Then Seth and Eve went towards paradise, and Eve saw her son, and a wild beast assailing him, and Eve wept and said: 'Woe is me; if I come to the day of the Resurrection, all those who have sinned will curse me saying: Eve hath not kept the commandment of God.' And she spoke to the beast: 'You wicked beast, do you not fear to fight with the image of God? How was your mouth opened? How were your teeth made strong? How did you not call to mind your subjection? For long ago you were made subject to the image of God.' Then the beast cried out and said: 'It is not our concern, Eve, your greed and your wailing, but your own; for (it is) on your account that the rule of the beasts hath arisen. How was your mouth opened to eat of the tree concerning which God commanded you not to eat? For this reason, our nature also has been transformed.'[5]

---

[5] This (modernized) quotation is from the translation of the earliest Greek version in *The Apocrypha and Pseudepigrapha of the Old Testament*, trans. R. H. Charles (Oxford, Clarendon,

On this account, not only is Adam's illness (and subsequent death) explained in terms of the Fall and the expulsion from the garden, so also is the transformation of the animals into predators.

The view that natural evil and corruption are to be attributed to the Fall persisted as the majority position in the Christian tradition into and through the Reformation as well. John Calvin, for example, argued that the totality of nature, nonhuman organisms included, is thwarted from attaining its ends because of the effects of the Fall and the subsequent curse. In his commentary on Romans 8: 20–2 Calvin writes as follows:

Since these creatures lack reason, their will amounts to their natural inclination, according to which the whole of the thing tends to its own nature and perfection; whatever then is held under corruption [from the Fall] suffers violence, nature being unwilling and repugnant. . . . God has given to everything its charge; and he has not only by a distinct order commanded what he wishes to be done, but also implanted inwardly the hope of renovation. For in the sad disorder which followed the fall of Adam, the whole machinery of the world would have instantly become deranged, and all its parts would have failed had not some hidden strength supported them. It is appropriate then for us to consider what a dreadful curse we have deserved, since all created things, both on earth and in the invisible heavens, which are in themselves blameless, undergo punishment for our sins; for it has come about that they are liable to corruption not through their own fault. Thus the condemnation of mankind is imprinted on the heavens, and on the earth, and on all creatures.[6]

All of these views contend that animal pain, suffering, and death are dependent upon the Fall of Adam. This was, of course, a much easier view to accept and defend in the medieval and modern periods, when theists believed that all such pain, suffering, and death occurred *after* the Fall. Yet even as early as the seventeenth century this standard view was regarded with increasing skepticism. Late seventeenth-century philosophers, theologians, and scientists were increasingly doubtful that all living organisms originated at roughly the same time. Puzzled by discoveries of fossils in apparently ancient geological formations, some began to hypothesize that these fossils signaled the existence of organisms which predated human creatures. As a result, the seventeenth century was witness to the rapid proliferation of cosmological hypotheses according to which the physical universe came to have its current contours through a long and slow developmental process. We will have the opportunity to consider these particular hypotheses in more detail in Chapters 5 and 6. But it is worth noting here that the prospect of an old universe developing progressively through

---

1913). It can also be found at <http://www.pseudepigrapha.com/pseudepigrapha/apcmose.htm>, last accessed November 2007.

[6] John Calvin, *Commentary on the Epistle of Paul to the Romans*, trans. John Owen (1849). Taken from the Christian Classics Ethereal Library at <http://www.ccel.org/c/calvin/comment3/commvol38/htm/xii.vi.htm>, last accessed November 2007.

time raised a serious problem for those who aimed to explain pain, suffering, and death in terms of the Fall. If fossil-laden geological formations were very ancient, predating the advent of human beings, then certainly death—and perhaps conscious pain and suffering as well—also preceded the advent of human beings and their Fall. Such conclusions appeared to many to be the undoing of the claim that death, pain, and suffering could be dependent on human misdeeds.

One of the earliest attempts to respond to the difficulty raised by the discovery of these apparently ancient fossils was rather straightforward: simply deny that these apparent fossil formations result from the death of organisms at all. We know that geological processes are capable of producing other deceptive formations: sometimes what we think to be gold turns out to be fool's gold, sometimes what we think to be diamonds turn out to be quartz. Similarly, perhaps unknown geological processes are capable of producing fossil-like formations which mimic or mirror the structure of organisms. Seventeenth-century naturalist John Ray, in his widely read *The Wisdom of God Manifested in the Works of Creation*, argued that these pseudo-fossils were indeed 'Productions of Nature in imitation of Shels and Fishes Bones, and not the Shels and Fishes Bones themselves petrified, as we have sometimes thought'.[7]

However, over the next century and a half most came to see the path of denial as unsustainable. The geological and paleontological evidence made it increasingly clear that the earth was quite ancient, and that it contained animals which died, and entire species which went extinct, long before Adam or any other human being walked the earth. With the publication of Darwin's *Origin of Species* in 1859 things took an even more dramatic turn. Not only did Darwinism acknowledge the reality of pain, suffering, and death prior to the advent of human beings, but pain, suffering, and death came to be seen as among the very instruments of creation itself. Species arise and thrive because they are better adapted to their environments than their natural competitors. Flourishing on the part of one species seemed to mandate suffering and death on the part of another. This was the way of nature from the beginning, and the Fall was impotent to account for it.

We might conclude from this, as many Christians did in the late nineteenth century, that attempting to explain pain, suffering, and death through the Fall is hopeless.[8] But perhaps things are not quite as bleak as the nineteenth-century critics made them out to be. In the remainder of this chapter we will look at ways in which post-Darwinians attempt to defend Fall CDs.

---

[7] John Ray, *The Wisdom of God Manifested in the Works of Creation* (London: 1691; repr. New York: Garland, 1979), 68. For more on seventeenth-century responses to such issues see Peter Bowler, *Evolution: The History of an Idea* (Berkeley, Calif.: University of California Press, 1989), 54.

[8] For a detailed discussion on the changing stance of Christian thinkers on the Fall in the late nineteenth century see Jon H. Roberts, *Darwinism and the Divine in America: Protestant Intellectuals and Organic Evolution, 1859–1900* (Notre Dame, Ind.: Notre Dame Press, 2001), 197 ff.

3.2 FOUR GENERAL PROBLEMS FOR FALL CDS

As noted in Chapter 1, a successful CD will be successful only if one is not warranted in rejecting it given one's warranted acceptances. Because of this, it will be useful to have before us an inventory of serious objections that beset Fall CDs before we get started. If the CDs considered here are not able to handle these objections adequately, we will be warranted in rejecting them. In this section we will look at four general objections that present the most serious hurdles for Fall CDs. In the following sections we will look at how the various proposed Fall CDs fare, especially in light of the first two objections. A full examination of the third and fourth objections would require separate volumes of their own. As a result, I will have a few words to say about them below, and set them aside when considering the specific Fall CDs in subsequent sections.

3.2.1 Objection 1: pre-Adamic pain and suffering

The first objection, noted briefly above, arises from the fact that nonhuman-animal pain and suffering seems to appear before the advent of human beings.[9] Let's call pain and suffering that predates the advent of the first human beings 'pre-Adamic pain and suffering' or 'PAP'. Why exactly is PAP troubling for Fall CDs?

Fall CDs typically involve two claims that are important when thinking about PAP. First, like all successful CDs they must give us reason to think that animal pain and suffering is an evil the permission of which is necessary for the obtaining of a certain outweighing good. Second, these CDs must hold that animal pain and suffering are *consequences of* the Fall. That second claim might appear to be nonnegotiable. But while Fall CDs have typically endorsed it, it is not absolutely necessary that animal pain and suffering be related to the Fall in this way for a Fall CD to succeed. As we will see in more detail later, the relationship between evils and the goods for which they are necessary conditions can be of two sorts. Some evils might be unavoidable *consequences* of states of affairs resulting directly or indirectly from the obtaining of outweighing goods. On this sort of explanation, the Fall gives rise to evil consequences in the same way that creaturely freedom gives rise to moral evil according to typical free-will

---

[9] The last line might be taken to indicate that theists adopting the Fall CD are or should be committed to the claim that a literal Adam would have been of the species *homo sapiens sapiens*. The reader should draw no such inference. If there was a literal Adam and a literal Fall having the sorts of consequences claimed in Fall CDs, Adam might have been one of a number of species of humanoid primate. For discussion of this question the reader should consult a pair of essays in Keith B. Miller (ed.), *Perspectives on an Evolving Creation* (Grand Rapids, Mich.: Eerdmans, 2003); namely, James P. Hurd's 'Hominids in the Garden?' and David Wilcox's 'Finding Adam: The Genetics of Human Origins'.

theodicies. On those theodicies, creaturely freedom is a good thing which is liable to misuse. If creatures in fact misuse it, the result is moral evil of various types. If there is no way to actualize a world with free creatures without permitting some moral evil as well, then one can argue that the goods of free creatures and their moral goodness outweigh the *consequent* evil they spawn.

However, some evils might instead arise out of *antecedent* conditions, the obtaining of which is necessary for securing outweighing goods. Explanations of this general sort are familiar to those acquainted with various types of 'soul-making' theodicies. According to these theodicies God permits certain evil states of affairs to obtain in order to give free creatures an opportunity to make morally significant choices and thereby cultivate virtues that otherwise could not be cultivated. The evil (antecedent) conditions do not arise as a result of the obtaining of some outweighing good, but rather as a precondition for the obtaining of that outweighing good.

Similarly, Fall CDs can come in consequent and antecedent varieties. Traditional Fall CDs contend that Adam and Eve freely committed acts of moral evil which resulted in *consequent* moral and natural evil. On these views PAP is a problem, since it occurs prior to the Fall and leaves one to puzzle over how these consequent evils could predate the events of which they are consequences. Consequent Fall CDs must explain how PAP and the Fall could possibly be related in this way. Antecedent Fall CDs can avoid this problem by arguing that PAP obtains in order to make possible conditions which allow for some other goods to obtain. We will look at one attempt to frame Fall CDs in this way in Section 3.3. However, antecedent Fall CDs will confront a couple of serious obstacles. First, it is hard to see what sort of good there could be which is such that PAP (or at least the permission of PAP) would be a necessary condition for its obtaining. Second, even if we can identify such a good, the defender of a Fall CD will have to show that the connection between PAP and the outweighing good is related to the Fall in a way that is not simply tangential. For example, if someone were to make the case that PAP was somehow a necessary condition for the emergence of creatures with powers to make morally significant free choices, and that the emergence of such creatures made possible (or even inevitable) the Fall, there would be no sense in which the Fall *explains* PAP. Rather, such an explanation would be a version of the free-will theodicy where the good of creaturely free choice would explain the antecedent evil of PAP *and* the consequent evil of the Fall. Thus, antecedent Fall CDs will bear the burden of showing how the Fall explains the antecedent condition of PAP, a condition which makes possible some greater good.

3.2.2 Objection 2: fragility

The second objection facing Fall CDs is one we might call the 'Fragility Objection'. Fall CDs typically posit an initial act of moral evil that explains the reality of natural evil, including animal pain and death. On these views, as we have seen, the Fall has certain natural consequences which include not only human corruption, but the distortion of the physical cosmos. As a result, natural evil is ultimately rooted in moral evil. But closer inspection reveals that something more is required here. In order for moral wrongdoing to leave such catastrophic consequences in its wake it must be the case that God created things so that the integrity of the natural order was, in some important sense, initially *dependent upon* the integrity of the moral order. And this fact itself stands in need of some sort of explanation. If God were omniscient, he would surely know that the natural order was fragile in this way. Unless there is some reason why the fragility of nature is necessary, or why making it fragile in this way makes possible certain outweighing goods, the fragility of nature itself seems to be a puzzling defect in creation.

This is a serious challenge for Fall CDs, whether they endorse the reality of PAP or not. What possible good reason could there be for creating the universe in such a way that the Fall of the first human pair could bring about a rewiring of brute nervous systems, thereby allowing for the possibility of pain and suffering? No easy answers jump readily to mind. As C. E. M. Joad quipped in reply to C. S. Lewis's defense of a Fall CD:

It is hard to suppose that the caterpillar feels no pain when slowly consumed; harder still to ascribe pain to moral corruption; hardest of all to conceive how such an arrangement [the explanation of pain in terms of Adam's moral corruption] could have been planned by an all-good and all-wise Creator.[10]

One might think that a similar objection could be lodged against all of the consequences that traditionalists take to come from the Fall, including the human proclivity towards sin. But notice that most such purported consequences directly concern human beings and are explained either as direct results of continued human sinfulness, or as divine punishments of human beings for their sinfulness. Neither mode of explanation can be employed to explain the reality of animal pain and death.

3.2.3 Objection 3: Paradisiacal Motivation Argument

In addition to worries about the extent to which Fall CDs can genuinely explain the existence of evil, especially natural evil, a number of critics have argued that there is something incoherent about the very idea of the Fall itself. According to the traditional conception of the Fall, the initial human pair fell from a paradisiacal state in which they were free and rational, enjoying the beatific vision

---

[10] C. E. M. Joad and C. S. Lewis, 'The Pains of Animals: A Problem in Theology', *Month*, 189 (1950), 95–104, repr. in Andrew Linzey and Tom Regan (eds.), *Animals and Christianity: A Book of Readings* (New York: Crossroads, 1989), 59.

and possessing everything a rational creature could want. Yet, despite being in this ideal condition, Adam chose to pursue what he knew to be objectively evil. Under such conditions, how could Adam coherently desire that which he knew was evil, especially knowing that choosing to do evil would dislodge him from his paradisiacal state?

We can put the objection in the form of an argument, the conclusion of which is that the choice by Adam to do something objectively wrong could not occur. If such an argument could be constructed from premises that we could not reject in light of our reasonable acceptances, Fall CDs of this sort would fail to meet the minimal standards of acceptability set out in Chapter 1. The Paradisiacal Motivation Argument formalizes the worry.

(1) If the first humans were rational and free and furthermore experienced union with God in the beatific vision, they would have everything such creatures could want and would thus be fully content.
(2) If the first humans had everything such creatures could want and were fully content, they would not have any motivation to do anything bad.
(3) If the first humans were not motivated to do anything bad, they would not do anything bad.
(4) Thus, if the first humans were rational and free and experienced union with God, they would not do anything bad.[11]

This objection against the coherence of the Fall is not new, of course, having been treated by nearly every major western theological figure. As a result, a full treatment of it exceeds the scope of this book. I will offer a few remarks on this objection here, which will have to suffice for my purposes in this chapter.

First, it is worth noting that defenders of Fall CDs need not hold that the first creatures capable of morally significant free choice enjoyed a condition of complete satisfaction and perfection, fully experiencing the beatific vision. Minimally, consequent Fall CDs need only hold that the cosmos has the sort of fragility described above and that some creatures with morally significant freedom at some point chose to commit moral evil. As long as those two conditions are satisfied, natural evil will have an explanation in terms of the wrongdoing of those free creatures. Antecedent Fall CDs similarly need only show that there is a connection between PAP—which makes possible some outweighing good—and the occurrence of the Fall. In either case Fall CDs need not be committed to the existence of Adam and Eve, nor a garden paradise.

However, defenders of Fall CDs who want to retain traditional claims concerning the initial paradisiacal state of the first human pair will need to address the Paradisiacal Motivation Argument. Both Premises (2) and (3) are vulnerable. A good deal of recent critical attention has been focused on Premise (3). The premise was famously defended in a pair of seminal essays by Peter van

---

[11] I thank Daniel Howard-Snyder for pressing this objection against Fall CDs.

Inwagen,[12] in which he argues that it is not possible for agents to freely perform actions towards which they have no pro attitude. What, van Inwagen asks, could an agent appeal to that would or could possibly justify the choice of an action of this sort? Such an agent would have to admit that while she had no reason or motivation to pursue a particular course of action, it was intentionally chosen nonetheless. Yet such explanations really amount to no explanation at all.

I have elsewhere defended a similar line of argument, though I now regard the view as problematic.[13] There are a number of ways to attempt to undermine the claim that it is impossible for us to perform actions towards which we have no pro attitudes. The most problematic cases for principles like van Inwagen's are those in which we regard agents as responsible for unreflective omissions. Standard cases of moral responsibility involve instances in which agents intentionally commit or omit particular actions. In those cases agents act on pro attitudes that lead them to perform or fail to perform an action. However, it is also true that we hold individuals responsible in some cases when they fail to perform an action in ways that are entirely unintentional or nonreflective. If I promise to drive you to an important meeting but fail to show up, you will want an explanation. Imagine my explanation is that I simply forgot. Does the explanation excuse me from responsibility? Typically not. You would be likely to treat me with indignation and let me know in no uncertain terms that I *should not have forgotten something so important*. But if van Inwagen is right, such indignation is misplaced, since, if the principle in question here is true, it would be impossible for me to have done anything other than fail to pick you up. In this case picking you up was impossible, since one of the necessary conditions of doing so was not met: I had no pro attitude concerning picking you up for the interview because I forgot the entire matter. Since picking you up was impossible, I cannot rightly be held responsible for failing to do so. Thus, your indignation is unwarranted.

Surely something is wrong here. And it is reasonable to suppose that what has gone wrong is the principle in question—the one needed in order to make Premise (3) plausible. If I can be held responsible for my unintentional omission (not picking you up), and being responsible for the omission entails that it was possible for me to do something other than omit this action (that is, to pick you up), then it was possible for me to pick you up. But since that is possible despite the absence of a pro attitude towards doing so, such pro attitudes cannot be necessary conditions for acting. If the reasoning is sound, Premise (3) is false. If it isn't, defenders of Premise (3) owe us an account of how we can be responsible for unintentional omissions.

---

[12] P. van Inwagen, 'When is the Will Free?', *Philosophical Perspectives*, 3 (1989), 399–422; 'When the Will is Not Free', *Philosophical Studies*, 75 (1994), 95–113.

[13] Michael Murray and David Dudrick, 'Are Coerced Acts Free?' *American Philosophical Quarterly*, 32 (April 1995), 147–61.

There are two ways in which defenders of Premise (3) might respond. The first is to argue that, despite common practice, we are not responsible for cases of unintentional omission. This response is implausible. The second response is to argue for responsibility for unintentional omissions not because they were avoidable at the moment they occurred (i.e. at the moment at which I was to have acted but failed to), but rather because of some prior omission or commission that was motivated and thus intentional. So perhaps I am responsible for failing to pick you up because when I thought to write myself a reminder to do so, I intentionally decided to rely on my memory (memory which I know to be quite faulty). On this scenario my unintentional omission is not free (and perhaps not culpable either). Yet I am nonetheless culpable for the prior intentional action which led to (or perhaps made inevitable) my subsequent unintentional omission. This response is more plausible, but still problematic. The problem is this: even in cases where we are unable to trace my unintentional omission to some prior intentional act, we still regard the omission as culpable. If, for example, you ask me why I forgot to pick you up and I tell you that I thought to write myself a reminder but then *forgot to do that*, it seems that I am nonetheless responsible for my failures, even though we have still not traced my omissions (the failure to pick you up and the failure to write the note) to any prior intentional act. As a result, I am culpable for the omission even though the explanation for my failure still involves no appeal to a prior intentional act or omission. So, Premise (3) and the principles that might be offered in its defense are problematic at best.

Premise (2) has historically been the most disputed premise in the argument. Abrahamic-theist thinkers have largely held that free and rational creatures can knowingly cultivate and act on pro attitudes for courses of action that are evil. The traditional Abrahamic-theist account of the Fall holds that the sin of Adam resulted from a form of pride according to which Adam wanted to be 'like God'.[14] Is it possible for creatures in the paradisiacal state to fall prey to a sin of pride of this sort? Many Abrahamic theists have argued that it is.

One reason for this is simply that there is nothing about satisfaction concerning one's current condition that entails that one would not find another condition to be even more enriching or satisfying. We can take ourselves to be fully satisfied, while recognizing that our full satisfaction falls short of maximal satisfaction. As a result, paradisiacal Adam could regard himself as fully satisfied while still regarding some other condition, equality with God perhaps, as even more satisfying. Recently, Alvin Plantinga has speculated that such a sin is not only possible but likely if the free creatures in question are created in the image of God. Plantinga reasons as follows:

Perhaps a high probability of such a fall attaches to free creatures (creatures with an area of autonomy) who are created in the image of God. God sets out to create beings in his

---

[14] This position is drawn from Gen. 3: 5.

own image: they resemble him in having will and intellect, and they recognize the lustrous beauty, glory, and desirability of God's position. God is himself the center of the universe; his creatures see the splendor and wonderful desirability of that condition. Perhaps, insofar as one is free, and sees the glory of this position and its enormous desirability, there is a powerful tendency to desire it for oneself. Perhaps there is a high probability that beings created in the image of God will also wind up resembling him in this: that they want to see and do see themselves as the center of the universe. Perhaps a substantial probability of falling into this condition is built into the very nature of free creatures who have knowledge of God's glorious status and do see it as indeed glorious and desirable. There are possible worlds in which there are free creatures with that kind of knowledge and affection who don't fall into this condition of sin, but perhaps these worlds form only a small proportion of the space of the totality of possible worlds containing free creatures. Fall isn't inevitable or necessary; nevertheless, perhaps its objective probability is very high.[15]

A complete discussion of the merits of Plantinga's views and similar views in the Abrahamic traditions extends beyond the scope of this chapter. It is worth noting, however, that responses like Plantinga's highlight the fact that there are a number of ways in which Premise (2) might be successfully challenged.[16]

3.2.4 Objection 4: Fall CDs and the value of creaturely freedom

Finally, most Fall CDs assume that the outweighing good which makes possible the permission of animal pain and suffering. Initially this assumption might appear uncontroversial. We highly value morally significant free action in ourselves and others. Indeed, most of what we take to be of greatest value in human existence revolves around our ability to engage in such action and to be the objects of such actions by others. As a result, permitted evils that are tied to the obtaining of such freedom are often taken to be explained by that freedom. But such explanations have limits. After all, as good as such freedom might be, it is not great enough to outweigh the permission of any and every evil we can imagine. Surely some level of permitted evil would be so great that the value of morally significant creaturely freedom would not outweigh it. If the price for morally significant free creatures involved permitting those creatures to live lives that were perpetually and unrelentingly filled with pain, misery, and devastation, the price would be too high; the good of creaturely freedom would not be outweighing, but would rather be outweighed. As a result, Fall CDs that make appeal to creaturely freedom as an outweighing good will need to defend the claim that such freedom is sufficient to outweigh the permission of the pain and suffering of animals throughout millions of years and trillions of generations.

---

[15] A. Plantinga, *Warranted Christian Belief* (Oxford: Oxford University Press, 2000), 212–13.
[16] A historical survey of challenges to Premise (2) is given in Williams, *The Idea of the Fall and of Original Sin.*

As I noted above, I will not specifically take up this objection in the remainder of this chapter. We will have opportunity to return to the question of the extent of the goodness of creaturely freedom in Section 4.1 and Section 5.1.2. We will also to have the opportunity to revisit the question of the badness of animal pain and suffering in Chapter 7. It will suffice for now that a complete defense of a Fall CD that appeals to the goodness of creaturely freedom will have to speak to this question.

We will now leave behind objections (3) and (4) and turn to a variety of Fall CDs which aim to explain animal pain and suffering in ways that bypass the first two objections noted above.

3.3 CONTEMPORARY FALL CDS: PAP DENIERS

One way for Fall CDs to avoid the problem of PAP is simply to deny its reality altogether. This was the most common form of Fall CD prior to the seventeenth century, since the most frequently endorsed cosmology had it that human and nonhuman animals were created together in the garden of Eden. By their lights, natural evil was strictly a postlapsarian phenomenon. As noted earlier, confidence in this view began to fade as early naturalists discovered apparently ancient geological formations containing numerous fossils of organisms. Yet, in spite of the evidence, some continued to defend the traditional Fall CD through the eighteenth century and right up to the present by denying the reality of PAP. We will look at two representatives of this view here.

The most radical flat deniers of PAP argue, contrary to the academic consensus, that the scientific, theological, and philosophical evidence taken together undercuts the very possibility of PAP. On this view, the totality of the evidence instead points to the existence of a universe only six to ten thousand years old, with organisms from each major phylum coming to exist all within a short period of time (less than three days to be exact) at the beginning of cosmic history. For these radical flat deniers the evidence available to us speaks with one voice, and that voice favors rejecting the reality of PAP. Less radical flat deniers argue that the scientific evidence, taken in isolation, suggests the reality of PAP, but the philosophical and theological considerations make it more reasonable to view that scientific evidence as misleading.

The reader might think that there is not much use in discussing views of this sort. After all, if we are looking for CDs that pass the sort of test set out at the end of Chapter 1, how can we take seriously a CD that hypothesizes that the universe and members of all the major phyla were created together no more than ten thousand years ago? Let me answer that question by reminding the skeptical reader that there are in fact *millions* of contemporary Abrahamic theists who are among the flat deniers. Those of us who disagree with their views on cosmology can do one of two things. First, we can choose simply to ignore them. If they can't get on board with the deliverances of contemporary science, one might say, then why bother with them? One reason to bother with them is that we are here discussing an argument, the evidential argument from evil, which is oftentimes aimed at those very Abrahamic theists. If they have beliefs which will make it more reasonable for them to reject than accept crucial premises in that argument, it is worth thinking about those beliefs and determining whether or not they pass muster. Perhaps we will, after thinking about those beliefs, discover that even if we grant these flat deniers their nonstandard cosmological and biological beliefs, there is something else about their view—something other than its awkward fit with contemporary science—that undermines it as an explanation for evil generally, or the evil of animal pain and suffering in particular. Thus, the second thing we might do with these flat deniers is engage them in reasoned dialogue, help them think carefully about their beliefs with charity, and see where the arguments lead. That is what philosophy is about. There is no cause to turn from that to ridicule or *ad hominem* here.

Our first and more radical species of flat deniers consists primarily of theologically conservative Christians and Jews who are unwilling to accept the broad outlines of Darwinism, choosing rather to stick with the predominant pre-nineteenth-century view that the universe is relatively young, and that all of the phyla were created within a three-day span at the beginning of cosmic history. The majority of those who hold such a view do so because they are persuaded that the Bible is divinely revealed, and that the biblical texts treat the creation narrative in Genesis as an account of actual cosmic history. Some point to the Genesis narrative itself, arguing that the view is warranted in light of the fact that the creation is described as having occurred in 'six days'. Some further point out in both the Hebrew and Christian Scriptures genealogies of figures whom we believe to be historical, Jesus of Nazareth for example, which include Adam among the list of ancestors. There are other resources internal to the text itself which signal that the Bible means to affirm that a fully-formed cosmos was created over the course of six days, sometime within the last ten thousand years.

Defenders of this view are not, however, merely motivated by the biblical creation narratives. Many advocates for this view go to great, though often quite unconvincing, lengths to make astrophysical and geological arguments for the view. In addition, these 'young-universe creationists' rely on philosophical motivations, one of which is especially relevant for our purposes. Consider, for example, these remarks from one of the most vocal young-universe creationists in the last fifty years, Henry Morris:

Perhaps the most serious problem (with the Darwinian picture) is theological. If we accept the geological ages at all, in effect we are saying that God used the methods and processes which exist in the present world to finally bring into the world the goal and culmination of His creative activity—man. This means, therefore, that at least a billion years of struggle, suffering, disorder, disease, storm, convulsions of all kinds, and, above all, death troubled the world before man ever entered the world and before any sin appeared in the world.

The Bible, on the other hand, teaches quite emphatically that there was no suffering or death in the world until after sin came in. Romans 5: 12 declares, 'Wherefore, as by one man sin entered into the world, and death by sin; and so death passed upon all men, for that all have sinned.'

Death by sin—there was no death in the world until sin was introduced. The present groaning, struggling creation of which we read in Romans dates Biblically from the time of the great curse God put on creation because of Adam's sin. So the whole creation now is under the bondage of corruption and decay and death because of man's sin. But if the concept of the geological ages is correct, there were geological ages and over a billion years of death in the world before any sin entered the world. Therefore, God must have used the principle of decay, suffering, and disorder. This is not the God revealed in the Bible—a merciful God, a gracious God, a God of order and power, not a God of confusion, random change and chance.[17]

Morris and other 'young-universe creationists' acknowledge the tension, using it to mount an argument not against theism, but against old-universe Darwinism. Given the conception of God they endorse, the sort of animal pain and death required by Darwinism is just not possible.

How does this more radical Fall CD accompanied by the flat denial of PAP fare? It is clear that the weight of empirical evidence available to us gives us overwhelming justification for rejecting any explanation of evil that trades on rejecting PAP. For that reason, this CD will not pass muster for most. Nonetheless, those young-universe creationists who also accept the Fall and who, given the information available to them, are warranted in rejecting the reality of PAP, are in a different position.[18] These theists might have a Fall CD which avoids the objection arising from PAP. For them, PAP is not a problem.

One can take a stance somewhat less extreme than the one endorsed by radical flat deniers (i.e. young-universe creationists). One could hold, for example, that the empirical evidence does, taken in isolation, strongly support the truth of Darwinism and reality of PAP. But in light of the theological problems raised by PAP—that is, tensions with the Genesis creation narrative or the problem of animal pain—one should discount substantially the weight of this empirical evidence. Defenses of this view date back at least as far as 1857 to Philip Gosse and his notorious and much lampooned work *Omphalos*.

Gosse is commonly ridiculed for his purported endorsement of the view that the entire fossil record was an elaborately planned ruse, set up by God to test the faith of strident scientists. In fact, Gosse makes no commitment himself on either the issue of the age of the universe or PAP in his work. Instead he

---

[17] Henry M. Morris, 'The Day-Age Theory', in Kelly L. Segraves (ed.), *And God Created* (San Diego, Calif.: Creation-Science Research Center, 1973), 72–3.

[18] For readers who endorse this young-universe-creationist position I highly recommend two treatments of the view by authors who have theological commitments that are otherwise the same as those of typical young-earth creationists: Davis A. Young, *Christianity and the Age of the Earth* (Grand Rapids, Mich.: Zondervan, 1982); Pattle Pun, *Evolution: Nature and Scripture in Conflict?* (Grand Rapids, Mich.: Zondervan, 1982).

highlights the fact that theists who accept the doctrine of divine creation are required to make certain theory-laden judgments about when *apparently* ancient natural objects, structures, and events are genuinely ancient and when they are not. Gosse argues that whenever a theist encounters a natural object he or she must decide whether to attribute its origins to the 'law of nature' or the 'law of creation'. If God sometimes directly creates things ('the law of creation') which can also arise by slow, natural processes ('the law of nature'), theists will need to be sensitive to the possibility that what appears to be a purely natural phenomenon is in fact an artifact of direct creation. If God were to create a mature tree, the tree would have a number of characteristics which typically signal a long developmental trajectory: full-grown leaves, roots, rings, etc. Upon encountering such a tree we would naturally assume that it came into existence through long, slow, law-governed processes. But since there is no direct empirical way to distinguish between complexity arising from ordinary law-like processes and instantaneous, divine creative processes, there will be no way to draw the line between cases of genuine evidence of age and merely apparent evidence of age, based on empirical data alone. How we ought to interpret the empirical evidence in such cases will have to be decided on more programmatic grounds. Gosse writes:

Admit for a moment, as a hypothesis, that the Creator had before his mind a projection of the whole life-history of the globe, commencing with any point which the geologist may imagine to have been a fit commencing point, and ending with some unimaginable acme in the indefinitely distant future. He determines to call this idea in to actual existence, not at the supposed commencing point, but at some stage or other of its course. It is clear, then, that at the selected stage it appears, exactly as it would have appeared at that moment of its history, if all the preceding eras of history had been real.... Let us suppose that this present year 1857 had been the particular epoch . . . which the Creator selected as the era of its actual beginning. . . . There would be cities filled with swarms of men; there would be houses half-built; castles fallen into ruins . . . These and other traces of the past would be found, *because they are found now*; [the world] . . . certainly would have presented all these phenomena; not to puzzle the philosopher, but because they are inseparable from the condition of the world at the selected moment[19]

In light of this, the theist is forced to acknowledge that apparent signs of age do not require us to take any particular stance on their veracity; it is an open question whether or not some of those signs of age are merely apparent. Thus, if there are good theological or philosophical reasons for denying PAP, then we have good reasons for rejecting the evidence which supports the claim that organisms predate the appearance of human beings.

One could endorse this view in an attempt to rescue a Fall CD from the problem of PAP. But the view faces a formidable difficulty. Popular accounts of Gosse's view represent him as holding that God puts evidence of age into

[19] Philip Gosse, *Omphalos: An Attempt to Untie the Geological Knot* (London: Voorst, 1857; repr. Woodbridge, Conn.: Ox Bow, 1998), 352–3.

our universe in order to deceive us or test our faith in revelation. As we have seen, this is not his view at all. Gosse thinks that apparent signs of age are an unavoidable by-product of divine creative activity, and that when we get clear on our theoretical commitments there will be nothing deceptive about the empirical data at all. Nothing in his view implies, he would claim, the objectionable opinion that God is a deceiver. However, it is not clear that Gosse can dodge the deception charge so easily. Imagine for a moment that the young-universe position is true. Further, imagine that an archeologist were to find the fossilized remains of Adam. Let's not worry in this example how the remains might be identified as Adam's remains. Would Adam's fossilized remains show misleading apparent signs of age? For example, would the skull fossil show the ossified fissures that are found in typical human skulls (i.e. those portions of cartilage which hold together the plates of the infant skull and ossify during maturation)? It doesn't seem that we have good a priori reasons for coming down either way on this question. It is true that the skull of a neonate has these cartilage fissures in order to allow compression of the skull as it passes through the birth canal (the ossification occurring later to afford the brain greater protection from injury). There is thus no reason why Adam's skull would *need* to have such complexity since *he* never passed through any birth canal. But it is also true that these fissures are structures *typical* of all human skulls. As a result, for God to create Adam's skull with such fissures wouldn't be *deceptive*. God simply elected to create Adam with or as a typical human body.

Things are quite different, however, when we consider, for example, the fossil-rich sandstone formations at Medicine Rocks State Park in Montana. It is much harder to see how the Gosse-type flat denier can dodge the charge of deception in cases like this. Sandstone does not *typically* contain such fossils. Nothing about the formation of natural sandstone implies or requires that fossil formations be found in them. So what necessitates or accounts for these misleading apparent signs of age? It is hard to escape the impression that such formations could only be the work of a creator that is a trickster or a deceiver.

Furthermore, both radical and less radical flat deniers fail to escape the second main objection for Fall CDs; namely, the Fragility Objection. There are at least two facets of the problem that are relevant. First, how could it be the case that the moral sin of Adam could yield the result that animals become subject to pain, suffering, and death? What transformation *could* animals undergo? Are animals originally unable to experience pain, only coming to have this capacity after the Fall? Or is it that they are originally able to avoid any type of injury but subsequently lose that ability? Even if either of these scenarios were credible—and they're not—we are still left with an even more nagging question: Why? It seems incredible that a perfectly good, omnipotent, and omniscient being couldn't set up the universe in such a way as to make this result avoidable? Any defender of the flat-denial positions owes us answers to these two questions, and none seem likely to be forthcoming.

The Gosse-type flat denier might claim, of course, that all of these puzzling and seemingly inexplicable facts do admit of a perfectly good explanation. Perhaps God's creating the deceptive fossils or permitting nature's fragility is necessary for bringing about certain overriding goods which require them.[20] Let's grant that if there are such goods, it is far from obvious what those might be.[21] Do we know that such deception does not in fact make possible certain overriding goods? We do not, and this is so for the same reason that we do not know that there are no outweighing goods to be had in the permission of apparently pointless evils; noseeum inferences are no better in this case than they were when we were trying to make out the evidential argument from evil in Chapter 1. Thus, our inability to fully explain away these puzzling facts does not itself undermine the possible truth of these CDs.

The defender of this CD is correct in noting that these worries do not serve to undermine the truth of the CD. However, this fact is not sufficient to vindicate the view. In Chapter 1 we saw that a successful CD will consist of hypotheses (a) which show how certain permitted evils might be necessary for securing outweighing goods, and (b) which one is not justified or warranted in rejecting in light of the claims one reasonably accepts. Flat-denier Fall CDs which are beset with all of these perfectly sensible and yet unanswered questions simply do not satisfy the first condition. The inability to answer these questions means that such CDs cannot, after all, 'show how certain permitted evils might be necessary for securing outweighing goods'. The defender of this CD has not shown that, nor even given a suggestion as to how it might be so. Radical flat-denier CDs thus fail in the absence of further defense.

3.4 CONTEMPORARY DEFENSES: PRECURSIVE CONDITIONS

Since most are convinced by the empirical evidence of the reality of PAP, few will be attracted to CDs that reject it. Marguerite Shuster, for example, remarks:

The evidence virtually compels assent to the assumption that death and the suffering that goes with it have been a reality since the beginning of the drama of life in this world. Nature has always been red in tooth and claw—sometimes in fantastically brutal ways that mock the very thought of a loving or even benign divine hand designing it thus.[22]

[20] In Chapter 5 I will consider further those conditions under which it would be permissible for God to constitute the cosmos so as to deceive us in certain respects.

[21] In Chapter 6 we will look at a view endorsed by Kenneth Miller and Michael Covey which attempts to argue that there are just such greater goods.

[22] M. Shuster, *The Fall and Sin: What We Have Become as Sinners* (Grand Rapids, Mich.: Eerdmans, 2003), 74.

However, Shuster argues, we might think about PAP and other 'pre-Adamic natural evils' not as evil consequences of Adam's Fall, but rather as conditions which obtained before the Fall but which were not, in those circumstances, evil. Thorns and thistles might have been a reality before the Fall, but they were not natural evils, since they did not serve, for example, to make agricultural production toilsome. For toilsome production to become a reality, human beings had to appear on the scene. Shuster thinks that in certain respects such conditions would be analogous to conditions that constituted the plagues that God visited on the Egyptians before the Hebrew Exodus. In at least some cases the plagues consisted of conditions that were, in themselves, benign or neutral; they constituted natural evils only when they were permitted to become 'intensified' and placed into a special context. There is nothing intrinsically evil about frogs or gnats. But a large number of frogs or gnats in a highly populated area is another story. On Shuster's view the 'intensification' occurs, or is allowed to occur, because humanity is benefited by enduring reminders of the degenerate condition of a world rife with sinfulness, or perhaps because such an occurrence constitutes an appropriate punishment for sinfulness. Alternatively, or perhaps in addition, the defender of this view might hold that natural evils of this sort are required in order to allow postlapsarian human beings to engage in soul-making, or to move human beings to realize how badly off they are in a world of sin where they are in many respects separated from God.

Views of this sort, as discussed earlier, depend on the claim that natural evils, including animal pain and suffering, do not arise as a consequence of moral evil, but rather as antecedent 'precursive conditions' necessary for some outweighing good. In this specific instance the claim is not that PAP is directly necessary in order for Adam to be able to exercise his freedom, and thus to sin. Rather, the claim would be that a universe which contains morally free creatures must also contain mechanisms that allow for correction and punishment of these creatures if and when their behavior transgresses certain moral boundaries. These natural conditions that preexist Adam would be among the necessary conditions for the operation of such mechanisms.

CDs like this might be able to account for some natural evil in terms of pre-Fall conditions that subsequently become intensified or wayward after the Fall. Perhaps pre-Fall thunderstorms never caused high winds or never led to the deaths of animals until after the Fall. However, what is at issue here is animal pain and suffering. Even if animal pain and suffering were 'less intense' before the Fall, this would not disqualify those states from counting as evil. The prelapsarian 'lower intensity' is just not relevant.

More relevant would be the position defended by a variety of Christian thinkers according to which God, in his foreknowledge, chose to prepare in advance a world with genuine evil and pain and suffering in anticipation of the fact that it would be the dwelling of fallen humanity. Emil Brunner, for one, argued that God, foreknowing the future Fall of humanity, would have created a natural environment suitable to humanity's future condition:

If then God knew beforehand that the Fall of man would take place, should not His creation of the world have taken *this* sort of man into account? Is it unallowable to think that the Creator has created the world in such a way that it corresponds with sinful man? Is not a world in which, from the very beginning, from the first emergence of living creatures, there has been a struggle for existence, with all its suffering and its 'cruelty,' an arena suitable for sinful man? We cannot assert that this is so; still less have we any reason to say that this is not so.[23]

Similar proposals have a long line of defenders among Greek Fathers of the Christian Church. Origen proposed a view, later developed by Gregory of Nyssa (in the fourth century), which runs along similar lines.[24] On this view fallen human beings were fated to be cursed with toilsome work in a creation which would not be immediately subject to their will. Such a natural environment would have to 'push back' against human initiative and require human beings to employ their rational powers fully to control it. Thus, for example, Gregory goes to great lengths to argue that God outfitted nonhuman animals with all sorts of offensive and defensive capabilities so that humans, who lacked them, would later be compelled to harness them for distinctively human ends. Birds have talons, bees have a sting, dogs have a strong bite, sheep have wool. These animals were part of the creation before human beings came on the scene, so that their various capacities, some of which would be used for survival and predation before human beings appeared, could be employed by humans when these animals were ultimately domesticated.

Not only did creating in this way force human beings to exercise dominion in toilsome fashion, it also allowed them to use their rational powers to subdue the brute forces of nature. Thus, having a natural environment which included pain, predation, and death served both to help human beings secure their good and to allow them to experience the punishment that the Fall carried with it.[25]

Above we noted that CDs of this sort explain the reality of evil not as a *consequence* of moral evil but rather as among the necessary antecedent conditions for a universe which provides morally appropriate conditions for postlapsarian free creatures. In this derivative sense the Fall necessitates that these antecedent conditions obtain. This view has the advantage of being able to avoid both of the

---

[23] E. Brunner, *The Christian Doctrine of Creation and Redemption*, trans. Olive Wyon (Philadelphia, Pa.: Westminster, 1950), 131.

[24] The view can be found in Origen's *Contra Celsum*, bk. 4, chs. 75 ff. The later discussion in Gregory of Nyssa is found centrally in *On the Making of Man*, ch. 7.

[25] In addition, Origen and a number of other early Christian theologians held that one result of the Fall and the cursing of humanity was that human beings, formerly immaterial spirits, became embodied creatures. A natural environment which allowed for pain, suffering, predation, and death further allowed embodied humanity to experience the natural consequences of its new, fallen condition. These views will be discussed in more detail in Section 3.5.

criticisms that afflict flat-denial views, since it need not deny the reality of PAP nor explain how the Fall could have natural evils among its causal consequences. This makes such views much more attractive.

Unfortunately, these advantages come at the price of making these CDs implausible for another reason. Fall CDs characteristically tie the reality of natural evil to creaturely freedom. Whether viewed as a consequence or an antecedent necessary condition, the goodness of (or derived from) creaturely freedom both requires and outweighs permission of the evils in question. Once we see this, however, it is clear that animal pain and suffering that is supposed to be explained by creaturely freedom is totally avoidable on these views, since nothing on these 'precursive conditions' views requires that the universe exist *before* human beings do. In other words, the view, as described, offers us no satisfying answers to the following questions: Why must the world have a natural history that precedes the existence of Adam at all? Wouldn't God secure all the relevant goods and avoid a massive array of evil simply by creating the universe in much the way the young-universe creationist believes it was created? If God were to so create it, none of the goods supposed to arise from animal pain and suffering would be lost, and a great deal of natural evil would have been eliminated.

It is open, at this point, for the defender of the Precursive Conditions CD to argue that there are independent explanations for the fact that the universe has a long history that predates the arrival of beings with morally significant freedom. In Chapters 4 through 6 we will examine a number of such proposals. Nonetheless, to adopt such independent explanations would amount to giving an entirely different sort of explanation for animal pain and suffering, or at least that portion of animal pain and suffering which precedes the Fall. There must be *some other* goods which justify God permitting that evil. Insofar as that is the case, the explanation we have is no longer properly characterized as a 'Fall CD' at all. Precursive Conditions CDs thus fail to provide an explanation for animal pain and suffering.

3.5 CONTEMPORARY DEFENSES: SATAN AND HIS COHORTS

For those who find the empirical evidence for an old universe compelling, and who cannot explain the existence of evil before the Fall of the first human pair, the only remaining option is to relegate the Fall to an event that occurred some time before the first human pair appeared on the scene. The most straightforward way to defend such a view while still drawing on resources intrinsic to the major western theistic traditions is to suppose that there are nonhuman free creatures which experienced a Fall prior to the Fall of Adam. Perhaps animal pain and suffering is to be explained not by the Fall of Adam, but by the Fall of Satan.

Christian theologians traditionally point to two texts in the Hebrew Scriptures as describing the Fall of Satan. Both texts have been understood to characterize Satan as a highly exalted angelic being who, through an act of pride, chose to rebel against God and was thereafter cast out from his position of power and authority. The two texts, from Isaiah 14 and Ezekiel 28, read as follows:

> How you have fallen from heaven,
> O morning star, son of the dawn!
> You have been cast down to the earth,
> you who once laid low the nations!
> You said in your heart,
> 'I will ascend to heaven;
> I will raise my throne
> above the stars of God;
> I will sit enthroned on the mount of assembly,
> on the utmost heights of the sacred mountain.
> I will ascend above the tops of the clouds;
> I will make myself like the Most High.'
> But you are brought down to the grave
>
> (Isa. 14: 12–15)

> You were the model of perfection,
> full of wisdom and perfect in beauty.
> You were in Eden,
> the garden of God;
> every precious stone adorned you:
> ruby, topaz and emerald,
> chrysolite, onyx and jasper,
> sapphire, turquoise and beryl.
> Your settings and mountings were made of gold;
> on the day you were created they were prepared.
> You were anointed as a guardian cherub,
> for so I ordained you.
> You were on the holy mount of God;
> you walked among the fiery stones.
> You were blameless in your ways
> from the day you were created
> till wickedness was found in you.
> Through your widespread trade
> you were filled with violence,
> and you sinned.
> So I drove you in disgrace from the mount of God,
> and I expelled you, O guardian cherub,
> from among the fiery stones.
> Your heart became proud
> on account of your beauty,
> and you corrupted your wisdom

because of your splendor.
So I threw you to the earth;
I made a spectacle of you before kings.
By your many sins and dishonest trade
you have desecrated your sanctuaries.
So I made a fire come out from you,
and it consumed you,
and I reduced you to ashes on the ground
in the sight of all who were watching.
All the nations who knew you
are appalled at you;
you have come to a horrible end
and will be no more.

(Ezek. 28: 12–19)

Nothing in these texts gives any indication about the time at which the Satanic Fall purportedly occurred. However, the tempting Serpent in the narrative of Genesis 3 is commonly understood to be an agent or an embodiment of Satan, indicating that some rebellious nonhuman moral agents were on the prowl in the universe prior to Adam's Fall.

On this CD sin, pain, and death were present before the advent of human beings, having been introduced as a result of an angelic Fall. Human beings later came on the scene with a redemptive task: to 'rule over' and 'subdue' a created order which had already been set on edge. However, the first human pair likewise failed at the task to which God put them, joining the angelic rebellion. In this way human beings also become partially culpable for the *continuing* reality of natural evil. Defending such a view Dom Trethowan writes:

Sin, then, started with the angels. They refused to *accept* grace—that is, the supernatural knowledge and love of God for which they were created. They preferred to remain as they were—God was not allowed to come into the foreground of the intelligences, to encroach on their self-sufficiency. Some of the Fathers put it like this: that the angels wouldn't stand for the Incarnation, for the putting of human nature above themselves. . . . Anyhow, the sin which the angels committed must have been a sin of pride—a refusal to toe the line. . . . One of the results, we may suppose, was a disorganization of the material universe over which, according to a reasonable theory, the angels had charge. It is a reasonable theory, because it seems to be a general law that the lower orders should be governed by the higher ones, that God's creatures should be arranged in a hierarchy, with a certain dependence of those below on those above.[26]

This view parallels the traditional Fall CD, except that the fallen agents are Satan and his cohorts. The Fall of Satan, on this view, initiated a chain of events in the natural world which led to a variety of natural evils, including animal pain, suffering, and death, either because Satan and these other demonic beings

[26] Dom Trethowan, *An Essay In Christian Philosophy* (London: Longmans, Green, 1954), 128.

surrendered their position as caretakers of the natural order, or perhaps simply as a natural consequence of the moral disorder introduced by their Fall.

This view has all the explanatory advantages of the traditional Fall CD for natural evil without the ahistorical liabilities.[27] Not only is there no reason to deny PAP, there is reason to affirm it. However, Satanic Fall CDs face their own distinctive difficulties. Some have argued that the view fails to meet even the minimal standards of a CD, since the lack of evidence for such powerful and unembodied spirits warrants our rejecting belief in them.[28] Would such an absence of evidence warrant our rejecting the Satanic Fall CD? Not straightforwardly. This critic of the Satanic Fall CD does not claim to be in possession of evidence which makes the existence of Satanic beings unlikely. Thus, even if the absence of evidence might warrant one in withholding on the claim that such a being exists, it would not warrant rejection of it.

Challenges of this sort should remind us, however, of the caveat discussed in Section 1.6, where we noted that whether or not a CD is successful will depend on the warranted acceptances one brings to the table, and what those acceptances further warrant us in rejecting. Since different individuals will have different warranted acceptances, CDs that are successful in deflecting the evidential challenge of evil for some might not be successful for others. This will be especially important when theists aim to draw upon elements of their theistic worldview that count among their warranted acceptances which are not shared by the nontheist. CDs of this sort can serve to preserve the reasonableness of theistic belief on the part of the theist in the face of evidential challenges raised by evil, by drawing upon beliefs that the theist reasonably holds and the critic of theism reasonably rejects. Of course, such CDs will be of no epistemic use to those who cannot reasonably endorse the distinctive claims. Because of this, the task of offering CDs might best be seen as dividing into two very different parts. On the one hand CDs that draw on acceptances that are warranted for the theist but not others will only serve to show how the theist can maintain reasonable theistic belief in the face of the particular sorts of evil. On the other hand CDs that draw on beliefs that are warranted for both the theist and the nontheist (or even for the nontheist alone) will show that the atheist cannot maintain reasonable belief in atheism on the basis of particular sorts of evil.

Since the absence of evidence for Fallen Satanic agents is not sufficient to warrant rejection of such beings, this CD can succeed even for those who do

---

[27] The view that natural evil should be explained by appeal to a Satanic Fall is defended by a handful of authors. C. S. Lewis appeals to the explanation specifically in the context of discussing animal pain and death (*The Problem of Pain* (New York: Collier, 1962), ch. 9). Others defend the more general hypothesis as it relates to all natural evil. See, for example, E. L. Mascall, *Christian Theology and Natural Science* (New York: Ronald, 1956), 301–2; Alvin Plantinga, *God, Freedom, and Evil* (Grand Rapids, Mich.: Eerdmans, 1974), 57–9.

[28] Quentin Smith, 'An Atheological Argument from Evil Natural Laws', *International Journal for the Philosophy of Religion*, 29 (1991), 159–74.

not share the theist's belief in the existence of beings like Satan. As long as the warranted acceptances of the nontheist don't justify outright rejection of the claim that Satan exists, this CD will succeed for the nontheist as well. But note that even for those who think that the absence of evidence for the existence of Satan does justify rejecting belief in his existence, this CD can still succeed for the theist.

Some might argue that we are warranted in rejecting the Satanic Fall as a way of explaining evil because it is egregiously ad hoc. Hypothesizing fallen beings to explain the reality of animal pain and suffering was, one might argue, a move cooked up after the Darwinian picture had become well entrenched and defenders of the Adamic Fall CD had begun to despair about the prospects of maintaining that view. In fact, however, the charge is mistaken. Since the late seventeenth century many Christians have argued that there are good reasons indeed to read the Genesis narrative as proposing two important and distinct stages in creative history. On this view the original creation became utterly corrupted as a result of the Fall of angelic beings and thereafter descended into chaos. The 'creation' narrative described in Genesis 1 is, in fact, largely a description of God's *refashioning* the original creation into the natural order we now find.

This view was popularized in the early nineteenth century by the Scottish theologian Thomas Chalmers, who used it as a way of explaining how one might reconcile the geological evidence of an ancient earth with the Genesis account of creation—the account which seems to indicate that the world was indeed less than ten thousand years old. Chalmers highlighted the fact that the first part of Genesis 1: 2 can be translated 'Now the earth *became* formless and void', and took this understanding to entail the presence of a temporal 'gap' between the original creation event and the events described in the verse. The existence of such a gap thus allowed for the possibility that there was some prior stage of it during which it exhibited a variety of order which was later destroyed. Chalmers thus understood Genesis 1: 1 to refer to this first stage of creation, which included the creation and Fall of some free preternatural beings. This phase was followed by the refashioning of the current order at the beginning of the present phase of cosmic history.[29] When this initial created natural world was refashioned into the current natural order, these preternatural beings persisted and corrupted this order as well, first and foremost by seducing human beings into sin.

The 'gap' version of the Satanic Fall explanation of animal pain and suffering has been defended recently by Gregory Boyd.[30] Boyd argues that only a CD of this sort can render natural evil explicable:

To be sure, according to Scripture the creation was originally created good, and the glory of God is still evident in it. . . . But something else—something frightfully wicked—is

---

[29] See T. Chalmers, *The Evidence and Authority of the Christian Revelation* (Hartford, Conn.: Sheldon and Goodrich, 1816).

[30] See his *Satan and the Problem of Evil* (Downers Grove, HI: InterVarsity Press, 2001), esp. pp. 293–318.

evident in it as well. Of their own free will, Satan and other spiritual beings rebelled against God in the primordial past and now abuse their God-given authority over aspects of the creation. The one who 'holds the power of death—that is, the devil' (Heb. 2: 14) exercises a pervasive structural, diabolical influence to the point that the entire creation is in 'bondage to decay' (Rom. 8: 21). If this scenario is correct, then the pain-ridden, bloodthirsty, sinister hostile character of nature makes perfect sense. If not, then despite the valid contributions of a number of thinkers on 'natural' evil, the demonic character of nature must remain largely inexplicable.[31]

Satanic Fall CDs can thus deflect the objection arising from PAP. In addition, on this view, unlike the Precursive Condition CDs, Satanic Fall CDs provide a coherent and non-ad hoc explanation for the obtaining of a pre-Adamic natural order. However, like our other Fall CDs, this view once again falls prey to the Fragility Objection. We are thus led to ask the very same apparently unanswerable question: How exactly are we to think about the transformation, caused by the Satanic Fall, which made it the case that animals which would not otherwise have experienced pain and suffering now do? And, as we saw before, even if there is an answer to this question, we are left with the still more vexing question of why God would create a universe which was subject to such catastrophic corruption on the occasion of a Fall of this sort. Such a universe seems defective indeed. No answers seem forthcoming. Thus, absent further emendation, CDs of this sort fail to meet the standards of acceptability set out in Chapter 1.

3.6 CONTEMPORARY DEFENSES: THE TRANS-TEMPORAL FALL

Inspired by Neoplatonism, the early Christian theologians Origen and Gregory of Nyssa adopted a view according to which human beings were originally created as disembodied immaterial entities. These immaterial entities only came to be embodied after engaging in some sort of sinful activity or another. In typically Neoplatonist fashion, Origen endorses a picture of creation in which God brings forth the created order by means of a series of emanations, where each emanation exemplifies a decreasing degree of goodness. On this view, the creation of human beings does not happen in the first instance by God creating a fully-formed and embodied man (Adam); rather, God first created an immaterial archetype of human beings that was capable of exercising genuine moral agency. It was not until the 'archetypal man' fell that human beings 'descended' into an embodied form. By becoming embodied, the archetypal man became multiply instantiated in numerous physical tokens. Through the descent into embodiment, human

---

[31] Ibid. 302.

beings acquired a disposition towards further sin, since, on this view, the body is the seat of the passions.[32]

None of this is, on its own, going to supply the seeds for a full-fledged CD for animal suffering. However, some twentieth-century commentators took inspiration from these 'transcendent Fall' accounts, arguing that the traditional understanding of the Fall is not far-reaching enough. Norman P. Williams, in his landmark study on the history of the doctrines of the Fall and of original sin, argued that only a view like Origen's could account for the radical evil we find in the natural world. On Williams's view divine creation of entities capable of moral agency must begin with the actualization of a World Soul. If we hypothesize the existence of such a World Soul, and a Fall on its part which results in, among other things, its fissioning into all the types of organic life we find in the world, this will explain the reality and the pervasiveness of evil experienced both by human and nonhuman organisms. Williams describes the view as follows:

> To explain evil in nature, no less than in man, we are compelled to assume a Fall . . . And to account for the vast and intimate diffusion of evil, selfishness and hate amongst all the multitudinous tribes of living creatures, we must place this ultimate Fall . . . at a point before the differentiation of life into its present multiplicity of forms and the emergence of separate species. . . . If we can assume that there was a pre-cosmic vitiation of the whole Life-Force, when it was still one and simple, at a point of time prior to its bifurcation and ramification into a manifold of distinct individuals or entelechies, we shall be in possession of a conception which should explain, so far as explanation is possible, the continuity and homogeneity of evil throughout all ranks of organized life, from the bacillus up to Man. This remote event . . . would then be the true and ultimate 'Fall.'[33]

Such a view represents a significant departure from the orthodox conception of creation found in the western theistic traditions. It also introduces a notion of the Fall which, while having some affinities with the views of the Greek Fathers, differs from these views in important respects. For Origen and Gregory of Nyssa the Fall is an event perpetrated by human beings or by 'the archetypal man' prior to embodiment. In this way their accounts more closely mirror the Genesis narrative, since the Fall springs directly from the moral wrongdoing of human beings (or at least the archetypal human). Williams, on the contrary, hypothesizes the existence of a divine emanation which is the primogenitor of all living organisms, human beings among them. He takes his own account to be superior, since it provides a natural way of explaining how all living things in the cosmic order can be corrupted by some initial act of moral wrongdoing.

While interesting as a historical curiosity, the trans-temporal Fall CD fails to offer resources that might help respond to the two key objections we have been considering. First, such a view will require the rejection of PAP. Second, the view does nothing to solve the concerns about fragility that have been raised

---

[32] An exposition of the view can be found in Origen's *De Principiis*, bk 2, ch 9.
[33] Williams, *The Idea of the Fall and of Original Sin*, 523.

for the accounts above. On this view the Fall of the World Soul leads not only to its corruption, but also straightaway to all of the embodied creatures which it subsequently spawns. This at least provides us with some sort of explanation of how the Fall could lead to such catastrophic corruption. However, it still gives us no indication of why God would create a universe liable to this sort of fracture.

3.7 SATAN, HIS COHORTS, AND EVOLUTION

We have found good reason to reject all of the Fall CDs considered so far. But the failure of these earlier views is instructive. What have we learned? First, any successful CD will have to take the reality of PAP seriously. Doing so requires accepting that the Fall occurred sometime prior to the origin of sentient life or perhaps the first living thing. Second, any such view will have to find a way to avoid the Fragility Objection. Perhaps, however, the fragility worry can be softened. The Satanic Fall CD considered earlier presumed that the Fall event itself was the culprit when it comes to natural evil. Something about the commission of the immoral act itself shattered the integrity of the natural order. The Fragility Objection seizes on this claim, arguing that the universe should not have been created in such a way that a single event like this, as monumental as it might be in sacred history, should have been allowed to yield such catastrophic results. This is the fragility which is regarded as objectionable.

Perhaps, however, natural evil need not be explained by appeal to a single pre-cosmic Fall by Satan and his cohorts. One might suppose instead that it is the pre-cosmic Fall combined with all of the subsequent moral evildoing which explains natural evil. In the same way that God has yielded substantial control over the terrestrial natural environment to fallen human agents, so, perhaps, God has yielded substantial control over the cosmic natural environment to fallen angelic agents. How much control over the cosmic environment can be ceded depends on what sorts of powers one takes these angelic beings to have. Could these beings, for instance, have exercised control over which natural laws obtain in our physical cosmos, over the quantity of matter the universe contains, over the speed with which habitable planets came into being, over the course of natural selection, over the genotype of various organisms or genotypic variation over evolutionary history? Could these beings be to blame for the fact that human beings often have bad backs, myopia, liability to cancer and heart disease? Could their activity explain the fact that animals react to potentially injurious stimuli with both avoidance behavior *and* qualitatively painful accompanying mental states? Are the fallen angels to blame for the fact that living sentient organisms are not naturally immortal? For the theist who is inclined to believe in the existence of powerful and yet fallen disembodied angelic beings, it is hard to be confident that the answers to these questions is no.[34] Furthermore, even the nontheist who merely lacks evidence for the existence of such beings is not in a position to reject such a position outright.

One might think that even this version of the Satan and his cohorts Fall CD is subject to a revised version of the Fragility Objection. On this view the worry is not that the integrity of the natural order hangs on the preservation of purity in the moral order. Rather, the problem is that God has populated the universe with free agents who can, through their free actions, carry out such wholesale natural destruction. According to this criticism, then, the world is fragile because so many sorts of goodness in the world are at the mercy of the free choices of a relatively small number of free creatures.

This objection cannot succeed without substantial emendation. First, our fragility objector owes us a substantive theory about just how much freedom ought to be accorded to free creatures, and how far the causal powers of these free creatures ought to extend. Second, this objector must have some way of showing that the range of freedom or the extent of the effects of free choices that this CD supposes these preternatural free agents to have is not itself a necessary condition for outweighing goods. It is hard to see how the objector could make good on either demand.

One could claim that the first demand places an unfairly high burden on the critic. To illustrate the problem, we might consider the following analogy:[35]

I phone in a delivery order to a local restaurant for a turkey meal. Thirty minutes later a dumptruck pulls up; the driver gets out, knocks on my door, and hands me a package with a couple of turkey legs, some breast meat, and stuffing and gravy on the side. He then asks: 'Where do you want the potatoes?'. I look at the truck: there's two tons of mashed potatoes, steaming hot. I object: 'That's too much'. He says, 'Well, now. Such an objection cannot succeed without substantial emendation. What you need here is a substantive theory about just how much potato ought to be accorded a customer who orders a turkey meal'. Your reply to the fragility objector is like his reply to my objection. I don't need a theory to tell me that *that* is too much. Likewise: the fragility objector doesn't need a theory to tell him that *that* is too much.

In reply we should note first that this particular objection is inapt. We can have a serviceable theory about how much potato should be accorded this customer: no more than one could reasonably expect to eat before it spoils. Of course we cannot do that in any precise or exact way. But we can make rough estimates. The objection might serve to show us that it is asking too much to demand that

---

[34] This view was first suggested to me in conversation with Alvin Plantinga. It may be the case that this is also the view of Gregory Boyd. His own description of his view makes it unclear whether or not it can escape the Fragility Objection in the way the view described here can.

[35] I thank Dan Howard-Snyder for this example.

the critic provide an account of exactly how much power should be accorded to free beings. But it is not asking too much to demand that some inexact and imprecise characterization of the relevant limits be set out. We know that two tons of potato is too much because no one could eat it without it spoiling. We know that Satanic power to influence the course of evolutionary history is too much power because . . . well, because what? That is the question that needs to be answered.

Even if the critic's objection that this CD accords too much power over nature to Satan and his cohorts fails in its current form, one can argue that the objection will gain some force if the critic can at least make plausible the claim that the free choices of creatures, or the causal ripples of those free choices, could be easily constrained in ways that prevent the most heinous forms of actual evil from occurring. In Chapter 5 we will consider an extended argument aimed at showing that it is not at all clear that such constraints could be implemented. Let me offer here a brief glimpse of that argument as a way of showing why I think this version of the Fragility Objection fails.

In order to think about the extent to which free choices and their causal consequences can be constrained, we need to gain some fix on what sort of causal environment is necessary for free choosing and free acting to occur. Among other things, free creaturely action must take place within an environment that has a robust and stable causal structure. Such a structure is required, in the human case for example, for us to be able to form intentions to act and to successfully carry out our acts. Unless moving our hand and arm in a certain way reliably brings about the motion of a ball we typically associate with throwing, we could never come to know that undertaking such motions would cause 'a throw'. And if we could never come to know that certain motions cause ball throwings, we could never intend to throw a ball. We would have no idea how to intend to do such a thing. Since such intendings are necessary conditions of free action, it follows that unless the environment in which we act contains a robust and stable structure, one which secures regular causal connection between our bodily motions and subsequent states of the world (trajectories of balls for instance), we could never intend to throw a ball. Executing the intention requires that the environment in which we act respond in nomically regular ways. Not only need there be stable regularities between bodily motions and causal consequences, there must also be stable regularities governing the forming of intentions and the consequences of those intentions. Unless my intending to raise my arm typically results in my arm going up, I can't intend to raise it, nor to do anything which I know requires the raising of it (shooting a free throw, for example).

If God structures the world so that there are stable, nomic regularities of these sorts, creatures who are capable of forming intentions that in turn cause bodily motions will have a great deal of power to affect the natural order. Conferring power on such creatures is a good thing, since, among other things, it makes possible morally significant free action. Unfortunately, even a small measure of causal power is sufficient to cause a substantial quantity of evil. If I have the capacity to learn about the workings of the natural world, by way of the study of chemistry for example, then even with very limited physical powers I can succeed in poisoning the reservoir, causing the collapse of the bridge, or setting the city ablaze. As a result, if God chooses to confer even modest amounts of causal power on free creatures who are capable of going wrong, it may be that those beings could and did freely choose to intervene in the processes of nature which led to the existence of animals. In doing so, they could also exercise substantial control over the structure and function of organ systems of these animals. If Satan and his cohorts did in fact act in this way, it would explain why nonhuman animals are susceptible to the pain, suffering, and death we have been seeking to explain.

3.8 CONCLUSION

Many theists share the view that explanations of evil which appeal to the Fall are no longer compelling, at least insofar as they are meant to explain things like animal pain and death. Jay McDaniel puts it as follows:

Earlier generations of Christians have explained the violence in creation by reference to a Fall that occurred in the distant past, itself initiated by human sin. But we cannot follow this route, for we have to acknowledge that there never was a time when life on our planet was free from violence. Predator–prey relations existed long before the early hominids appeared. Millions of years before human sin, there was a 'dark side.'[36]

No doubt it is true that the discovery of the long ages of terrestrial prehuman evolutionary history rendered many of the traditional appeals to the Fall implausible. However, as we have seen, it is too strong to claim that every attempt to explain animal pain and suffering by appeal to the Fall of free creatures is doomed to fail. Not only can one construct an explanation of animal pain that satisfies the conditions of a CD, in fact the CD described in Section 3.7 has some support in Christian revelation and the history of Christian thought.

It is probably true that few will go so far as to regard this CD as a full-fledged theodicy. But that isn't relevant here. The important question is rather: do our warranted acceptances justify rejection of this CD? The account described in Section 3.7 gives us good reason to think at least for some of us that the answer is no. As a result, Fall CDs which account for animal pain by appeals to the Fall of Satan and his cohorts provide us with a defensible CD for animal pain and suffering.

[36] Jay B. McDaniel, 'Can Animal Suffering be Reconciled with Belief in an All-Loving God?', in Andrew Linzey and Dorothy Yamamoto (eds.), *Animals on the Agenda* (Champaign/Urbana, Ill.: University of Illinois Press, 1998), 162.

4

Nobility, Flourishing, and Immortality:
Animal Pain and Animal Well-being

The idea that animals do not experience physical pain comparable to our pain . . . 'has never satisfied anyone without something to gain.' That assumption may now once and for all be discarded as rubbish. . . . Modern science has now confirmed what mankind suspected all along with a prima facie case that of course animals suffer, of course they have emotions, and of course they are conscious beings. That is not an expression of sentiment. It is not a statement of ideology. It is neither an avowal nor a denial of any tenet of religion or philosophy. It is a statement of fact, objective reality as best we can discern it. Three centuries after Descartes likened the crying of animals to 'broken machinery,' no serious person can say that anymore.

Matthew Scully[1]

In Chapter 2 we looked at a serious defense of the position which, according to Matthew Scully, no serious person defends. No matter how much scientific evidence one might marshal in favor of the neo-Cartesian view, and no matter how successful we might be in deflecting the philosophical, empirical, and moral objections to the neo-Cartesian view, few people are likely to find it satisfying as an explanation for all (or perhaps even any) of the apparent animal suffering the world contains. Perhaps this is so because the evidence against the view is stronger than I have been willing to admit. Perhaps, as suggested at the end of that chapter, it is rather that our human cognitive architecture ineluctably leads us to attribute the relevant sorts of mentality to other organisms. Further, despite the fact that we possess little or no evidence that would warrant our rejection of the Satanic Fall CD defended in Chapter 3, that CD does not seem likely to gain widespread acceptance except among theologically conservative western theists. In light of that, the responses we have considered to the evidential problem raised by animal suffering are not likely to be adequate for many to meet the demands set out for a successful CD.

---

[1] M. Scully, *Dominion* (New York: St Martin's Press, 2002), 294–5.

In this chapter and the following two we will assume that the neo-Cartesian stance is false and that nonhuman animals are susceptible to real and morally significant states of pain and suffering. We will further assume that the qualitatively rich mental life of at least some nonhuman animals does in fact motivate their behavior. Operating under these assumptions we will consider two general classes of 'outweighing goods' that might potentially provide a morally sufficient reason for permitting the evils of animal pain and suffering. More specifically, in this chapter we will look at purported outweighing goods which directly benefit animals themselves, and in the following two we will turn to consider outweighing goods which require animal suffering but which do not benefit animals themselves. Defending animal suffering by appeal to goods of the latter sort, as we will see, presents some unique challenges. These challenges arise from the claim that the justification of evils must not only explain how those evils are required to bring about outweighing global goods, but must also explain how those evils either benefit the victims of evil or are at least accompanied by appropriate compensation for the victim. The sorts of evils we are considering in this chapter allow us to bypass these worries, since, on this view, the permitted evils are allowed for the sake of securing outweighing goods for the animals themselves.

What sorts of goods might there be which (a) directly benefit animals, (b) have pain and suffering as necessary prerequisites or concomitants, and (c) serve to outweigh the animal pain and suffering the actual world contains? Here we will consider three possibilities, two of which, I will argue, provide us with sufficient ingredients for constructing a satisfactory CD for animal suffering. First, we will consider a position defended recently by Richard Swinburne. Swinburne argues that animals have a capacity for pain and suffering which confers a type of moral significance, or perhaps nobility, on animals and on certain types of their behavior. Moreover, the goodness of this moral significance outweighs the suffering animals in fact endure, and further would be unattainable without the possibility of that pain and suffering. I will argue that this explanation of animal suffering does not succeed.

We will then consider two other CDs which have had a variety of defenders historically. According to the second CD pain is not merely instrumentally beneficial, but is instead necessary for the survival and well-being of sentient, embodied organisms (like animals) which live in a nomically regular natural environment. Finally, we will consider the view that the capacity to experience pain and suffering allows animals to experience something analogous to soul-making, the value of which is manifest in their existence as resurrected beings in eternity.

4.1 THE SIGNIFICANCE OF ANIMAL ACTION

In Chapter 3 we considered a brief defense of the view that the capacity for free choice, and especially the capacity for freely choosing between good and evil courses of action, is a great good. But perhaps there is a sort of goodness manifested in action even when that action is not freely chosen. Richard Swinburne has argued that there is a distinctive variety of outweighing goodness available in the actions of animals, that essentially involves the reality of animal pain and suffering.[2] If Swinburne is correct then the world, and animals themselves, are better for being capable of instantiating this sort of goodness. This view would provide us with at least the ingredients for a CD of the sort we are seeking in this chapter; namely, one according to which the outweighing goods accrue to the animals themselves.

The process of acting and the actions which constitute the process can be good in two ways: intrinsically and instrumentally. They are good instrumentally when they serve to bring about good consequences. The intrinsic goodness of acting and actions varies with the type of activity at issue. Actions can be intrinsically good, first, simply in virtue of the fact that they involve an agent making a causal contribution to the obtaining of some event through the exercise of its causal powers. The measure of goodness that attaches to an action in virtue of being an exercise of causal power might seem meager at best. Nonetheless, there is a long-standing tradition, perhaps most notably defended by theists themselves, of regarding the ability to exercise causal power as a property that confers goodness on its bearer. The underlying intuition here is the same one which licenses the move by Anselmian theists to regard omnipotence as a 'great-making property' of God. On this conception power to effect states of affairs in the world is, all on its own, a great-making property of a substance. Exercising those causal powers manifests that goodness.

In addition, the process of acting and the actions performed display a more profound measure of intrinsic goodness when they are *intentionally* caused; that is, when the agent performs the action because he or she means to do it. What is more, it seems that intentional action is better still when the agent is, as Swinburne puts it, 'fully behind it'. An agent is fully behind an action when the desires that explain the agent's act are unconflicted or unopposed. Swinburne labels such actions 'spontaneous'. Better still, finally, are cases in which agents freely choose to do what is good *for the right reason*. Actions of this sort are good because by acting freely the agent becomes ultimately responsible for the good action performed and thus becomes a fit subject of moral praise. Swinburne stipulates that most nonhuman animals lack anything like free choice. Yet since animals are capable of spontaneous and intentional good action, their activities can exhibit the intrinsic good which attends actions of this sort, thereby contributing to the goodness of the animals themselves and the world as a whole.

There are a variety of ways that this sort of account of the goodness of animal action might be used to leverage at least a partial CD for animal pain

---

[2] Swinburne's account is set out in *Providence and the Problem of Evil* (Oxford: Oxford University Press, 1998), 171–5, 189–92.

and suffering. The one adopted by Swinburne contends that the capacity for experiencing pain and suffering is a necessary condition for animals to be able to engage in the full range of spontaneous and intentional actions possible for them. On this account, if animals were incapable of experiencing these mental states, a variety of good action types would be unavailable for them. For example, absent the capacity to experience loss, either through death or through real pain and suffering, animals could not possibly have the sorts of mental states required for their actions to count as instances of sympathy, affection, courage, patience, and so on. Swinburne defends this claim as follows:

Yet an animal cannot go on looking for a mate despite failure to find it unless the mate is lost and the animal longs for it; nor decoy predators or explore despite risk of loss of life unless there are predators, and unless there is a risk of loss of life . . . And there will not be a risk of loss of life unless sometimes life is lost. Nor can an animal intentionally avoid the danger of the forest fire or guide its offspring away from one unless the danger exists objectively. And that cannot be unless some animals get caught in forest fires. For you cannot intentionally avoid forest fires, or take the trouble to rescue your offspring from forest fires, unless there exists a serious danger of getting caught in fires. The intentional action of rescuing, despite danger, is believed to exist. The danger will not exist unless there is a significant natural probability of being caught in the fire.[3]

In addition, for animals to be capable of engaging in intentional action of this sort, they need to know the consequences their actions are likely to have. For an animal to intend to rescue its offspring, it must believe or otherwise have available to it an awareness of the fact that acting in a certain sort of way will probably yield the intended outcome. For me to hail a cab I need to know that the way to do so is to wave my arm as the cab goes by. Knowing this allows me to form the intention to 'wave my hand in order to hail the cab'. But unless I believe that moving my body in a certain way reliably results in that which I aim to bring about, I can't intend to bring about those results through my actions. Thus, for animals to act courageously or sympathetically, for example, they must know that some of their actions will prevent or forestall the occurrence of certain evils. And to know this they will have to have beliefs or be aware of the fact that the obtaining of certain conditions will cause other animals harm. Having these beliefs (or coming to such an awareness) will, however, involve animal suffering.

It is a great good that animals are not mere digestion machines with pleasurable sensations attached to the digestive process; but that they struggle to get food, save themselves and their offspring from predators and natural disasters, seek mates over days, and so on. But they can only do these things with some knowledge of the consequences of their actions, and they could only acquire this by learning and seeking (as opposed to just being born with it) and it could only amount to very well-justified knowledge, if it is derived from experience of the actions of others, of the unintended effects of their own actions, and of

[3] Swinburne, *Providence and the Problem of Evil*, 171–2.

the effects of natural processes. . . . animals must suffer if some animals are to learn to avoid suffering for themselves and their offspring. If deer are to learn how to help prevent their offspring from being caught in fires, some fawns have to be caught in fires for the deer to see what happens. . . . Otherwise, it will all reasonably seem a game . . . And then animals will be deprived of the possibility of serious and heroic actions.[4]

There is much to be suspicious about in this two-pronged proposal from Swinburne. Central to his position is that it is good for creatures to be able to act intentionally, and better that they can act intentionally to bring about good states of affairs. The latter are triply good since they involve the intrinsically good exercises of causal power and the intentional pursuit of a good end, while at the same time they are instruments for securing the resultant good outcome. The two intrinsically good features of such action provide benefits at the global level as well as for the animal itself. The third is an instrumental good which provides benefits at the global level, and perhaps sometimes for the animal itself.

In order to assess Swinburne's position, we must consider whether or not the purported intrinsic goods at work here are goods after all. While certain animal actions can be counted good in virtue of bringing about good consequences, the question we are considering here is whether or not the goodness of animal action can justify animal pain and suffering. Swinburne proposes that it can, since many good actions only count as good because they spring from desires and/or beliefs that the animal has. Thus, the action of the mother seeking to play the decoy while her young ones escape is good in part because it is one in which the mother is *aiming* to do something good. The beliefs and the desires of the mother direct her to put herself in harm's way so that her offspring can escape danger. The fact that the offspring escape danger is instrumentally good, and the fact that the mother brings it about that they escape danger is a further instrumental good. But, Swinburne claims, it is also good—intrinsically good—that the mother's action of bringing about this end was mediated by her mental states.

But this cannot be all there is to the story. For we can imagine that these types of instrumental and intrinsic good are available even in a world in which there is no possibility of pain and suffering. For example, Swinburne himself notes that some higher animals seem to be capable of play and courtship. If this is right, these behaviors, when motivated by an animal's intentional states, would yield the same types of intrinsic and instrumental goods noted in the last paragraph. But of course when one animal seeks to play with or court another there need be no background possibility that instances of pain and suffering are likely to be forestalled by this behavior. The possibility of the good state of affairs the animal seeks to bring about is all that is necessary for these goods to be actualizable. As a result, such goods could be manifest even in a world without the prospect of pain and suffering.

---

[4] Ibid. 189–90.

Perhaps Swinburne can grant this while still insisting that certain subspecies of intentionally generated goods would be lacking were the possibility of animal pain and suffering absent. Consider the virtue of courage for example. If there really were no threat to her offspring, the mother could not act courageously by intentionally playing the decoy. To seek the good of courageously 'playing the decoy' the mother would have to believe that 'by acting this way, I safeguard the lives of my offspring'. Further, if there were no real threat to the mother in acting as decoy, there would be nothing courageous in her action. All of that seems right. Yet none of this requires that animals be capable of experiencing pain and suffering either. Animals perform decoy behaviors to prevent death to their offspring, even at the risk of their own death. Perhaps this is a good thing, and perhaps it is a good thing in part because the mother intentionally pursues it. But none of this requires animal *pain* and *suffering*. It only requires that the offspring, and the mother, face the prospect of some sort of loss (of life, of bodily integrity, etc.). There is no reason to think that all such losses will be intrinsically connected to pain and suffering.

We might be able to construct cases in which the only good an animal secures for another is protecting it from pain and suffering, and in which the good of an animal's action consists, at least in part, in the pursuit of that good. If we succeed, we can at least say that actions of that type will be unavailable to animals in a world where pain and suffering are absent. But even if we succeed in coming up with such action types the question remains: Is it worth having a world filled with animal pain and suffering to secure a world in which this narrow range of esoteric goods is possible? I suspect most will think it is not. Of course, even if goods of this sort cannot on their own serve to explain the reality of pain and suffering, they might provide a partial account of the goods that animal pain and suffering can secure. We will return to consider this possibility in more detail in Chapter 7.

4.2 THE GIFT OF PAIN

In the late 1940s Dr Paul Brand was recruited to India to help serve the crippling needs of patients with leprosy, or Hansen's disease.[5] Hansen's disease results from a bacterial infection and its consequences are debilitating and lifelong. As the disease advances patients experience paralysis and degeneration of digits and limbs, with an accompanying loss of pain sensation. As a result of the paralysis, many patients are left with hands deformed into the shape of useless claws, a defining characteristic of those with the disease. Brand began work on some pioneering procedures aimed at reversing the effects of the paralysis and restoring

---

[5] The following account of Brand's work is drawn from Philip Yancey and Paul Brand, *The Gift of Pain* (Grand Rapids, Mich.: Zondervan, 1997).

functionality to the hands and feet of his patients. However, he found the battle against the degeneration was exacerbated as functionality was increased. Many of those who suffer from Hansen's disease are afflicted with skin lesions that involve swelling, blisters, and open sores which lead further to the degeneration of the underlying tissue and bone. Paradoxically, the more successful Brand was at restoring some measure of function to a hand or a foot, the more he found those same patients returning to his clinic with even more festering lesions on the supposedly 'restored' area. Until that time, no one had successfully explained the cause of the lesions and the subsequent degeneration of digits and limbs. While it was originally hypothesized that the culprit was the bacteria, the discovery of antibiotics later demonstrated that even when patients were given a course of treatment which rendered them free of the pathogen, tissue degeneration continued.

Brand's patients were almost all exclusively quarantined in a 'leprosarium', where they lived and received treatment without hope of ever being released. He describes one patient, Sadan, who came to the leprosarium with severe deformities in his hands and feet as a result of the disease. Through a series of hand surgeries, physicians were able to restore substantial functionality to his hands. In fact, Sadan went on to work as a typist. Yet, despite this success, the condition of Sadan's feet declined significantly. Several doctors had recommended that his legs be amputated below the knees as a way of halting the progressive degeneration and the accompanying infection which threatened to take over the rest of his body.

Brand continued to treat Sadan's feet, now shortened by half and covered with ulcers. Yet despite the regular change of dressings and aggressive use of antibiotics, his condition worsened. He describes one defining visit with Sadan, when he returned to the clinic to have his dressing changed for the tenth time in a single day. Because the disease had destroyed his ability to feel pain, Sadan sat stoically with a look of resignation on his face as Brand unwrapped the bloody bandages. Finally coming to the realization that Sadan would never recover from his horrifying condition, Brand grudgingly agreed that Sadan's lower legs should be amputated. After re-bandaging Sadan's foot, he walked him down the hospital corridor to the door. As he watched Sadan walk down the steps and across the sidewalk, he noticed something important. Despite the fact that Brand has just spent half an hour cleaning out a grossly abscessed wound on the ball of his foot, Sadan was walking without even a hint of a limp. During the whole course of his treatment, he continued to walk in a way that put his full weight on the damaged tissue they had been so carefully treating.

Sadan was able to do this only because his disease had robbed him of the capacity to feel any pain in his feet. Anyone else would have been unable to walk on such horribly crippled feet at all. But Sadan, blind to the injury he was inflicting on himself with each step, continued to press the inflamed and infected skin, muscle, and bone into his unforgiving shoes.

Brand went on to show conclusively that all of the tissue injury and degeneration experienced by patients with Hansen's disease was caused by injuries that patients had quite unwittingly incurred because of this inability to feel pain. Sometimes, the circumstances leading to an injury could be easily avoided. For example, patients were cautioned about picking up any cup containing hot beverages, since they would frequently scald the skin on their hand without realizing it. Yet other injuries were much harder to avoid, even when patients gave painstaking attention to their activities.

Living tissues must be able grow and react to injury in such a way that they either prevent further damage or regenerate or both. This in turn requires that these tissues have the capacity for recognizing noxious stimuli and for responding appropriately to them. For example, one of the most common defense mechanisms against noxious stimuli is inflammation. When tissues are exposed to a powerful noxious stimulus, being hit by a baseball for example, the body first reacts by causing inflammation in the area. This sort of inflammation not only allows a greater amount of blood flow in the affected area, thus enhancing the oxygenation of the tissues and flooding them with immune cells, but it also increases pressure on pain sensors, or nociceptors, which makes them correspondingly more sensitive. As a result of the greater sensitivity, we feel even greater pain when the same area receives further noxious stimulation. The result is that we are more protective of the damaged tissue, which in turn allows it to heal and regenerate.

It is this cascade of events that causes us to limp when we experience tissue damage in our foot or leg. The tenderness caused by the inflammation makes the affected area especially sensitive, leading us to alter our gait, thereby preventing us from putting pressure on it. It was this sort of reaction that was lacking in Sadan and which thus prevented his healing.

Physiological reactions of this sort are, in fact, more pervasive and influential than we consciously realize. Even repeated low-level noxious stimuli, those that we experience when we clap our hands repeatedly or run a kilometer, generate the same inflammation reaction. In both cases inflammation begins to occur after a very short time. We avoid injury in these cases because our body, quite unconsciously, detects the increasing pressure and pain sensations and leads us to alter our clapping pattern or gait.

When Brand finally left India to continue his research at a center dedicated to Hansen's disease in the USA, he launched a series of studies focused on the inflammation reaction to noxious stimuli. Using a device which measured increased temperature and inflammation in tissues, he tested the patterns of noxious stimulation on the feet of normal subjects walking long distances. Comparing the patterns to inflammation at different stages of a lengthy walk he demonstrated that by shifting our gait we distribute the repeated pounding of our feet so that no single area becomes injured. However, when patients with Hansen's disease go for a similarly long walk, they come back with inflammation, blisters, and ulcerations caused by a failure to make just such minute adjustments.

Reflecting on Brand's work provides support for a CD of animal pain and suffering which seems intuitive and obvious. On this intuitive and obvious CD, animal pain and suffering is permitted by God because that ability to experience pain and suffering is necessary for living organisms to survive and flourish in a physical environment governed by physical laws.[6] If it is good for God to create animals in the first place, then it is good for those animals to be susceptible to feelings of pain. Such explanations seem, however, to face a number of significant hurdles.

Those who aim to defend a CD of this sort must offer some reason to think, first, that it is good for there to be physical organisms which are capable of sustaining injuries to their bodily integrity, and second that it is good to place those corporeal organisms in potentially injury-causing nomically regular environments. Once those two conditions are met, an advocate of this CD would further need to defend the notion that there are not other, better ways to promote the end of preserving the integrity of the animal organism, without pain and suffering. I will use most of this section to address this final and most formidable issue. What of the first two?

Since the second of these claims is instrumental to the CD developed in Chapters 5 and 6 I will postpone a full discussion of it until then. Let's grant, for now, that one can substantiate the claim that a nomically regular physical world is indeed good. What then of the first claim?

In reflecting on the doctrine of creation, many theists have argued that God engages in the act of creating out of the overflowing abundance of his own good nature. This allows God both to bring into existence creatures that are capable of sharing in the divine goodness and thereby to make that goodness fully manifest. It is common in the Christian tradition further to hold that these two goals are achieved, at least in part, by God producing a creation that is *diverse*. St Thomas Aquinas, for example, defends the goodness of such diversity as follows:

For He brought things into being in order that His goodness might be communicated to creatures, and be represented by them; and because His goodness could not be adequately represented by one creature alone, He produced many and diverse creatures, that what was wanting to one in the representation of the divine goodness might be supplied by another. For goodness, which in God is simple and uniform, in creatures is manifold and divided and hence the whole universe together participates in the divine goodness more perfectly, and represents it better than any single creature whatever.[7]

For St Thomas this means that it is good to have creatures of various sorts, including non-embodied intellectual creatures (angels), embodied intellectual creatures

---

[6] This view is endorsed but not defended at any length by Nancey Murphy and George Ellis in their *On the Moral Nature of the Universe* (Minneapolis, Minn.: Fortress, 1996), 211–13.

[7] Summa Theologiae I 47, a.1, resp, Fathers of the English Dominican Province, trans. (Wheaton: Christian Classics, 1981).

(human beings), embodied nonintellectual creatures (plants and animals), and so on. The nineteenth-century Yale theologian George Park Fisher similarly argued that such diversity is of value not because of the opportunity for appreciation that it affords creatures, but simply because it reflects the self-expression of God:

Every gem and every blossom manifests in its very structure a purpose, even without reference to the impression it is adapted to make on human observers. But one of the motives of their creation may be the self-expression, for its own sake, of the Author of their being.[8]

The seventeenth-century philosopher (and Lutheran) Gottfried Leibniz argued that by creating in this fashion God demonstrates the various ways in which the divine attributes (existence, goodness, knowledge, power, creativity, etc.) might be manifested in limited respects by finite, created things:

Every substance is like a complete world and like a mirror of God or of the whole universe, which each one expresses in its own way, somewhat as the same city is variously represented depending upon the different positions from which it is viewed. Thus the universe is in some way multiplied as many times as there are substances, and the glory of God is likewise multiplied by as many entirely different representations of his work. It can even be said that every substance bears in some way the character of God's infinite wisdom and omnipotence and imitates him as much as it is capable.[9]

Western monotheists have used these sorts of considerations to argue that a creation which contains a diversity of kinds of things, and perhaps a spectrum of increasingly good things, is most befitting for a perfect and loving God. If along that spectrum we find organisms that are living, sentient, and corporeal, it will be good for those organisms to be capable of feeling pain as a mechanism for protecting bodily integrity.

Or at least it will be good that they can feel such pain only as long as there is not some other way of protecting their bodily integrity without these qualitatively undesirable phenomenally conscious mental states. It is at this point that critics are most likely to think this CD runs aground. It seems, on first consideration, that the bodily integrity could be secured without permitting any pain and suffering at all. God might, for example, have created animals like robots which, without a trace of sentience, are capable of recognizing the presence of environmental threats. Thus, for all it seems, God could have created organisms with a mechanism which sufficed to signal the presence of noxious environmental stimuli to creatures without making the deliverances of that mechanism *painful*. Perhaps all that would be needed is something like an internal equivalent of a fire alarm. Upon encountering potential (or actual) danger, whistles and warning lights could go off in an organism's head signaling: 'Danger! Take action!'.

---

[8] George Park Fisher, *The Grounds of Theistic and Christian Belief* (New York: Scribner 1919), 54.

[9] G. W. Leibniz, *Discourse on Metaphysics*, ix. This translation is from Leibniz, *Philosophical Essays*, ed. Roger Ariew and Daniel Garber (Indianapolis, Ind.: Hackett, 1989).

No doubt we can imagine designing robots which are capable of recognizing dangers in the environment and responding so as to avoid them. But we are now assuming that the neo-Cartesian position is false—that is, we are assuming that it is a good thing for God to create corporeal, *sentient* organisms. Can organisms of this sort, that is organisms which manage their behavior largely through the mediation of sentient or phenomenally conscious mental states, survive without some sort of mechanism which produces pain? One can imagine the critic pressing the claim that even in sentient organisms sentience is quite irrelevant when it comes specifically to the practice of detecting and avoiding potential dangers. If the only reason that pain is adaptive is that it produces appropriate avoidance behaviors, those behaviors would be adaptive even if they were executed as unconscious reflex reactions. Were things to in fact function this way, the adaptive behaviors we typically associate with pain would remain in place but would no longer be *mediated by sentient states* of the organism. Even if animals are not robots, it can still be true that some animal behaviors take place without sentient states being involved. Indeed, plenty of animal behaviors do—digestion, respiration, not to mention that alteration of our gait that mitigates inflammation as described earlier. Why can't the same be true of injury-avoidance behaviors?

Neurophysiologist John Eccles argued that this imagined arrangement would be less advantageous than one in which pain behaviors were mediated through sentient or conscious states, for two reasons. First, he claimed, the *hurtfulness* of pain forces one's entire being to attend to the noxious stimulus. Once my skin is severely cut, I forget all about my busy schedule and run for a bandage. The ability to harness the attention of the whole being in this way is likely to be adaptive in many cases, since it prevents us from ignoring serious injuries when in pursuit of highly desired ends. Second, Eccles claimed that the hurtfulness of pain 'sears the painful experience into our memories', helping us avoid future noxious stimuli in a way that reflex behaviors never could.[10]

However, neither of these explanations seems plausible. It might be true that it is adaptive for organisms 'to direct the whole of their attention' toward sources of noxious stimulation, or at least toward the most serious of these sources. But why is this more likely to occur when sentient or conscious states are involved? If the reflex pain behavior were sufficient to take command of the body in this way, that alone would suffice. In fact, numerous examples are available of cases in which organisms 'direct the whole of their attention' to crucial bodily demands even when sentient states play no role. One need only consider basic bodily functions—secreting insulin or changing our heart rate during exercise—to find examples of adaptive mechanisms not mediated by sentient or conscious states. One might respond that while basic bodily *functions* of this sort can go on unconsciously, the same would not be true when it comes to *behaviors*. But

---

[10] J. C. Eccles, *The Human Psyche* (Berlin: Springer-Verlag, 1980).

again, this critic would be wrong; even behaviors can sometimes be mediated unconsciously in ways that are highly adaptive. All of us have had the experience of walking along the sidewalk and, at an inattentive moment, stepping on the very edge of the curb. As pressure is applied to the foot and it begins to buckle, the ligaments in the ankle stretch sending a signal to the brain which slackens the tension in the thigh muscle, causing us to tumble over to avoid tearing the ligaments in our ankle apart irreparably. In this way, those sensors in the ligaments have successfully commanded the 'whole of my attention' in a way that produces adaptive avoidance behaviors but does not involve conscious or sentient states. The second reason fails as well, since, as we saw in Chapter 2, future avoidance behaviors do not depend on the ability of present noxious stimuli to produce mental states with a qualitatively undesirable character.

Yet despite all of this there are some very good reasons for thinking that at least some injury-avoidance behaviors could not successfully be rigged up to operate in reflex fashion. One reason is that the adaptiveness of pain behaviors is context-dependent. Perhaps in some circumstances it is adaptive for me to pay heed to a noxious stimulus of a certain sort while in other circumstances it is not. If I step on a tack it is appropriate for me to stop and pull it out of my foot before taking any more steps. But we surely would not want this sort of behavior hardwired into our behavioral repertoire as a reflex. After all, if I am being chased by a hungry grizzly and happen to step on a tack, I had better keep running! Hardwired pain-related behaviors would detract from the flexibility required to adapt to the complex environmental conditions organisms encounter.

It is not, however, the mere context dependence that is important here. All sorts of behaviors and functions are context-dependent. What is important is rather the fact that pain provides the organism with a desire that must be weighed against any desire to perform actions which would serve to induce or sustain the noxious stimulus. Sentient beings are capable of engaging in intentional action and such actions are motivated and directed by desires. In cases where desires are unopposed, intentional action aimed at satisfying those desires is inevitable.[11] *Hurtful* pain constitutes or generates a countervailing desire that provides the intentional agent with an occasion to weigh the threat to its bodily integrity against the importance of satisfying the desire motivating its action. When I step on the tack, the pain induced provides me with incentives for doing something that mitigates the pain; namely, stopping my run. Unless I have some other aim that I judge to be more important than protecting myself from further injury to my foot, like avoiding the bear, the pain provides me with an all-things-considered motivation to thwart the earlier course of action (the running) and to remove the cause of the noxious stimulation. Any corporeal organism that engages in intentional action must have some mechanism that

---

[11] This claim is not entirely uncontroversial. I have defended it in Michael Murray and David Dudrick, 'Are Coerced Acts Free?', *American Philosophical Quarterly*, 32 (April 1995), 147–61.

allows it to recognize the potential for such risks. And this mechanism must provide the agent with countervailing desires that force an assessment of the value of staying the course and incurring the risks, or stopping short.

Indeed, the mechanisms mediating conscious pain sensations in human beings seem honed to function in ways that assist us in making these relative judgments, sometimes in ways that it might have been difficult to anticipate. For example, one might think that as the perceived threat increases in severity, pain must always increase proportionately. Yet in cases where the risk of injury or death is very high *and* where achieving a particular goal is extraordinarily important, our nociceptive system responds not by making the din of pain deafening, but rather by shutting down altogether. In cases where someone is in a heightened state of awareness or excitement, for example, because she is fleeing from a perceived danger, or pursuing an urgent goal, inhibitory mechanisms block the activity of the nociceptive pathways below levels of stimulus activation that are proportionate to the degree of heightened excitement. As a result, soldiers injured in battle or athletes injured in sporting events often don't feel the pain of their injuries until long after they have been induced. The awareness and importance of the goals play a role in mediating the organism's avoidance behaviors. In the cases described here, the mediation takes place at an unconscious level. In cases where less all-consuming goals are at stake, our nociceptive systems function as advertised: warning us of potential threats to our integrity and of the severity of those threats.[12]

An imaginative critic might concede that some system needs to be in place which provides us with countervailing considerations in cases where my pursuit of certain goals puts my bodily integrity at risk, but contend that this could be done in ways that don't involve *hurtful pain*. Two suggestions come to mind here. First, perhaps our injury avoidance could work with carrots rather than sticks. On this scheme intentional agents would be motivated to avoid injury not because so doing removes or mitigates pain, but rather because it *induces or enhances pleasure*. Second, perhaps injury avoidance could be motivated not by inducing hurtful pain, but rather, as suggested earlier, by inducing *beliefs* in me that unless I address the source of noxious stimulation I am putting myself at some risk.

While injury avoidance through pleasure seems initially preferable, it is not hard to see why it cannot work. Our injury-avoidance mechanisms work more like fire alarms than radar. If they were radar-like they would succeed in detecting *potential* risks in the environment: merely looking at the fire and thinking about putting my hand in it would induce mental states that provide incentives for me

---

[12] For a more developed account of the way in which phenomenally conscious pain-sensory and pain-inhibitory mechanisms might play an adaptive role for organisms which engage in conscious goal-directed behavior see Virginia Hardcastle's *The Myth of Pain* (Cambridge, Mass.: MIT Press, 1999), 130–43.

to avoid the action. Being fire alarm-like, the incentives for avoidance only arise when we actually engage or come in contact with the threat; for example, actually putting our hand in or very close to the fire.[13] This mode of operation seems rather efficient, since there are so many potential threats in our environment we would otherwise be bombarded with noxious sensations. Fire-alarm injury avoidance works when the mental states that are induced are hurtful. In order to function by inducing states of pleasure it would have to be the case that when we stick our hand in the fire we find it strongly pleasurable to remove it. Would such a mechanism work? It hardly seems so. To see why not, imagine the prospect of having children rewired with such an injury-avoidance mechanism. If they were to experience powerful feelings of pleasure when removing their hands from fires, one would expect them not to avoid injury, but rather to spend their afternoons sticking their hands in fires and removing them! Not exactly adaptive behavior.[14]

What about the avoidance mechanism that works by inducing belief? Brand's work, it turns out, is also relevant to our consideration of this alternative, and it shows us why it would not work. He conducted a number of re-engineering experiments with Hansen's-disease patients, attempting to mitigate the degenerative effects of the disease through gloves and socks which were appropriately responsive to applications of excessive pressure. In this way, if a patient squeezed a piece of iron too hard, or grabbed a thorny branch, or stepped on a tack, the transducers on the apparatus would signal a potentially injurious stimulus. As Brand explains, the experiments were not a success:

We had grandly talked of retaining 'the good parts of pain without the bad,' which meant designing a warning system that would not hurt. First we tried a device like a hearing aid that would hum when the sensors were receiving normal pressures, buzz when they were in slight danger, and emit a piercing sound when they perceived an actual danger. But when a patient with a damaged hand turned a screwdriver too hard, the loud warning signal went off, he would simply override it . . . and turn the screwdriver anyway. Blinking lights failed for the same reason. Patients who perceived 'pain' only in the abstract could not be persuaded to trust artificial sensors. Or they became bored with the signals and ignored them. The sobering realization dawned on us that unless we built in a quality of compulsion, our substitute system would never work. Being alerted to the danger is not enough; our patient had to be forced to respond. Professor Tims of LSU said to me, almost in despair, 'Paul, it's no use. We'll never be able to protect these limbs unless the signal really hurts.' . . . We tried every alternative before resorting to pain, and

---

[13] While this is largely true it is not true across the board. There are, after all, a few avoidance systems in human beings that work more like radar. For example, human beings have a well-documented 'contagion-avoidance' mechanism. The mechanism displays itself in our hardwired aversions towards contact with certain potential sources of pathogens; most notably, contact with waste products and corpses. For example, humans have a powerful aversion towards contact with objects that have knowingly come in contact with fecal material, no matter how many times they have been cleaned. Contagion-avoidance in this way is more radar-like. The example comes from Pascal Boyer, *Religion Explained* (New York: Basic, 2001), 215.

[14] I thank David van der Laan for first suggesting this problem.

finally concluded that Tims was right: the stimulus has to be unpleasant, just as pain is unpleasant.[15]

In fact, Brand explains that development of such devices was ultimately abandoned because the human subjects would find ways to circumvent their function. He describes one patient, Charles, fitted with a device that was capable of causing pain via a strong shock to the armpit (a place where pain sensation is typically possible for those suffering with Hansen's disease, since the pathogen which causes the disease usually afflicts cooler tissues). But the device failed to yield the desired avoidance behaviors:

[Charles] wheeled the bike across the concrete floor, kicked down the kickstand, and set to work on the gasoline engine. I watched him out of the corner of my eye. Charles was one of our most conscientious volunteers, and I was eager to see how the artificial pain sensors on his glove would perform. One of the engine bolts had apparently rusted, and Charles made several attempts to loosen it with a wrench. It did not give. I saw him put some force behind the wrench, and then stop abruptly. The electric coil must have jolted him. . . . Charles studied the situation for a moment, then reached up under his armpit and disconnected a wire. He forced the bolt loose with a big wrench, put his hand in his shirt again, and reconnected the wire. It was then that I knew we had failed. Any system that allowed our patients freedom of choice was doomed.[16]

These considerations give us some very good reason for thinking that mental states which are not *hurtful* would fail to generate the necessary and adaptive behavioral responses in organisms that engage in intentional action.

All of this gives us very good reason for thinking that physical pain and suffering will be inevitable for corporeal, sentient beings living in a nomically regular world. They further give us reason for thinking that *psychic* suffering and pain will be part of such a world. Intentional behavior is behavior that is motivated by desire and aimed at an end. It is a conceptual truth that achieving or attaining an intended end is something that the agent regards as good and, as such, will be attended by feelings of pleasure, satisfaction, and joy. Correspondingly, when I am thwarted in my attempts to achieve or attain my end, this failure will be attended by frustration or anger or other mental states characteristic of feeling pained. Since my ability to achieve or attain my intended ends is inevitably going to be contingent in a nomically regular world, it is inevitable that there are some intended ends I will fail to secure, and as a result it is inevitable that I will sometimes experience mental states which constitute being pained. And what is true of me is going to be true of the many other animal organisms which are capable of engaging in intentional action.

As a result, the claim that pain and suffering are required to preserve the integrity of sentient physical organisms engaged in intentional action is one we cannot reject outright. Indeed, contrary to initial expectations, this CD is one that we are not warranted in rejecting given our acceptances.

---

[15] Yancey and Brand, *Gift of Pain*, 194.   [16] Ibid. 195–6.

4.3 ANIMAL SOUL-MAKING AND IMMORTALITY

Many Christian thinkers have argued that animal immortality plays an important role in explaining the reality of animal pain and suffering in the earthly life. Perhaps there is a connection between the earthly life of animals, filled as it is with pain and suffering, and a blissful, eternal existence for those animals in the divine presence. Keith Ward emphasizes what he takes to be the crucial importance of animal immortality:

Theism would be falsified if physical death was the end, for then there could be no justification for the existence of this world. However, if one supposes that every sentient being has an endless existence, which offers the prospect of supreme happiness, it is surely true that the sorrows and troubles of this life will seem very small by comparison. Immortality, for animals as well as humans, is a necessary condition of any acceptable theodicy; that necessity, together with all the other arguments for God, is one of the main reasons for believing in immortality.[17]

Although not directly affirmed in the texts of the major theistic traditions, the notion that at least some animals are immortal is consistent with these traditions. For example, select eschatological texts in the Hebrew Bible acknowledge the existence of nonhuman animals in the *eschaton*, as, for example, the following text from Isaiah:

> And the wolf will dwell with the lamb,
> And the leopard will lie down with the young goat,
> And the calf and the young lion and the fatling together;
> And a little boy will lead them.

Later Isaiah continues:

'The wolf and the lamb will graze together, and the lion will eat straw like the ox; and dust will be the serpent's food. They will do no evil or harm in all My holy mountain,' says the LORD.[18]

In addition, many biblical theists have inferred that since animals are part of the original (prelapsarian) creation, they must make an important contribution towards the divine plan for creation as a whole. Thus, we have equally good reason to affirm the eternal existence of both human and nonhuman animals.

Even if these texts affirm the existence of animals in a future heavenly kingdom, we still have something short of an affirmation of the immortality of those animals that are part of the *present* creation. It might be the case that the animals that exist currently are resurrected and transformed in the future. But it might also be the case that in eternity God simply creates new and different

---

[17] Keith Ward, *Rational Theology and the Creativity of God* (New York: Pilgrim, 1982), 201–2.
[18] Isa. 11: 6 and 65: 25 (New American Standard Bible).

animals. If the latter, then there is nothing about the presence of animals in heaven that could explain or account for the animal pain and suffering we have been discussing.

One text that is cited in support of the continuing existence of animals that are part of the present created order is Romans 8: 19–22. There St Paul writes:

For the anxious longing of the creation waits eagerly for the revealing of the sons of God. For the creation was subjected to futility, not willingly, but because of Him who subjected it, in hope that the creation itself also will be set free from its slavery to corruption into the freedom of the glory of the children of God. For we know that the whole creation groans and suffers the pains of childbirth together until now.

Methodist founder John Wesley argued that this text implies that the future, liberated creation must contain the very same animals that inhabit the current, corrupted natural order. Only this way could the present animals be 'set free' from 'slavery to corruption'. The only other way to have animals as inhabitants of the eternal kingdom would be for the animals of the present order to be annihilated, with new animals being created *de novo*. But this would, Wesley argues, be inconsistent with the language of the passage, since, as he notes, 'annihilation is not deliverance'. Thus, the same animals which populate the universe here and now must be the ones compensated for the suffering of this life in eternity:

As a recompense for what they once suffered, while under the 'bondage of corruption,' when God has 'renewed the face of the earth,' and their corruptible body has put on incorruption, they shall enjoy happiness suited to their state, without alloy, without corruption, and without end.[19]

Most pre-Reformation Christian thinkers rejected the notion of animal immortality, since animals were held to lack the sorts of souls capable of surviving bodily death. While it was common to regard animals as ensouled, these souls were taken to be corporeal 'principles of organization', which worked exclusively in and through the physical organism. As a result, animals were regarded as unable to survive death and the dissolution of their bodies. St Thomas Aquinas, for example, argues as follows:

No operation of the sensitive part of the soul can be performed without a body. In the souls of brute animals, however, there is no operation superior to those of the sensitive part, since they neither understand nor reason. This is evident from the fact that all animals of the same species operate in the same way, as though moved by nature and not as operating by art; every swallow builds its nest, and every spider its web. The souls of brutes then are incapable of any operation that does not involve the body.[20]

---

[19] Wesley's remarks on animal resurrection come from the sermon, 'The General Deliverance', in *The Works of John Wesley ii*, ed. A. C. Outler (Nashville, Tenn.: Abingdon, 1985), 437–50.
[20] *Summa Contra Gentiles ii*, ed. V. Bourke (Notre Dame, Ind.: Notre Dame Press, 1995), 82.

The conclusion? Animal existence is directly tied to the continuing existence of the animal body. One could take issue with the soundness of such arguments. For example, one might think that animal souls are incapable of surviving without a body, while still holding that animals can be immortal in virtue of the fact that they are brought back into existence by means of a resurrected body.[21] But the soundness of such arguments is not our central concern here. What is important is noting that once Christian thinkers distanced themselves from arguments of this sort, the door was opened to the possibility of animal resurrection and immortality.

As a result, numerous Reformation and post-Reformation figures endorsed the notion of animal immortality. John Calvin, commenting on the text of Romans 8 above, says:

Paul does not mean that all creatures will be partakers of the same glory with the sons of God, but they will all share in their own manner in the better state, because God will restore the present fallen world to perfect condition at the same time as the human race.[22]

Likewise, Martin Luther appears to have held that at least some animals are immortal. When asked about animal immortality, Luther is reported to have remarked, concerning his own dog, Tölpel:

Peter said that the last day would be the restitution of all things. God will create a new heaven and a new earth and new Tölpels with hide of gold and silver. God will be all in all; and snakes, now poisonous because of original sin, will then be so harmless that we shall be able to play with them.[23]

Unfortunately, even if there is substantial warrant in the Christian tradition for the claim that some animals are immortal and thereby able to enjoy a blissful eternal existence, it is not clear how this might be used to develop a CD for earthly animal pain and suffering. Indeed, it appears initially that the prospects for developing such a CD are grim. What we are looking for is a way of explaining a particular type of evil which shows why permitting it (or some equivalent evil) is necessary for securing some correspondingly equal or greater good. Animal

---

[21] Arguments concerning the possibility of resurrection and individual continuity have generated some interest recently. The standard position, defended by Peter van Inwagen, in 'The Possibility of the Resurrection', *International Journal for the Philosophy of Religion*, 9 (1978), 114–21, has it that no physical organism could survive dissolution and reconstitution of the sort that would have to be proposed to avoid St Thomas's conclusion. Recent critics of van Inwagen have argued that identity through such changes may be possible after all. See, for example, Dean Zimmerman, 'The Compatibility of Materialism and Survival: The Jumping Elevator Model', *Faith and Philosophy*, 16 (April 1999), 194 f. A discussion of related issues can be found in Wennberg 2003: 321 ff.

[22] John Calvin, *Calvin's Commentaries: The Epistles of Paul the Apostle to the Romans and to the Thessalonians*, ed D. W. Torrance and T. F. Torrance (London: Oliver and Boyd, 1961), 173.

[23] Scott Ickert, 'Luther and Animals: Subject to Adam's Fall?', in Andrew Linzey and Dorothy Yamamoto (eds.), *Animals on the Agenda* (Champaign/urbana, Ill.: University of Illinois Press, 1998), 91.

immortality would be a great good for the animals. But how is permitting the pain and suffering in the earthly life a *necessary condition* for it? Since animals seem incapable of anything on the order of soul-making, it does not seem that the reality of animal pain and suffering can bring about or enhance the quality of life experienced by animals in eternity. If the outweighing good that results is not something of the order of soul-making, what could it be?

Wesley and others are of the opinion that since nonhuman animals are subject to pain, suffering, and corruption in this life, there must be some future state in which they can be compensated for that suffering, perhaps by being made the recipients of eternal bliss. It is certainly reasonable to think that were animals to be victimized in this way they would need to be so compensated. But that does not add up to a successful CD for animal pain and suffering. This picture instead leaves us with an important, nagging question; namely, 'Why does God allow any animal pain and suffering in the first place?'. Unless there is some good reason to allow the pain and suffering, the compensation will not be sufficient to excuse God's permission of it. We can imagine someone agreeing to be the victim of a certain sort of evil, with the understanding that this evil will be compensated for afterwards by a vastly outweighing good. But one would never agree to such an arrangement if told that the outweighing good could be had without the evil. If the evil is not in any way needed to secure the outweighing good, the evil is in fact gratuitous. So far as we can tell on this account, the same is true here. That is, animals can be the recipients of the gift of blissful immortality whether they have been allowed to be the victims of pain and suffering or not. So while the eternal reward might be sufficient compensation, it will not excuse God's permission of this evil unless there was some good reason to allow it. The theist cannot take comfort here merely in the fact that animals might be granted a postmortem blissful existence.

It may be that the outweighing good which requires the permission of the pain and suffering of nonhuman animals is one that does not directly benefit the animals themselves of course. We will consider CDs of that sort in the following two chapters. But here we are considering CDs where the resulting and outweighing goods do directly benefit the victims. Is there any other way to employ the prospect of animal immortality to construct a CD of this sort?

4.3.1 Animal suffering and immortal bliss

Although theists commonly argue that pain and suffering are necessary conditions for humans to be capable of developing certain virtues (courage, charity, etc.), these 'soul-making theodicies' lose plausibility when we attempt to apply them to the case of animals. Nonetheless, one might argue that there are other ways that a period of earthly pain and suffering could enhance the resurrected condition of animals that don't involve soul-making. Consider the following analogy. Athletes who exercise regularly do so for a variety of reasons. Some do it to stay trim.

Some do it for the love of competitive sports. Others do it for the euphoric feeling that they experience at the end of a vigorous workout. Those in this last group freely admit that the workouts themselves often contain a great deal of pain and suffering, and yet they insist that the ultimate feeling of euphoria is an outweighing good that makes the pain and suffering worth it.

Imagine that sports physiologists discover the mechanism which accounts for these euphoric feelings and offer these athletes the following options: continue to experience the euphoria as a result of the daily workout, or hook yourself up to the euphoria machine every morning and press the button instead. Which would they pick? I suspect many, perhaps most, would reject the machine, since the euphoria experienced as a result of this particular variety of pain and suffering is satisfying in a way that the machine-induced pleasure is not. What is it exactly about the prior suffering that contributes to this overall greater satisfaction?

A variety of possible answers suggest themselves. Perhaps, first, the suffering endured during the workout heightens the anticipation that the athlete feels as she struggles towards the euphoric state. Perhaps instead the endured suffering provides the athlete with the sense that the resulting goods have been secured through his or her own efforts. Or perhaps, finally, the contrast between the pain and suffering of the workout and the subsequent euphoria makes the pleasurable feelings more intense than they would otherwise be. Perhaps it is a combination of these. Perhaps it is none.

Whatever the explanation is, such considerations open the door to the possibility that in order to experience fully the bliss of postmortem existence animals will have to experience some pain and suffering in a prior earthly existence. For this to be the case, it must also be the case that animals have the necessary cognitive capacities to experience the states that make such an outweighing good possible. Can any of the explanations that we applied to the athlete above be applied in the case of nonhuman animals and their experience of postmortem bliss? The comparisons at first do not seem promising. For example, it seems evident that we cannot reasonably take the animal's anticipation of postmortem bliss to provide the outweighing good. Likewise, we can't plausibly claim that the goodness of animals' experience of postmortem bliss is enhanced by their recognition that their own efforts were involved in securing the good. The reason for this is simple: there is nothing—as far as we can tell—about the pain and suffering of the animals that meaningfully contributes to the bliss they would experience postmortem.

Of the three explanations applied to the case of the athlete only the third seems potentially relevant here; that is, perhaps allowing animals to experience some measure of pain and suffering in the earthly life would serve, by contrast, to enhance the goodness of this ultimate state. The plausibility of this explanation is enhanced when we recognize that, proportionately, the suffering of the earthly life is infinitesimal in comparison to eternal bliss. Further, the goodness of the postmortem state might be *very* substantially enhanced, since the contrast provides animals with a vastly greater appreciation for that state in which they are exempted from pain, death, and predation.

Explanations of this last sort are instances of a general type of explanation often found in attempted explanations of evil. The type is usually described with slogans proclaiming that it is impossible to appreciate (or to appreciate fully) good without corresponding or prior experience of evil. Explanations of this sort, however, are troublesome. Surely the theist cannot endorse the claim that appreciation of the good is *impossible* without experience of evil. God has such an appreciation. And for traditional Christians the original human pair and the angels had or have a similar appreciation. Further, even if it were the case that all persons except God, angels, and the original human pair are unable fully to appreciate good without evil, *this fact too* seems to be a flaw in design. Why couldn't God have succeeded in creating sentient creatures with the capacity for such appreciation absent the experience of evil? As the above examples show, experiencing this sort of evil is not a necessary condition for experiencing the later great good of eternal bliss in the divine presence. So what other reason might there be?

4.3.2 Sentience, pain, and meaningful immortality

In considering ways in which animal pain and suffering can be explained by appeal to a meaningful immortal existence, there are still more exotic options available. It is a very great good for sentient and conscious organisms to be able to enjoy eternal well-being in the divine presence. This is evident in the case of conscious beings capable of morally significant free action, as human beings are. But it is equally true in the case of animals with less robust capacities, including those animals that are capable of intentional but unfree action, and those which are sentient but not capable of free or intentional action. As a result, we can suppose that if there are good reasons for creating such beings, God would desire that these beings share in eternal beatitude.

But perhaps there are also good reasons why these animals must first be part of a created earthly order, prior to their enjoying eternal beatitude. In that case, the very capacities that make it possible for these animals to enjoy this beatitude might function during their earthly life in such a way that the possibility of experiencing pain and suffering is unavoidable. Thus, perhaps when an animal gets a thorn in its paw the thorn causes the animal to feel pain because God has created these animals with the requisite capacity for pain and suffering, a capacity that, in the future, makes possible the very great good of the enjoyment of God.

We can see how this explanation of the reality of earthly animal pain and suffering is supposed to work by considering the following analogy. During a snorkeling trip I drove to a remote beach with a fantastic reef within swimming distance of the shore. The weather was brutally hot and so, before venturing from the parking area across the sand, I put on my flippers to keep my feet from being scalded by the sand. Anyone who has tried to walk with flippers knows that this is perilous business. In order to keep from tripping over the end of the flippers and falling head first into the sand, I had to goose-step towards the water. Unfortunately, my goose-step is less fully coordinated than that of the average goose, and so I crashed to the ground and ended up with a mask full of sand. If someone had asked me why I was wearing flippers, I would have told them that it is very hard, and much less fun, to go snorkeling without them. And the reason I wore them across the sand was that I was also hoping to keep my feet from burning. No doubt other footwear would have been more effective if my only aim was to cross the sand. But it wasn't. And so, in order to get to the very great good of snorkeling, I had to put myself in the position of being able to trip and fall. Notice that the flippers that I needed to snorkel did not require me to fall. They rather set up conditions that made the falling possible.

For all we reasonably accept, animal sentience and consciousness are like flippers. God outfits animals with these capacities because they will allow the animals to experience fully the goodness available to them in the divine presence. But for other reasons, still to be specified, the animals were needed to participate in the prior earthly life. That prior earthly life set up the conditions that made pain and suffering possible, though they themselves did not require it. Nor was actual pain and suffering instrumental in securing the greater postmortem goods for which sentience and consciousness were created.

For this CD to be successful, we would have to have some good reason to think that there were good or outweighing reasons to allow animals to have an earthly existence in which actual pain and suffering were possibilities. Perhaps the following:

It is good for God to create human beings in an environment where soul-making is possible. In such an environment human beings must have freedom, and must be in a position to exercise it. This in turn requires that they be placed in an environment which is law-like or 'nomically regular', in order to be able to form intentions to bring about such-and-such states of affairs in the world, i.e. to act intentionally. It is quite reasonable to suppose that human beings living in a nomically regular environment will be essentially dependent on nonhuman animals in a variety of ways. If they are not necessary for food, they are at least a necessary part of an ecosystem which provides humans with food, since they appear to be necessary for the functioning of the ecosystem in much the way they seem to be in the actual world; i.e. for spreading pollen and seeds, for replenishing atmospheric carbon dioxide, and so on. For these and other reasons, embodied, physical humans cannot live without animals. As a result, God creates the animals but also invests them with the capacities which make them well suited to a meaningful and fulfilling eternal future.

On this view animal pain and suffering really serves two goods which might be seen as jointly outweighing: the good of an eternal life of bliss, and the good of allowing human beings to live in an appropriately nomically regular environment during their earthly life. In the next two chapters we will see how a CD might be developed which appeals only to the latter of these goods. Notice, however, that a CD of this sort could also serve to supplement CDs of the sort considered in Chapter 3. There we considered the possibility that animal suffering is, in some way, due to the Fall of angelic or human creatures. On those views animal pain and suffering were not possible without a moral fall. But we might consider a view according to which animals were created with the capacities for experiencing pain and suffering. On that view those capacities would have remained dormant without the Fall. But because of the Fall, the created order is transformed in such a way that actual pain and suffering are experienced.

As a result, animal immortality can be relevant when it comes to animal pain and suffering in the earthly life, both for the sake of animals themselves, and for the sake of the good of human beings. Understood this way, the reality of animal immortality and the prospect of eternal beatitude for them provides us with a second successful CD for animal pain and suffering in which animals themselves are the recipients of an outweighing good. Nonetheless, the majority of the 'greater-good'-type explanations for animal pain and suffering have focused on goods which do not accrue directly to the animals which suffer. We turn to examine such explanations in the following chapters.

5

Natural Evil, Nomic Regularity, and Animal Suffering

It may not be a logical deduction, but to my imagination it is far more satisfactory to look at such instincts as the young cuckoo ejecting its foster-brother—ants making slaves—the larvae of the ichneumonidae feeding within the live bodies of caterpillars—not as specifically endowed or created instincts, but as small consequences of one general law, leading to the advancement of all organic beings, namely, multiply, vary, let the strongest live and the weakest die.

(Charles Darwin[1])

Like many of his late nineteenth-century colleagues, Darwin found it hard to believe that animal pain and suffering could be accounted for in terms of goods that accrue to the animals that suffer. For Darwin it seemed evident that the pain-wracked and unjust course of organismic history failed to confer outweighing benefits on its victims. If all of this animal suffering was to serve any outweighing goods, those goods would have to be found among subsequent generations of organisms—perhaps our own—or in the general goodness of organismic 'advancement'.

In Chapter 4 we considered attempts to show Darwin wrong on this score. There I argued that some of the explanations of animal pain and suffering which focus on outweighing goods enjoyed by or affecting animals themselves can indeed provide us with successful CDs. In this chapter and the next we turn to explore the 'Darwinian' position that animal pain and suffering, if justifiable at all, is justified as a necessary condition for outweighing goods which either are enjoyed by creatures other than those that suffer or serve to enhance the goodness of the universe at the global level. This approach to animal suffering has been much more common not only in the late nineteenth century but throughout the history of theological reflection on animals. This is a less than surprising fact, since animals have typically been regarded not as ends in themselves but rather

---

[1] Quoted in Neal C. Gillespie, *Charles Darwin and the Problem of Creation* (Chicago, Ill.: University of Chicago Press, 1979), 127.

as instruments for achieving the aims of God or 'rational' creatures.[2] Since, on this view, the very purpose of animals is to serve the needs of others, we would expect that their suffering must be explicable in terms of goods that accrue to others.

As an historical aside it is interesting to note that many of the explanations of animal suffering that we will explore in this chapter and the next were widely defended by those theologians, philosophers, and scientists of the later nineteenth century who were the first to face squarely the fact that the paleontological evidence signaled a terrestrial natural history filled with a colossal amount of 'organic evil'. Some of these explanations are based on scientific or philosophical positions that are no longer regarded as plausible. Others are worth revisiting. Unfortunately, the history of these discussions has not been traced with as much detail or clarity in the secondary literature as it deserves. As tempting as it is, I cannot attempt to piece together a detailed reconstruction of the relevant nineteenth-century discussion here, though it is a project that is certainly to be commended to able historians. I will, however, accord myself a bit more latitude in this chapter to explore positions that were defended in this period that are less clearly able to jump the epistemic hurdle we set down earlier for successful CDs, that is, being such that we are not warranted in rejecting them given our justified acceptances. In some cases I think such rejection will be clearly warranted, but most of these positions will be intriguing or instructive enough to repay careful visits nonetheless. This will be true of *most* of these positions, not all. I will be up front in admitting that some of the views I will recount below are included simply because I find them interesting or bizarre.

5.1 'NOMIC REGULARITY' CDS

5.1.1 Moral versus natural evil

As noted in Chapter 3, theists attempting to give explanations for God's permission of evil have traditionally divided that evil into two broad types: moral evil and natural evil. What both types have in common is that token instances of each type involve creaturely harm.[3] The two types differ in that for every

---

[2] Though this view is not universal and is not regarded as a central theological commitment by any of the major theistic traditions.

[3] In the case of moral evil this will sometimes involve an agent causing morally blameworthy harm to another. However, there will be other types of cases as well. For example, in some cases moral evil will involve an agent causing itself morally blameworthy harm, the obvious cases being self-mutilation and suicide. It will also include less obvious cases such as those in which one agent bears a deeply felt hatred towards another but never acts on it. Bearing such hatred is itself a moral evil, and while the target of the hatred is not harmed by it, the bearer is, since such sustained hatred erodes one's character.

moral evil at least one free creature can be rightly blamed, at least in part, for that evil, while in the case of natural evil no free creature can be rightly blamed for it.

Which side of this divide does animal pain and suffering belong on? If we accept any of the CDs discussed in Chapter 2 we will have to admit that all of it falls on the moral side, since, on these CDs, animal pain and suffering is attributable to the free actions of human beings or Satan and his cohorts or some combination of these. For those who reject this view, such pain and suffering will likely straddle the types. *Some* animal pain and suffering is undoubtedly culpably caused by free creatures. But evils visited on animals by free creatures, as numerous as they may be, are utterly dwarfed (at least in quantity) by the evils that have been experienced by animals through the countless ages of organic natural history.

In these two chapters we will set aside the possibility that animal pain and suffering might be attributed to a fall by human beings or preternatural beings endowed with free choice. We will also set aside those instances of animal pain and suffering directly attributable to the actions of free creatures (wanton hunting, torture, factory farming, etc.). The remaining instances will fall into the category of natural evil. Once we think about animal pain in this way, it is natural to ask whether or not the strategies typically deployed by theists to explain natural evil generally can be applied to animal pain and suffering in particular. To answer this question we will first have to think a bit about how natural evils are explained, and then see if those explanations can be extended to the cases of interest here.

Before we look at the possibility of constructing CDs for animal pain and suffering considered as natural evils I would like to raise one general complaint about arguments against theism based on natural evil. The complaint is only of marginal importance here, since it will not be directly relevant to any argument or evidence for atheism grounded in animal suffering. However, it will be especially relevant to any argument which attempts to use the totality of natural evil, of which animal suffering will be a part, as evidence for atheism. The complaint concerns just what we should take to count as a natural evil.

Critics of theism are wont to point to any occurrence or state of affairs that we typically describe as a 'natural disaster' as an instance of natural evil. But our characterization of natural evil won't strictly speaking allow this. The reason for this is that at least in many cases the evil that results from such natural disasters is in part attributable to the actions of free creatures. Consider a case in which I am hiking in some rocky terrain and come across a section of the trail that passes by an unstable rock wall. Let's further imagine either that I am sufficiently knowledgeable about geology to see that the rock wall is unstable or that there are signs warning of the dangers of falling rocks ahead. If I proceed along the trail and am injured or killed by falling rocks, the injury or death would certainly not count as natural evil, since the evil here results in part from my freely choosing to do something I know to be risky. As a result, the evil of being injured or killed by the rock is at least partially attributable, causally and morally, to me. Similarly, if I choose to build a home on a known fault line, or in the likely path of hurricanes, and my home is later destroyed by an earthquake or a hurricane, the resultant evil is not, strictly speaking, a natural evil, since it is in part attributable to my (poor) choices.

One might object, of course, that the problem with these 'semi-natural' evils is that God makes them possible in the first place. Why would God put us in a position where we are capable of being harmed by falling rocks, or capable of building homes which are subject to destruction by catastrophic natural forces? There are two things to say in response. First, the question is simply a variant of the question of why God allows us to choose between doing good and evil in the first place. Providing us with the ability to do good and evil *just is* providing us with the ability to cause good or harm (to ourselves or others). And the cases we are discussing here are simply further instances of the general phenomenon.

Second, there are good reasons for the theist to think that God would put free creatures in a position where being able to cause goods and harms of this particular sort is on balance better than not being able to do so. How might an argument for this claim go? We might argue that it is a good thing that the world be governed by regularities which make these sorts of harms possible, and that this regularity is good enough to outweigh those harms. If it is good to have a world with free creatures and good that such a world be governed by physical regularities, there will be occasions where those free creatures might willfully throw themselves in front of 'lines of causation' that cause them harm.

However, whether the critic of theism finds this pair of responses helpful or not, the complaint stands: much of what is typically regarded as natural evil is in fact moral evil. This is not to deny that there *are* some genuinely natural evils. Indeed, some evils will still count as wholly natural evils even in cases where creaturely free acts have contributed to their occurrence in some central way. This is because my complaint is relevant only to evils that result from natural processes of which creatures ought to have been aware. If I build a house on the beach in Miami, I know that at some point it will be damaged by a hurricane. When that day arrives, the damage will count as one of these semi-natural moral evils. On the other hand, if an earthquake were to devastate Philadelphia tomorrow, home owners there could hardly be blamed. Philadelphia has never experienced such an earthquake, nor does anyone think it liable to. Thus, my complaint is not intended to amount to an argument that there is, after all, no genuine natural evil, but rather that there is probably a great deal less than one is initially inclined to believe. This in turn means that there is less evidence available for mounting an argument for atheism from natural evil than one might have initially believed. Of course, as I noted, this complaint will not have a substantial bearing on the central concern of this book: the reality of animal pain and suffering. Some animal pain and suffering can be blamed on creaturely free action. But it is clear that, unless CDs like those developed in Chapter 2 are correct, a great deal, indeed the vast majority, cannot.

As noted, the fact that most animal pain and suffering counts as natural evil should lead the theist to wonder whether or not she can deploy explanations aimed at other types of natural evil generally to explain animal pain and suffering. The most common sort of explanation of natural evil has it that natural evils are necessary by-products resulting from the creation and conservation of a physical world which operates in a regular or law-like manner. I will call such a world *nomically regular*. CDs that appeal to nomic regularity in this way hold that this feature of a world is either intrinsically good or good because it serves to secure other goods that outweigh the evil by-products. Such a CD will have to show both that nomic regularity is good or secures outweighing goods and that there is no set of natural laws which can yield a better balance of intrinsic or instrumental goods over evils. This is the general strategy. We will see along the way that there are some special difficulties involved in applying this general strategy to the case of animal suffering in particular.

This approach to animal suffering was taken by a number of theologians confronting this problem in the wake of the acceptance of Darwinism. The nineteenth-century theologian and geologist George F. Wright, one of the most prolific writers on the topic, argued that the problem of animal suffering is, in this way, like another problem faced by traditional theists: the problem of the reprobation of the damned. For Wright, 'The reprobation of the wicked may come in as a circumstance subsidiary to the general ends of the moral system that is created', and the suffering of animals could be viewed likewise 'in terms of the requirements of *the general scheme*'.[4] By 'the general scheme' Wright means here the general order of the natural world which is required to serve the particular ends God has for creation.

In the remainder of this chapter we will assess the success of this approach to animal pain and suffering by considering three questions in turn. First, why would one think that nomic regularity is a good feature of a universe in the first place? Second, even if it is, do we have good reason to believe that no nomically regular world has a substantially better balance of good over evil than the actual world? And, finally, can the goods under consideration outweigh the type of natural evil in question; namely, animal suffering? In addressing this third question we will raise one further question; that is, what reason do we have for thinking that the good of nomic regularity would have animal pain and suffering as one of its unavoidable by-products?

    [4] Emphasis added. Quoted in Jon H. Roberts, *Darwinism and the Divine in America: Protestant Intellectuals and Organic Evolution, 1859–1900* (Notre Dame, Ind.: University of Notre Dame Press, 2001), 132–3.

5.1.2 What is nomic regularity?

Whether or not the observation plays any role in explaining evils, theists must accept the claim that nomic regularity is either something that God values highly in creation or it is an inevitable by-product of something else valued highly. Nomic regularity is, of course, a pervasive fact about the natural order and it seems to be a fact that comes at a high cost. It is plain to atheists and theists alike that God might secure a world with a great deal less evil by sometimes, or perhaps often, intervening in the course of natural events to prevent or thwart (at least most large-scale) natural evils. The fact that he does not do so demands some sort of explanation. The explanation, whatever it is, will have to involve some account of why the preservation of nomic regularity is good and important.

Before we look at accounts of what makes nomic regularity good, we will need a more detailed characterization of what exactly it is. The phrase itself intimates that nomic regularity has something to do with the processes in the natural world being liable to description by law-like statements that admit of few or no exceptions. One way for the universe to be nomically regular would be for it to be entirely deterministic. Were the universe to function this way, the state of the universe at each instant would determinately follow from the state of the universe at the previous instant in conjunction with the exceptionless laws true in the world. But this isn't the only way a universe could be nomically regular. The universe would be nomically regular if some or all of the laws of nature were probabilistic or 'chancy', as long as the probabilities were well-behaved. Radioactive decay provides a good example. The half-life of the most common isotope of uranium is roughly 4.5 billion years. A 9-billion-atom sample of uranium will thus have half of its atoms decay over 4.5 billion years, at the rate of approximately one atom per year. On the most widely accepted way of thinking about radioactive decay, the process of radioactive decay is not a deterministic one. If one were fully acquainted with every natural fact about the universe at a given instant, one could not predict whether or not any atom in our sample would decay in the next instant. At best we can say that in the course of the next year the odds are that one atom will decay. Nonetheless, this process is governed by or subject to description in terms of well-behaved probabilistic laws.

For those to whom the indeterminism of radioactive decay is news, it is important to realize that the unpredictability of the decay in these cases is not due to the fact that we have substandard or flimsy powers of prediction. Nor is it based on the fact that we have a less than fully complete description of the universe and its workings at our disposal. The unpredictability is rather based on the fact that in some respects nature behaves in a fundamentally indeterminate manner. Certain events occur without sufficient causes. This fact, however, does not preclude indeterministic events from conforming to well-behaved patterns. Because of this, a universe with nondeterministic processes such as radioactive decay can qualify as nomically regular as long as those processes can be described by laws which include determinate probabilities. We may not be able to predict whether or not a particular uranium atom will decay at any given instant, but we can predict that one atom in our 9-billion-atom sample will decay this year, etc.

Nomic regularity and the good of creaturely freedom

Is nomic regularity good and, if so, what *sort* of good is it? It is commonly held that nomic regularity is at least an instrumental good, since it provides a necessary condition for the overriding good of genuine moral agency or free will. Since free will is a very great good indeed, it is reasonable to suppose it to be sufficient to outweigh a great deal of natural evil that arises as a by-product of having nomic regularity.

Of course, the connection between nomic regularity and moral agency or free will is not exactly straightforward. If freedom most fundamentally involves being able to make a choice between competing and available alternatives, the presence or absence of a nomically regular external environment seems irrelevant. To see the relevance, we need to consider exactly what makes freedom the great good that it is for creatures. The first thing that makes it a great good is that it introduces the possibility of moral goodness in the universe. For creatures to be potential fonts of moral goodness those creatures must have the ability to choose between alternative courses of action where, at least in some cases, the choice is between morally good and morally evil alternatives. The second thing that makes it a great good is that it confers on creatures the capacity to make a difference in how things go in their world. In order to be able to do this, creatures must be situated in an environment in which their choices lead to results which are, at least typically, of the sort the agent intends. That is, the agent must be able to make choices, and those choices must be capable of being translated into actions which in turn make a difference for how things go in the world. *Valuable freedom* then involves both freedom *to choose* and freedom *to affect the course of the world* in virtue of such choices. Let's call these two components of valuable freedom 'free choice' and 'effective choice' respectively.

It is possible to imagine worlds in which free and effective choice are detached. Indeed, some have argued that such detachment is preferable. To see why, consider the view defended by some that free choice is a good primarily because it allows creatures to cultivate virtuous (or vicious) characters (i.e. the 'soul-making' explanation of evil). On this view creatures are placed in a world where they are torn between incentives and desires to do both good and evil. Free choice is afforded to these creatures in order to give them an opportunity to choose to do good and thereby become creatures who are habitually disposed towards good-doing, i.e. who are virtuous. In order for it to be possible to cultivate virtue, the creature must be subjected to certain evil states of affairs, caused by other free creatures or by the operations of nature itself, and must be allowed to respond to these evils by choosing to act virtuously or failing to do so. If the creature acts virtuously, she does a morally good thing and further contributes towards the cultivation of her virtue. If not, she will, either by inaction or by the active pursuit of evil, cause harm and contribute towards her own viciousness.

If the possibility for 'soul-making' is what makes freedom the great good that it is, then it seems that God might arrange things in such a way that this good is permitted without allowing misused freedom to cause harms when evil is chosen, simply by putting us in a 'virtual playpen'.[5] In a virtual playpen creatures would be permitted to make free and morally significant *choices*, but whether or not those choices would be *effective* would further depend on the content of what we will. If we choose to do good, God permits the choice to issue in the intended consequences. If we choose to do evil, God allows the evil *choice* but blocks the negative consequences of our choice. However, God could not simply block the negative consequences. What would it look like if he were to do so? I intend to pull the trigger to shoot you but suddenly find that my finger is paralyzed, or that the bullets have all vaporized, or . . . I intend to steal the car but when I rear back to throw the brick at the car window to gain entry I suddenly fall asleep, or I find that windows are unbreakable when struck during attempts at theft, etc. Would this suffice? In one sense it would. Were the world so configured, I would not be able to bring about any evil beyond my evil choices. But it is further true that in such a world I would not be able to make evil choices at all since the totality of my experiences will make it evident that doing evil is impossible.

In such a scenario choosing to do evil would be like choosing to fly. When I was five years old, I and a few other boys at Towpath Elementary School decided that we wanted to fly. At recess we assembled at the top of the concrete wall at the edge of the playground. One after another we jumped off the wall, flapping our arms as hard as we could, each crashing to the ground in disappointment. Of course, as the first few plopped to the ground, some of those still to jump were convinced that those who failed to fly failed only out of lack of strength or skill. But after twenty minutes of consistent failure and sore behinds we all decided that flying was not in our future. To the best of my knowledge, no one in that group has since been tempted to fly off of a concrete wall. Indeed, I suspect none of my kindergarten companions *could* now even form the intention to fly off the wall. They know by their experience that doing so is as impossible as leaping to the moon or swallowing the ocean. If God were simply to block the evil consequences of our actions, choosing evil would be no more possible for us than choosing to fly or choosing to jump to the moon is for us in the actual world.

As a result, were the playpen world to be actual, God would need to block the consequences of our evil choices, all the while allowing us to live with the illusion

---

[5] See, for example, David Lewis, 'Evil for Freedom's Sake', in Lewis, *Papers in Ethics and Social Philosophy* (Cambridge: Cambridge University Press, 2000).

the action we had chosen had been carried out. In the course of our making evil choices God would thus provide us with experiences that made it *seem* as if those choices had been effective, but where, in fact, the effects of the choice were illusory. There is real moral evil in such a world, since the choice itself is a morally evil one. But there is *less* moral evil, since the evil consequences are never realized and, perhaps best of all, no one except the evildoer is ever harmed by those evil choices. Would such an arrangement be preferable?

One might object that the playpen world casts God objectionably in the role of a deceiver, since he would be leading the murderer or the car thief to believe that they had murdered someone or stolen a car, when in fact they had merely formed an intention to do so (and been subjected to an illusion that they had actually done so). But if such deception is the only way to allow the possibility of evil-choosing freedom without allowing harm to others, perhaps the deception is itself an evil necessary for this outweighing good.

There are good reasons, however, to doubt the coherence of virtual playpens. How can it be possible, for example, for free creatures to remain in genuine contact with one another after an extended period of making evil choices with these illusory consequences? Were I to be in the playpen, I would have to be under an illusion every time I came to apologize to someone whom I thought I had wronged. God would have to cause me to go mute every time I intended, in conversation, to refer back to some occasion on which I had—or so I thought—wronged you. Or, even worse, God would have to make me believe that I spoke words which referred to such a prior occasion when I did not. Presumably, there would have to be corresponding adjustments to how you perceived me on occasions like this. That is, when I elected to make reference to the occasion when I wronged you, you would either have to hear me say something else, or watch my lips move without hearing sounds, or . . . If I stole your car or your watch, what would things be like for me when we met again and you were driving the car or wearing the watch I believed I stole? I would have to become blind to the world as it really is. In order to keep all of these illusions working, I would be plunged deeper and deeper into a solipsistic world until I became utterly disconnected from the real world.

Let's suppose that I am wrong about that and that such a world is possible after all. The important question at issue here is whether or not it matters that a world have both *free* and *effective* choice. The critic is arguing that it does not, since the world would be better if evil could be chosen but not executed. While such a world would be better in the sense that the willed evil consequences of evil choices never actually arose, something rather important, indeed an outweighing good, is lacking in such a world. To see what that good is, let's consider what would be absent were God to conduct business similarly in the case of morally *good* choices. In that case, creatures would make free choices, but God would prevent those choices from having any effect on the ways things really go in the world, whether those choices were good or evil. Instead God only allows the creature to experience the illusion of carrying out the choice. In this world, while you might think you have comforted your friend in her grief, or given sacrificially to help someone in need, instead you have merely *made a choice* to do so. Everything after that was illusion. Something is sorely lacking here, and it is part, perhaps the largest part, of what makes freedom valuable in the first place. What is good about free choice is not simply that I have the ability to choose among a list of items on a mental menu. Rather, what is good is that I have the ability to exercise my causal powers in my environment by means of my choices. I have the capacity to choose to show love to my spouse or my child, *and to do it*. I have the ability to choose to sacrifice for the sake of my friend, *and to do it*. Would we think that creatures in this world have been deprived of a great good? Indeed we would. Being able to choose is a great good. Being able to effect states of affairs in the world in virtue of our choices is even better. And the greater goodness of the latter is not simply due to the utility of whatever the good consequence might be. It is due also, perhaps largely, to the fact that *I* can affect it.

Thought experiments like this show us why it is free *and* effective choice that we value. It is the ability to choose and to have that choice affect the way things happen in the world beyond my own skin that matters. And this is something I value even in cases where the choice I make is an evil one. Undoubtedly, the 'playpen' arrangement would permit the possibility of at least one good beyond the good of the act of freely choosing, i.e. the good of 'soul-making'. But the thought experiment of the last paragraph shows us that such truncated freedom would surely not be worth trading for, even for the sake of gaining a world in which evil choices were all subject to the confines of the playpen.

All of this serves to show that freedom is valuable because it is both free *and* effective. Once we see this, we are in a position further to see that certain conditions must obtain in a world in which creatures have freedom of this sort. First, free and effective choice requires that creatures be capable of bringing about causal effects beyond their own skin. But not any old causal powers will do. It must be the case that corporeal creatures with this sort of choice are capable of causing specific types of bodily movements which reliably result in the obtaining of specific cascades of events outside of the body. If not the former, then those creatures would be incapable of causing effects in the world at all. And if not the latter, creatures could not cause effects intentionally.[6]

The first of these claims is obvious. But what about the second? In order for us to bring about states of the world intentionally, by way of our choices, we must be able to form intentions to bring about states in the world, and

---

[6] Strictly speaking these claims apply only to free creatures with bodies. Perhaps it is also possible for there to be disembodied free creatures. If there are, those creatures would at least need to be able to causally affect states of affairs in the external world. This would require some sort of nomically regular connection between the forming of intentions and the causal effects in the world, even if the relation obtains without the mediation of a body.

we must have reason to believe that by undertaking certain bodily movements we make it likely that those states of the world will come about. Neither of these things is possible in a world without nomic regularity. We could never form intentions of this sort in a non-nomically-regular world, since we would never have seen any correlation between what we will to happen in the world and what does happen in the world. Unless I can come to count on the fact that when I wield the ax it splits the wood (as opposed to causing nuclear fusion among the atoms in the wood), or that when I eat the apple it provides me with nutrition (as opposed to causing me to go blind), I cannot form intentions to split the wood or eat an apple in the first place. And, of course, even if I somehow could form an intention to split the wood, or provide my body with nutrition, I wouldn't have a clue how to go about it in a world that was not nomically regular.[7] Bruce Reichenbach defends this position as follows:

Without regularity of sequence, agents could not entertain rational expectations, make predictions, estimate probabilities, or calculate prudence. They would not be able to know what to expect about any course of action they would like to take. Whether or not such action would be possible, or what they would have to do to have God bring it about, whether it could occur as they planned (supposing agents could plan, which is doubtful), what the consequences would be—all this would be unknown and unknowable. Hence, agents could not know or even suppose what course of action to take to accomplish a certain rationally conceived goal. Thus, rational agents could neither propose action nor act themselves.

But proposing action and acting on that proposal are essential for an agent's determination as a moral being. 'Good' is predicated of a moral agent when proper intentions come to fruition in right conduct: 'bad' when improper intentions result in wrong conduct. But since they would be unable to rationally conceive what actions to take in order to achieve certain goals, and since they could not perform the actions, a world . . . [without regularity] would prevent moral agents from formulating or carrying out their moral intentions. In effect, it would become impossible for agents to be moral beings.[8]

Much earlier in the twentieth century F. R. Tennant argued similarly:

It cannot be too strongly insisted that a world which is to be a moral order must be a physical order characterized by law and regularity. The theist is only concerned to invoke the fact that law-abidingness . . . is an essential condition of the world being a theatre of moral life. Without such regularity in physical phenomena there could be no probability to guide us: no prediction, no prudence, no accumulating of ordered experience, no pursuit of premeditated ends, no formation of habit, no possibility of character or of culture.[9]

---

[7] T. J. Mawson has made this argument forcefully in 'The Possibility of a Free-will Defense for the Problem of Natural Evil', *Religious Studies*, 40 (2004), 23–42.

[8] B. Reichenbach, *Evil and a Good God* (New York: Fordham University Press, 1982), 103–4.

[9] F. R. Tennant, *Philosophical Theology* (Cambridge: Cambridge University Press, 1928), ii. 199–200.

Free and effective choice is a good, and nomic regularity is a necessary condition for it. However, insofar as nature is nomically regular, the laws governing the hardness of matter and the conservation of energy, laws that permit me to use my hammer to drive nails, will also allow the hammer to crush my thumb. The same will hold true with respect to laws that make possible all sorts of conditions which lead to natural evils. The same laws that allow me to chew my food also allow the bear to tear my flesh. If nomic regularity is a great enough good to outweigh the evils that result from not disrupting it, God will allow that nomic regularity and the natural evil it generates.[10]

This first instance of the instrumental goodness of nomic regularity focuses on its importance as a necessary condition for allowing morally significant agency. Thus, there is an important sense in which this involves an attempt to explain natural evil in terms of morally significant freedom, but in a way different from that considered in Chapter 3. In that chapter the reality of evil was to be explained in terms of free beings using their freedom to bring about consequent evils. In this case antecedent conditions required to make free and effective choice possible have unintended and ineliminable evil side effects. We can label these two different ways of relating freedom and natural evil *consequent free-will CDs* and *antecedent free-will CDs* respectively.

Nomic regularity and the good of intellectual inquiry

In the nineteenth century a number of Christian thinkers argued that nomic regularity provided a necessary condition for a quite distinct variety of good: the good of the intellectual satisfaction that comes from scientific inquiry. Commenting on the general trend towards seeing the goodness of God in nomic regularity in this period, Jon Roberts remarks:

The world disclosed by science made theological sense only if intelligible, lawlike processes were seen as witnesses to the providential concern of a God whose will was immutable. In this connection, many Protestants placed a great deal of emphasis on the familiar claim that intelligible events enabled God's children to interpret the cosmos. This ability afforded them intellectual gratification, a clearer apprehension of the wisdom of God, and assistance in their efforts to make their way in the world.[11]

The most sustained defense of the view that nomic regularity is instrumental for securing the good of intellectual satisfaction was mounted by the nineteenth-century geologist and theologian George Frederick Wright. Wright argued that intellectual goods are as significant as moral goods, and that nomic regularity serves the aims of both. As an eminent geologist, Wright had experienced firsthand the pleasures of intellectual inquiry and discovery, and the corresponding pleasure

---

[10] Note that the world can be nomically regular even if God sometimes intervenes to disrupt the laws of nature. The only condition on such interventions would be that they should not undercut the possibility of the goods nomic regularity is intended to bring about.

[11] Roberts, *Darwinism*, 144.

of seeing the 'handiwork of the creator' in the complex order stamped into nature. Such pleasures require that there should be a well-ordered universe to discover, and intelligent beings there to discover it.

The tendency of mind which leads us to seek for the bond of unity and order which appears in the similar and analogous phenomena is among the noblest impulses and the highest endowments of the soul. The gratification of that tendency *must* constitute an important part of the reason of our existence. The adaptation of the creation to this tendency of our minds is among the most important of nature's contrivances.[12]

Indeed, for Wright, these intellectual pleasures were sufficiently good that they offset the natural evils that might occur as by-products of the nomic regularity of nature:

[T]he comprehensive end of creation is the 'highest good of being in general'... the sensational happiness of all organic creatures... is an element to be considered in that general good of being. The pleasurable sensations of the intellect, investigating and interpreting the ways of God as displayed in the creation, are likewise a part of that good included in the end for which all things were made... In other words, it may reasonably be supposed that it is of more account to God's creatures as a whole that the universe be capable of interpretation, and that the method of God in his works be manifested, than that any amount of temporary good should occur during the earlier stages of the process of development.[13]

The 'temporary goods' which he has in mind in this passage are the physical pleasures that would be derived from God occasionally intervening to prevent the laws of nature from causing the pain and suffering resulting from natural evil. Since intellectual pleasures are indeed greater goods than physical pleasures, it is worth having a world in which intellectual pleasures are possible, even at the cost of some physical pain and suffering. Wright puts the point as follows:

The doctrine of final causes has been too often associated with low forms of utilitarianism. The paleontologist, for example, finds the cast of a Trilobite in the bed of what was an old Silurian sea. The purpose of that low organism is by no means exhaustively explained when we have taken a measure of the sensational happiness he derived from his monotonous existence. The light so well adapted to his marvelous eyes, the agreeable temperature of the waters, the slimy food on which he lived, all this, and more, brought him some degree of pleasure; and this is to be considered part of the final cause of his existence. But a far higher purpose is served in the adaptation of his complicated organism and of the position of his tomb in a sedimentary deposit to arrest the attention and direct the reasoning of a scientific observer. The pleasure of one lofty thought is worth more, and so fitted to be with the Creator an object of design, than a whole herd of sensational pleasures. A page of Darwin has to a single reader more 'value in us' than all the elements had to the whole race of trilobites in Silurian seas. Yet the latter, with their marks in the rocks... when correlated with general laws of production and preservation, may have

---

[12] George Frederick Wright, *Studies in Science and Religion* (Andover: Draper, 1882), 243.
[13] Ibid. 194–5.

been necessary before ever the thought which illuminates the page of the naturalist could have been engendered.[14]

Theists like Wright were well aware of the fact that certain sorts of intellectual satisfaction are available to creatures like us outside the domain of natural science. Mathematicians and logicians are just as likely to find intellectual satisfaction in their a priori investigations as are scientists in their investigations of nature. But those in the Judeo-Christian tradition, like Wright, were equally aware of the fact that the Hebrew and Christian Scriptures are replete with references to the fact that God's existence and nature are manifest in the workings of the physical universe. Psalm 19: 1, for example, reads 'The heavens declare the glory of God; the skies proclaim his handiwork'. For those familiar with these texts, it seemed obvious that the intellectual investigation of the natural world was an equally important source of intellectual and spiritual satisfaction. But for the heavens and skies to be capable of delivering these goods they would have to bear the earmarks of rationality and design. As a result, a world suitable to reflect the divine creator and to provide delights in intellectual endeavor must be nomically regular.

Nomic regularity and created-order goods

It is common in the Christian tradition to hold that creaturely diversity is an intrinsically good feature of creation since by it the divine goodness is multiplied in creatures. In Chapter 4 we saw that from the thirteenth through nineteenth centuries philosophers and theologians in the Christian tradition argued that diversity of types and degrees of goodness of organisms served to manifest the goodness of God directly.

It seems reasonable to suppose that a world with such varied types of organisms would further require a high degree of nomic regularity. Embodied creatures cannot successfully reproduce, acquire adequate nutrition, constitute a suitably interdependent ecosphere, and so on, unless the physical world in which they are embodied is appropriately nomically regular. Without such nomic regularity it would be impossible for animals to behave intentionally in ways necessary to survive and propagate. For example, we saw earlier that intentional actions on the part of human beings would be impossible in a world that was not largely nomically regular. Things are no different when it comes to action in the case of nonhuman animals. Without nomic regularity, it would be impossible to create animals capable of successfully navigating in their environment, whether their patterns of behavior were learned or instinctual. Animals could not learn, for example, that to behave in certain ways would serve to catch prey or that drinking from the river would slake their thirst. Nor could these patterns of behavior be programmed into animals instinctually, since an irregular world would be

---

[14] Ibid. 204–5.

unresponsive to such programming. Responsiveness of this sort would require nothing short of nomic regularity.

Augustine took such regularity in the cosmic order to be at least part of the explanation for the reality of the evils that afflict the animal kingdom:

One might ask why brute beasts inflict injury on one another, for there is no sin in them for which they could be a punishment, and they cannot acquire any virtue by such a trial. The answer, of course, is that one animal is the nourishment of another. To wish that it were otherwise would not be reasonable. For all creatures, as long as they exist, have their own measure, number, and order.[15]

Thus, one reason to think that a suitably diverse creation would require nomic regularity is that it seems that organisms in such a world would have to be suitably dependent upon each other and upon an environment that pushed back in dependable ways.

Nomic regularity as intrinsically good

In addition to thinking that nomic regularity is an *instrumental* good, many have argued that a world which is nomically regular is *intrinsically* more valuable than one that is not. This sentiment has been defended by a variety of theists over the last two millennia. But it is notable that ardent defenses of it are especially prominent during historical periods characterized by rapid and radical scientific advance. Both in the seventeenth century and in the nineteenth century theists impressed with the revolutions in mechanistic physics and later in biology were led, as we saw earlier, to argue that the goodness, wisdom, and bounty of God are manifest through the variety of effects he can bring about by nomically regular means. Leibniz, to give just one example, defines the goodness of the created order in terms of 'as much variety as possible, but combined with the greatest possible order'.[16] Leibniz also argued repeatedly that a universe that required regular miraculous intervention by God—a universe that was not nomically regular—would speak ill of its creator. In response to Newton's hypothesis that God must intervene periodically in the course of nature to maintain the orbits of the planets, Leibniz wrote:

Sir Isaac Newton, and his followers, also have a very odd opinion concerning the work of God. Acceding to their doctrine, God Almighty wants to wind up his watch from time to time: otherwise it would cease to move. He had not, it seems, sufficient foresight to make it a perpetual motion, Nay, the machine of God's making, is so imperfect, according to these gentlemen; that he is obliged to clean it now and then by an extraordinary concourse and even to mend it, as a clockmaker mends his work; who must consequently be so much the more unskillful a workman, as he is more often obliged to mend his work

15 Augustine, *The Literal Meaning of Genesis*, trans. and annot. John Hammond Taylor (New York: Newman, 1982), i. 92.

16 G. W. Leibniz, *Monadology*, §58, in Leibniz, *Philosophical Essays*, ed. R. Ariew and D. Garber (Indianapolis, Ind.: Hackett, 1989), 220.

and set it right. According to my opinion, the same force and vigor remains always in the world, and only passes from one part of matter to another, agreeably to the laws of nature, and the beautiful pre-established order. And I hold, that when God works miracles, he does not do it in order to supply the wants of nature, but those of grace. Whoever thinks otherwise must needs have a very mean notion of the wisdom and power of God.[17]

Fellow seventeenth-century philosopher Nicholas Malebranche held that nomic regularity in the world essentially follows from God's perfect wisdom and goodness. When we look to judge the overall perfection of the world, he claimed, we must do so by considering two dimensions. First, we must assess the overall goodness of the product, including all the good and evil states of affairs, free and natural, which the world contains. To this we must add, second, the goodness or lack of goodness of the *means* that God employs to bring about that product. Since the latter is as reflective of the divine nature and attributes as the former, it is the sum of the two which constitutes the overall goodness of the world. As crude as this procedure of summing the two variables appears to be, it is explicitly endorsed by Malebranche:

A work that has a degree of perfection equal to eight, or which bears the character of the divine attributes to a degree equal to eight, and that is produced by ways that express the divine attributes only to a degree equal to two, expresses them overall only to a degree equal to ten. But a world that is perfect only to degree six, or which expresses the divine attributes only to degree six, and that is produced by ways that express them once again to degree six expresses the divine attributes to degree twelve. Therefore, if God chooses one of these two works, he will choose the less perfect one because the less perfect work together with the ways bears the character of the divine attributes to a greater degree.[18]

Similar sentiments were expressed in the nineteenth century as Christian thinkers begin to endorse versions of Darwinism. In this regard Henry Ward Beecher remarks:

If single acts would evince design, how much more a vast universe, that by inherent laws gradually builded itself and then created its own plants and animals, a universe so adjusted that it left by the way the poorest things, and steadily wrought toward more complex, ingenious, and beautiful results! Who designed this mighty machine, created matter, gave it its laws, and impressed upon it that tendency which has brought forth almost infinite results on the globe, and wrought them into a perfect system? Design by wholesale is grander than design by retail.[19]

---

[17] *The Leibniz–Clarke Correspondence*, ed. H. G. Alexander (Manchester: Manchester University Press, 1956), 11–12.

[18] N. Malebranche, *Abrégé, du traité de la nature et de la grâce*, in Malebranche, *Oeuvres complètes de Malebranche*, 20 vols., ed. A. Robinet (Paris: Vrin, 1958–67), v. 9.1085. The translation is from Steven Nadler, 'Spinoza in the Garden of Good and Evil', in Elmar Kremer and Michael Latzer (eds.), *The Problem of Evil in Early Modern Philosophy* (Toronto: University of Toronto Press, 2001), 83.

[19] Henry Ward Beecher, *Evolution and Religion* (New York: Fords, Howard and Hurbert, 1885), 114.

It is important to see that Malebranche and Beecher are not arguing that nomic regularity serves to bring about some greater good. The point instead is that there is something grand, beautiful, and artful about a universe which contains within it everything that is necessary in order for it to yield the results God intends for it. God could cause every event that we see in the natural world directly. But a powerful and rational designer would, like the owner of the rug factory, display his power and reason far more manifestly in a universe which is itself a machine-making machine. A universe which achieves the ends God has for it in this self-contained fashion does as much to express the glory of its creator as do the end-products of the creative process. Because this feature of the universe is good simply in virtue of the fact that it reflects the creator's goodness, it is in-itself good.[20]

5.1.3 Is there no better world?

In *Love and Death* Woody Allen expressed a sentiment shared by many who press the argument from evil: 'if it turns out that there is a God, I don't believe that he is evil. The worst that can be said is that he's an underachiever'. Is God an underachiever when it comes to the amount of natural evil he allows to creep into the nomically regular universe? That is, do our justified acceptances warrant rejecting the claim that there is no significantly better world in this respect?[21] One might quite naturally think so. After all, it seems that God might have made hurricane-force winds physically impossible, or have made laws of fluid dynamics that preclude the possibility of tsunamis. And even if such changes were not possible, God could certainly intervene in the course of things with greater frequency to prevent hurricanes and tsunamis. This would detract

---

[20] This way of putting it makes it appear as if goodness of this sort is only instrumental, since the machine-making machine which is the universe is good only because of the fact that it does something else: reflects the creator's goodness. However, the underlying view of goodness here is one according to which goodness consists of the relation of resemblance to the divine being. Thus, reflecting the divine goodness is just what goodness consists in. Similar views have been defended by some contemporary theists. Those interested in this position should consult the following: Howard J. Van Till, 'The Creation: Intelligently Designed or Optimally Equipped?', *Theology Today*, 55 (1998), 362, and Peter van Inwagen, 'The Problem of Evil, the Problem of Air, and the Problem of Silence', in *God, Knowledge, and Mystery* (Ithaca, NY: Cornell University Press, 1995), 83–4.

[21] It is worth mentioning here that a number of theists have argued that *even if* there is reason to believe that there are significantly better worlds, this alone is no reason to think that these explanations for evil fail. To assume the contrary would be to assume that God is obliged to create the best possible world he can create. But there is reason to think that God has no such obligations. Indeed, if there is available to God a continuum of worlds such that for each world God could create there is a better one, then God cannot be obliged to create the best one. Perhaps then God is simply obliged to create any of the worlds that surpass a certain standard of moral acceptability. For more on this see, for example, Daniel and Frances Howard-Snyder, 'How an Unsurpassable Being Can Create a Surpassable World', *Faith and Philosophy*, 11(1994), 260–8, and Michael Murray and Michael Rea, *Introduction to the Philosophy of Religion* (Cambridge: Cambridge University Press, 2008).

from nomic regularity to *some* extent no doubt. But wouldn't prevention of the Johnstown Flood or Hurricanes Andrew and Katrina be worth the price of a small case of irregularity? Would such irregularity serve to make the world nomically irregular enough to prevent it from exhibiting the sorts of good that come from regularity? Let's consider these two sorts of criticisms; that is, the criticism that the natural laws could have been better, and the criticism that there should be more evil-preventing interventions.

Could the laws which govern our physical universe have been configured to yield a substantially better overall balance of good? It is hard to know how to begin answering such a question. To show that such a world is possible the critic would need to describe a nomically regular world which (a) contains goodness of the sorts (either the same sorts or equivalent or better sorts) and amounts found in the actual world and which (b) contains substantially less natural evil than the actual world. This task seems hopeless. To pull it off we would first need to spell out a reasonably complete list of the goods the actual world contains. We may be well acquainted with some of these. Are we acquainted with all of them? I haven't the slightest idea—and no one else does either. It must at least be the case that this alternative world contains important goods like living beings, intelligent beings, free beings, beings capable of sustained relationships of love and friendship, along with the external and internal conditions necessary to permit and support the existence of such goods. There are surely more goods as well. But even if we were able to construct a very long list of goods, all the goods we could think of after lots of trying, it is hard to know how we could ever have much confidence that we had arrived at a reasonably complete list.

What is more, even if we were able to overcome this hurdle, it is hard to know how to secure a better balance of goods over evils without a very clear idea of what the constraints of world design might be, and how those constraints would lead both to securing equally great goods and eliminating evil. It is important to see that merely giving a superficial description of a world which contains slightly less evil will not serve the critic's purposes. Rather, the description would have to show how one could, using the same constituents and laws as in our world, or using entirely alien constituents and laws, construct a world that is realizable, stable, and capable of supporting goodness. Surely it is simply beyond our powers to do something like this. And even if it were in our power to do it, it would be very unlikely that we could have much confidence in the fact that we had succeeded at it.

Not only must the critic confront the fact that describing such an alternative world is seemingly beyond our capacities, she must also confront the claims of numerous scientists that there are many respects in which the physical parameters governing our world could not, after all, be significantly different from what they are in fact. Instead it appears the universe is fine-tuned in such a way that were the basic physical parameters that govern the structure and behavior of matter to differ in very small ways, there would be no universe at all or, at least, no life at all. As a result, even minor changes in the fundamental workings of the world might result in a universe that existed for such a short span of time that it would be unable to give rise to or support the existence of any living things at all. Just how much flexibility is there in world design? Just how might the structure of the world be altered in the service of reducing natural evil without obliterating the possibility of a world altogether? We don't know the answer for sure. But we do know that a large number of parameters must be fixed within narrow constraints. This gives us at least good, positive reason for thinking that the task of describing better universes constituted of different laws and components might well turn out to be futile.[22]

Perhaps trying to construct better universes from whole cloth is not an option. But can't the critic argue that the universe would be better were God to intervene with greater frequency in order to prevent a greater share of natural evil? God could, perhaps, establish a policy of steering all tornadoes away from homes? Would such a world contain substantially less evil? Of course. Would this result in a massive disruption in nomic regularity—massive enough, say, to undermine some of the goods God aims to bring about through permitting the regularity in the first place? For example, would such disruption suffice to undermine the free and effective choices of free creatures? It seems not. And we can imagine similar thought experiments concerning other sorts of natural evil.

One might respond to this objection in Malebranchian fashion, arguing that although such intervention would not undermine the instrumental role nomic regularity is supposed to play, it nonetheless directly detracts from the goodness of the world because it detracts from the intrinsic good represented by nomic regularity itself. I suspect few will think that the destruction wrought by tornadoes is worth the cost of a small additional amount of unnoticed (indeed, perhaps undetectable) nomic regularity.

However, the defender of the nomic-regularity CD need not retreat to this less plausible response. All naturally evil states of affairs are naturally evil because they constitute harm to some being or beings capable of being harmed. If God were to seek to minimize the relative quantity of natural evil, he would be seeking to reduce the overall quantity of harm done to creatures. However, divine justice requires, among other things, that God's dealings with creatures be evenhanded. Such evenhandedness entails that when creatures are treated a certain way in certain circumstances, other creatures in similar circumstances will be treated in like fashion. If justice requires such evenhandedness, then were God to prevent destruction from tornadoes, he would surely be obliged to prevent similar destruction of property caused by hailstorms, tropical-storm wind gusts,

---

[22] For a brief survey of the relevant physical parameters and the cosmic implications of changing them see Murray and Rea, *Philosophy of Religion*, ch. 5. More detailed treatments can be found in Paul Davies, *Mind of God* (New York: Simon & Shuster, 1993) and John Leslie, *Universes* (New York: Routledge, 1996).

and so on. It is, of course, not at all easy to say what 'similar destruction' might amount to. There might be all sorts of cases that would have the appearance of being similar but which might figure in a set of necessary conditions for securing outweighing goods of which we are wholly unaware. Nonetheless, the evenhandedness condition requires that if God is going to preserve one sort of sentient creature from a certain sort of harm by fiat, other similar sentient creatures similarly situated will be preserved from similar harms. Given this, we have good reason to expect that minimal interventions would quickly multiply to such an extent that there is a high likelihood that any intrinsic or instrumental goods which were to come from nomic regularity would be in jeopardy.[23]

Thus, it seems that if we are to try to describe a world with the same constituents and laws with substantially less evil is unlikely to succeed. As a result, nothing we accept gives us good reason to reject this CD for natural evil.[24]

5.2 AN ACCOUNT OF ANIMAL SUFFERING?

As we have seen, we might be able to explain at least some natural evil as an unavoidable by-product of an overall good and nomically regular world. Such a position has three components. First, nomic regularity is instrumentally or intrinsically good. Second, nomically regular worlds which can sustain varied and robust quantities of good will contain the potential for natural evil. Third, no other world has a significantly better balance of good over evil than the actual one. Thus, any world governed by nomic regularity and which contains as much good as this world contains (for example, containing the goods of being capable

[23] It is worth noting that the evenhandedness reply is more or less plausible depending on which sort of good we take nomic regularity to be a necessary condition for. For example, if the good in question is that it permits free creatures to learn how the natural order functions in order that they might engage in intentional action, the evenhandedness reply only goes so far. As Daniel Howard-Snyder points out, if that is what is at stake, God can regularly intervene to prevent events that would lead to the pain and suffering of nonhuman animals as long as 'it didn't happen around us'. Fair enough. Of course, as noted in the text, violations of nomic regularity will undermine the intrinsic goodness of nomic regularity as identified by, for example, Malebranche and Leibniz. For Howard-Snyder's discussion of this matter see his 'God, Evil, and Suffering', in Michael Murray (ed.), *Reason for the Hope Within* (Grand Rapids, Mich.: Eerdmans, 1998), 96–7.

[24] Perhaps one might think that victory has been declared too quickly. In order to reasonably believe that the cosmos could have been configured to yield a better balance of good over natural evil, must one be able to fully specify the conditions that would lead to such a better balance—or can one simply rely on a bare intuition that things could be better on this score? It seems that I assume the former. Michael Rea has argued, in correspondence, for the latter. In fact, I think rather that it is neither. What the critics of theism need is some reason to think that things could be better on this score than they are. Do they have that? The answer is that they do only if they can show, at least for some token instance, that the natural world could have been set up in such a way that evil could be avoided without incurring an overall worse balance. This would not require describing an alternative possible world in fine-grained detail. But it would require an account that gives us good reason to believe that the suggested alteration could be pulled off without actually incurring the cost of a worse overall balance. It is this, however, that cannot be done.

of supporting the existence of complex living organisms and providing some
of those organisms with free and effective choice) would have at least as much
natural evil as this one. If this is right, then perhaps, like the harm caused by
avalanches and AIDS, animal pain and suffering is one of the unintended natural
evils that are by-products of having a robust and nomically regular natural world.
Is this sufficient?

The most difficult task in constructing such a CD comes in showing how
nomic regularity might be argued to have permission of the specific evil of
animal suffering either as a necessary condition or as an unavoidable by-product.
Does nomic regularity, and the goods it yields, somehow require *that*? There
is certainly no intrinsic connection between the two. After all, a world could
be utterly nomically regular and as complex as you please without having any
sentient creatures at all. Such a world would be regular, and would lack natural
evil altogether. As a result, there will be no way to argue that the intrinsic
goodness of nomic regularity, taken on its own, is sufficient to explain animal
suffering. One thing this shows us is that a successful CD will require that we
focus on the instrumental goodness of nomic regularity. If there are goods which
will serve to outweigh the evil of animal suffering, it will have to be found among
these instrumental goods.

Perhaps some will think that I have dismissed the 'intrinsically good nomic
regularity' view too quickly. After all, with certain plausible emendations, perhaps
more can be said for this view. For example, the theist might plausibly wish to add
that God would, antecedently at least, desire to create a universe which contains
beings made in the divine image, and who are capable of free and effective choice.
If there is good reason why such beings need to be embodied, they will need to be
situated within an ecosystem that will require the existence of other organisms (as
sources of food, or as resources required to supply oxygen for respiration, etc.).
In particular it might require that there be animals that have capacities sufficient
for them to experience pain and suffering. For example, it might require animals
that are suitable evolutionary precursors to human beings. If such precursors
were necessary, they would have to be animals with fairly well-developed central
nervous systems, perhaps nervous systems which are capable of sentience of a
sort that allows for the experience of pain and suffering. Or, perhaps it requires
animals that are of sufficient size to provide suitable sources of food for those
organisms capable of morally significant agency. Larger organisms of this sort
might plausibly be supposed to require something like a central nervous system
to oversee the functioning and behavior of the organism. And it is plausible
to suppose that there must also be nociceptors which allow these organisms to
detect noxious stimuli in the environment, etc.

Once we include these sorts of emendations, we have in fact begun to construct
an explanation of animal pain and suffering that treats nomic regularity as an
instrumental good. That is, by adding these additional points, the argument
now amounts to the claim that nomic regularity is required in order to allow

for something else, for example for the existence of creatures capable of morally significant agency, which makes nomic regularity and the by-products it yields in this complex set of circumstances worth it. We will turn to CDs of this sort shortly. But we can note here that even if they are successful, their success is going to depend largely on seeing nomic regularity as an instrumental good. Can the instrumental goodness of nomic regularity suffice as the outweighing good for the purposes of this CD?

The CDs we have been discussing here are, as noted earlier, all variants of a theodicy commonly employed to offer explanations for natural evil more generally. On that theodicy there is something good about nomic regularity which makes the permission of certain sorts of evil unavoidable. We have looked at four candidate goods here: (i) the intrinsic goodness of nomic regularity, and the instrumental goods of: (ii) free and effective choice, (iii) intellectual satisfaction, and (iv) created-order goodness. Two of these four, the second and third, make sense only against the background claim that the cosmos contains beings like us (corporeal beings capable of morally significant free action and of rational inquiry). The other two depend on the created order exhibiting certain sorts of dynamic and static stability respectively. These facts should initially make one skeptical about the prospect of developing a CD of animal suffering which will be up to the task. We can see why by considering first whether or not regarding nomic regularity as a good aimed at free and effective choice might provide the outweighing good we need.

5.2.1 Nomic regularity and the good of free and effective choice

Above I have argued that there are good reasons for thinking that nomic regularity is required in a world capable of sustaining free and effective choice on the part of creatures. I have also argued that we have no reason to reject the claim that there is no world that is overall significantly better than the actual world that would also lack natural evil of the types and quantities found in the actual world. Can the theist reasonably claim that in securing such a nomically regular environment *animal pain and suffering* in particular will likely follow? It seems not. A complete CD of animal suffering of this sort faces two insurmountable hurdles. The first hurdle is that such an account, like many Fall CDs, does not seem to have the resources to explain why there is so much prehuman-animal pain and suffering—an analogue of the problem of PAP raised in Chapter 3. Even if it were true that sentient nonhuman animals were somehow necessary preconditions for or by-products of securing the goods of free and effective choice for beings like us, it is hard to see how this requires the existence of animal pain and suffering *before human beings appeared on the scene*. Since there would be no beings like us around to reap the benefit of nomic regularity, the pain and suffering experienced by nonhuman animals as a result of it could not plausibly be thought of as necessary conditions for goods that accrue to us. Thus, if we are to imagine that this is the sort of good God aims to secure in bringing about a world which allows for the possibility of animal pain and suffering, it seems that it would be overwhelmingly better for God to have created human beings and nonhuman animals all at the same time, that is, in much the way young-universe creationists understand the Genesis creation narrative.

What is more, even if we could make a plausible case that free and effective choice by creatures like us requires the existence of animals which preexist human beings, it is hard to see how this good could further require that these prehuman animals have second-order mental states of the sort that make animal pain and suffering morally salient, as discussed in Chapter 2. Recall that the CDs under discussion in this chapter are of a general sort usually used to explain the existence of natural evils such as the devastation caused by hurricanes or earthquakes. On such CDs nomic regularity might sometimes require that bits of matter come into contact with other bits of matter in a way that results in harm to creatures. Applying this to the case of animals, one might argue that nomic regularity could plausibly explain why some animals must sometimes be subjected to bodily harm. But *even if this is right*, this CD must explain further why the sort of harm necessitated by nomic regularity must include *morally salient phenomenally conscious second-order mental states*. It is hard to see how this could be done in this case.[25]

We should also notice that there is nothing about this CD which explains exactly what role nonhuman animals play in the economy of the universe in the first place. Perhaps if there are reasons for God to create nonhuman animals in the first place—say, because they enhance the diversity of creation in a way that makes it intrinsically better—then these animals would, like any other physical entity, be subject to possible damage if they accidentally wander into nomically regular causal processes. Yet a CD like this will only have something to offer us if it can explain the most serious issues that arise when we consider animal suffering in the first place.

There are, then, two problems faced by nomic-regularity CDs which seek to explain animal suffering in terms of the goodness of free and effective choice for beings like us. Those two problems are:

(1) The Prehuman Suffering Problem; i.e. PAP;
(2) The Nature of Animal Mentality Problem.

As we will see, these two problems arise for the other instrumental-good CDs as well (i.e. those grounded in the goods of intellectual satisfaction and created-order goods).

---

[25] Again at least it is hard to see how this can be done without availing oneself of the resources afforded by other CDs. For example, one might supplement this CD by making appeal to the view, defended in Chapter 4, that the capacity to have morally salient second-order mental states of pain and suffering is a necessary condition for embodied organisms maintaining their organismic integrity.

5.2.2 Nomic regularity and the good of intellectual satisfaction

As we saw before, the most notable defender of the intellectual-goods CD, George Wright, felt the need to address the Prehuman Suffering Problem. In the text cited earlier, in fact, he notes that the pleasures of intellectual discovery extend to prehuman natural history as much as they do to present natural processes, and that these intellectual pleasures are sufficiently outweighing goods. As a result, it is a good thing for the natural processes which led to the present arrangement of things to have a lengthy history for us to study with care and in detail.

For this account to have any chance of success we would have to have reason to think, first, that the suffering of the animals whose natural history we can now reconstruct is outweighed by the intellectual pleasures found in the reconstruction. Second, we would need reason to think that the overall goodness of the intellectual pleasure of reconstructing an accurate evolutionary history is superior to the goodness that would arise from our reconstructing a natural history based on deceptive appearances of a natural history of the sort we might have if, for example, young-universe creationism were true. On this view it is good or perhaps necessary for the universe to exhibit apparent signs of age despite the fact that the universe is quite young. Finally, we must again confront the question of whether or not this account explains why animal harm must be accompanied by morally salient mental states. Let's consider these in turn.

Is it reasonable to believe that the suffering of animals throughout prehuman history is outweighed by the intellectual pleasure of those who were fated to discover it? One might think that such questions are impossible to answer. Indeed, one might wonder to what extent goods and evils of these sorts are even commensurable. If they are commensurable, it is hard to know exactly what metric might be applied in making the comparison. As a result, a defender of the intellectual pleasures might argue that we just are not in any position to make confident assertions about intellectual pleasures being unable to outweigh animal pain.

This defense of the intellectual-pleasures CD initially seems wholly unsatisfying. We can imagine all sorts of inane experiments which involve a great deal of animal suffering, the only aim of which is to answer some silly or ridiculous question. (How many decibels is the yelp of a tortured dog?) Surely we would regard such experiments as morally indefensible. The pain and suffering of these animals undoubtedly *is* commensurable with the intellectual pleasures derived from them, and we have no problem seeing that these goods are not outweighing. From this we can conclude that the intellectual pleasures of a few curious scientists are just not sufficient to outweigh the pain and suffering of a large number of animals in the case of the study of evolutionary natural history either.

A defender of the intellectual-pleasures CD who wants to insist on the incommensurability of these goods and evils might respond to such an argument as follows. In considering the case of the deranged (dog-torturing) scientist we are led to draw a certain correct conclusion, but not on the grounds supposed by the argument. The example invites us to conclude that the scientist's actions are immoral *because the good of his intellectual pleasure was not sufficient to outweigh the pain and suffering of the animals (the tortured dogs for example)*. The defender of this CD might argue that though we are correct in arguing that the scientist's actions are immoral, the *reason* for the immorality of his action has nothing to do with our relative assessments of the goods and evils. Rather, his actions are evil because he intentionally chose to inflict pain and suffering on the animals. He shouldn't have undertaken the experiment because, in carrying it out, he acted from an immoral will. But that conclusion is insufficient for us to draw any conclusions about the relative goodness of his intellectual pleasure and the badness of the dogs' pain and suffering. As a result, such thought experiments cannot be used to show anything about the potential for scientists' intellectual pleasures to outweigh the pain and suffering of animals throughout evolutionary history.

While this response would succeed in explaining away our moral revulsion at such experiments without making any appeal to the relative weights of the goods and evils involved, it is nonetheless insufficient. One can easily amend the original thought experiment in ways that show that we find the evils of animal suffering and specific goods that accrue to human agents to be commensurable after all. For surely there are *some cases* where the benefits of subjecting dogs to pain-inducing research might indeed be justified by the outcomes such research will yield. If such an experiment would likely lead to a cure for heart disease in humans, we would praise such research and, perhaps, award the one who undertook it the Nobel Prize. In this case we would judge the overwhelming good of curing heart disease to outweigh the pain and suffering of the dogs if in fact the pain was truly necessary for the research to yield its results.[26] Such cases make it clear that we can at least sometimes make judgments about the commensurability of these goods and evils after all. With our confidence thus restored, we can fairly conclude that we should judge the intellectual pleasures of the scientist to be insufficient, on their own, to outweigh the pain and suffering of animals in evolutionary history.

Even if one could somehow defend the claim that intellectual pleasures would provide sufficiently outweighing goods, this CD faces a further difficulty. On this CD the possibility of animal pain and suffering is supposed to be an *unavoidable* precondition for beings like us being able to enjoy the intellectual pleasures that attend certain sorts of rational inquiry. In other words, if the very same

---

[26] There are, of course, some who do not find such judgments plausible at all. For them, it is evident that the goods that might accrue to human beings do not justify the suffering inflicted on innocent, sentient animals. There is no need to quarrel about who is right here. The important thing is that the critic is equally confident in her ability to draw conclusions about how to weigh the relevant goods and evils involved. And this shows that she too judges the goods and evils in question to be commensurable.

intellectual pleasures could be had without any animal pain and suffering, it would be impermissible for God to allow that pain and suffering to occur. Is this possible? It seems so. All that would be required is that God create the universe in the way that the young-universe creationists think he did: fully formed and with all of the apparent signs of age which it actually exhibits. This possibility was, as we saw in Chapter 3, raised most famously by Philip Gosse in *Omphalos*.[27] Let's call such a world an 'omphalic world'. If creating an omphalic world were possible for God, this would surely be preferable in light of the fact that it prevents prehuman animal suffering while allowing the same measure of intellectual satisfaction to the paleontologist.

A defender of the intellectual-satisfaction CD might complain, first, that an omphalic world would undermine the possibility of intellectual 'discovery' altogether, since coming to believe falsehoods hardly counts as *discovering*.[28] But worse is the fact that any intellectual pleasures secured in this way come at the high cost of making God a deceiver in massive proportions. Let's consider these responses, starting with the second.

It is not clear that it would always be a bad thing for God to make the world in such a way that we are naturally led to believe false things about it. In Chapter 2, for example, we saw that human beings are highly liable to make attributions of mentality to animals that are phylogenetically close to human beings. One would imagine that this trait would be adaptive (and, even if not adaptive, highly desirable) since it would make it far less likely that we could bring ourselves to believe that our fellow human beings, beings that look and act like us, are automata or zombies and thus not fit objects of our moral concern. Having such a trait is rather likely to lead us to feel an appropriate moral sympathy towards others, leading further to the kindness displayed in selfless behaviors that some evolutionary biologists and sociobiologists have argued are adaptive.[29] However,

---

[27] Philip Henry Gosse, *Omphalos: An Attempt to Untie the Geological Knot* (London: Voorst, 1857; repr. Woodbridge, Conn.: Ox Bow, 1998).

[28] Interestingly, Gosse argues in *Omphalos* that this claim is mistaken. Gosse claimed that the universe is to be understood in terms of a single underlying law which not only governs the operations of nature, but which also acted as God's guide in structuring the universe at creation. Thus, when the geologist considers geological strata or fossils, he is uncovering the laws of the universe no less on the young-earth-creation hypothesis than on the hypothesis that the apparent history of the universe is real: 'the acceptance of the principles presented in this volume, even in their fullest extent, would not, in the least degree, affect the study of scientific geology. The character and order of the strata; their disruptions and displacements and injections . . . and all the other phenomena, would be *facts* still. They would still be, as now, legitimate subjects of examination and inquiry. I do not know that a single conclusion, now accepted, would need to be given up, except that of the actual chronology. And even in respect of this, it would be rather a modification than a relinquishment of what is at present held; we might still speak of the inconceivably long duration of the processes in question, provided we understand *ideal* instead of *actual* time;—that the duration was projected in the mind of God, and not really existent' (ibid. 369).

[29] As one example, defended by a pair of group selectionists, see David Sloan Wilson and Eliot Sober, *Unto Others: The Evolution and Psychology of Unselfish Behavior* (Cambridge, Mass.: Harvard University Press, 1999).

this trait also leads us into error when we attribute mental states to robots or dolls. We would not typically regard these as fodder for atheistic arguments, in large measure because cases in which we make these false judgments are generally inconsequential. Rather than insist on nondeception at all costs, the following more sober principle seems in order:

Permissible Deception: It is permissible for God to establish conditions which are inherently liable to dispose us to false belief as long as either there is a substantial outweighing benefit to be had by the obtaining of the conditions, or the cases in which we are led to the false judgments are inconsequential.[30]

This principle is plausible but it does not rule out the possibility that God creates the world in such a way that its prehuman history exhibits merely apparent signs of age, especially if the intellectual benefits that result from the false appearances are great and, correspondingly, the animal suffering that would have otherwise been required to secure it is also great. Since both of those seem to be true, there seems nothing untoward about God conducting the affairs of creation in this way.

Worse still is the fact that Wright's hypothesis seems unable to address the second major worry for CDs treating nomic regularity as an instrumental good, that is, there is nothing on this hypothesis that mandates that the animals in evolutionary history have morally relevant and qualitatively undesirable second-order mental states. Thus, the CD based on intellectual goods must ultimately be judged unsuccessful.

5.2.3 Nomic regularity and created-order goods

What of our third variant of the nomic-regularity CD? On this third view nomic regularity is an instrumental good aimed at the realization of a creation which fully manifests divine goodness, perhaps by generating creatures which constitute a 'great chain of being'. As noted earlier, advocates of this view argue that the goodness of the creation is enhanced by the fact that it contains diverse types of beings. Among the diversity of types are organisms with increasingly robust sorts of mental capacities. As a result, we might expect that some organisms will be capable of simple (first-order) control and access consciousness, while others, as discussed in Chapter 2, will have a simple capacity for second-order awareness of first-order mental states of the sort that some ethologists such as Gordon Gallup attribute to primates capable of forming self-concepts. Still other organisms, like human beings, will have, in addition to second-order

---

[30] Richard Swinburne has defended a similar principle, the 'Principle of Honesty', according to which 'God has an obligation not to make a world in which agents are systematically deceived on important matters without their having the possibility of discovering their deception' (*Providence and the Problem of Evil* (Oxford: Oxford University Press, 1998), 139). Swinburne uses the principle to argue, among other things, that God would not place us in what I called earlier a 'virtual playpen'.

awareness, the capacity to reason abstractly, and to deliberate and choose freely. This is not meant to provide an exhaustive characterization of the nodes on the continuum of mental capabilities. Instead, it shows that there will be nodes on the continuum which include animals capable of second-order awareness, and thus of pain and suffering, but whose mental capacities will be insufficient to support morally significant agency. If this is right then combined with the general approach we find in nomic-regularity CDs we can say that animal suffering is an unavoidable by-product of creating a world aimed at maintaining two distinct sorts of goods: (1) creaturely diversity of a sort that allows for a robust manifestation of the divine nature in creatures, and (2) nomic regularity. The first of these explains why animal sentience, and thus *real* pain and suffering, is possible. The second explains why it is actual, since, this CD assumes, there is no other world with different constituents or laws which is capable of supporting a world of the sort characterized by (1) with a better overall balance of good over evils.

This CD succeeds where the others have failed. That is, it gives us reason for thinking that real animal pain and suffering might be required in a world manifesting these goods of created order. However, it also fails where the others succeed. That is, even if organismic diversity is a key ingredient in a universe which appropriately manifests the divine goodness, it is hard to see any good reason why this should come about by means of the pain, suffering, death, and waste endemic to the evolutionary process. The problem here is not merely the problem of prehuman-animal suffering. The problem is rather the evolutionary means that brought this diversity into existence in the first place. Perhaps the end products manifest the divine nature in profound ways. But it is a contingent fact that the end products come to be through evolutionary means. And it is these evolutionary means that raise the greatest share of our difficulty, since it is the pain, suffering, and death in natural selection that is at issue.

5.3 TWO EMENDATIONS TO THE NOMIC-REGULARITY CD

So far the attempts to use CDs grounded in the instrumental or intrinsic goodness of nomic regularity have been unable to supply adequate replies to the two key objections they face. For those CDs which claim that nomic regularity secures goods for beings like us (creatures capable of free and effective choice and intellectual satisfaction), these CDs are unable to explain the existence of prehuman-animal pain and suffering. The remaining CDs, intellectual satisfaction and created-order goods, fail to explain why the goods in question—the goods nomic regularity is supposed to help secure—cannot be had without the reality of morally salient pain and suffering endemic to natural selection. But the defenders of CDs grounded in nomic regularity are not yet out of resources. In what follows we will consider two emendations suggested by other philosophers which might be thought to circumvent these difficulties.

5.3.1 The problem of massive irregularity

To salvage the free-and-effective-choice CD or the intellectual-satisfaction CD, one will have to supply reasons for thinking that it would be better, all things considered, for the universe to contain the prehuman suffering it seems to contain (i.e. reasons for thinking that it would not be better for God to have created the universe in the way described by young-universe creationists). One way to defend this claim is to argue that the literal Genesis creation scenario would make for an overall worse world in virtue of the fact that it would be massively nomically *irregular*.

Peter van Inwagen argues that worlds can be 'massively irregular' in more than one way. First, they can be irregular in virtue of an overwhelming number of miraculous interventions in nature. Second, he writes:

It would also be possible for a world to be massively irregular in a more systematic or 'wholesale' way. A world that came into existence five minutes ago, complete with memories of an unreal past, would be, on that account alone, massively irregular.[31]

What is true of the five-minute-old universe will hold true of any universe created fully formed at some finite time in the past complete with complex yet misleading apparent signs of age. Thus, were God to create the world 'fully formed' in the sense that, for example, it contained tokens of creatures of every basic kind, he would be creating a massively irregular world. From this we might conclude, though van Inwagen does not, that the only way to have a world that is not massively irregular in this wholesale way is to have it evolve from an initial singularity in a way similar to that described by contemporary advocates of big-bang cosmology.

The supposition that a universe that is not massively irregular would progress from a chaotic initial singularity to subsequent stages which contain pockets of remarkable order is important.[32] For if nomic regularity required such a universe, it would require that complex organisms like us develop by way of processes that allow for gradual accumulation of organismic complexity. As a result, this emendation would provide an explanation of why God might elect to bring about the variety of types of organisms in the world, including complex organisms like

[31] P. van Inwagen, 'The Problem of Evil', 78.

[32] The chaotic nature of the initial singularity here does not refer to the structure of the laws that govern the universe at the time. Rather, it refers to the way in which the matter and energy in the universe are configured. Forces of nature operating in the early universe make it possible for simple matter to emerge. The subsequent operation of those forces allows for the formation of stars and their successors, which further make possible higher elements. The forces of nature in turn make possible the existence of life-sustaining planets and life itself. In this sense, the universe moves from initially chaotic to ordered states over time.

us, by way of the slow-moving yet nomically regular processes of evolution and natural selection.

The key to this amendment is the claim that a universe that is created fully formed at some time in the recent finite past is massively irregular in a way that the universe evolving from an initial singularity is not. Exactly how is the evolving universe superior on this score? It must either be that the evolving universe is not irregular at all, or that it is irregular, but not *massively* irregular. We might think such a universe is not irregular in any respect if we further accept the notion that we can give a thoroughly satisfying explanation of the origins of the universe without appeal to supernatural creative action. There are a number of cosmological models which propose that the universe can bootstrap itself into existence in this way.[33] On these models fluctuations in the quantum vacuum can give rise to the matter necessary to generate the known universe without running afoul of any thermodynamic principles. We might think then that we have a nomically regular story of the universe that goes right back to its origin.

However, these accounts are confused at least in so far as they all assume that the quantum vacuum out of which matter arises is not something which itself requires an explanation. Sometimes this claim is masked by the fact that the quantum vacuum is referred to as 'nothing'. But surely 'nothing' here means only an absence of material stuff. The quantum vacuum must be *something* in light of the fact that it has certain capacities and dispositions, and that its behavior is subject to description (or regulation) by natural laws. Surely *nothing* can neither behave nor be described or governed by laws. Thus, even if the theist were to favor such models, she would have to admit that something comes to be in a non-nomically regular way; namely, the quantum vacuum out of which the matter of the universe emerges.

In addition, even if we could provide a satisfactory explanation of the origins of the universe that did not run afoul of nomic regularity, it is hard to see how such a picture could commend itself to the traditional theist who endorses the notion of creation *ex nihilo*. Such a doctrine is simply inconsistent with the idea that we can give a complete and satisfying nomically regular explanation for the origin of the universe.

So perhaps any created universe will have to admit at least as much irregularity as is required in order to get an initial state or the initial conditions of the universe. In light of this, can we still make the case that at least the big-bang universe is less irregular than the fully-formed, young-universe-creationist universe? Perhaps one might argue that creating a world complete with animals having false memories and trees having rings signaling an apparent process of growth would be more irregular than creating a 'mere' space-time or a 'mere' quantum vacuum. The irregularity here would spring from the fact that the laws of nature tell us that certain complex states arise by such-and-such means, and

---

[33] For a brief survey of these views see Davies, *Mind of God*.

these complex states would, in the fully-formed universe, have arisen *without* such complex means. Given the complexity, variety, and number of states that a fully-formed universe would have to contain, its degree of irregularity would be much greater than that of a creation consisting of empty space-time or an initial singularity.

Perhaps that is right—although one might reasonably claim that the laws of nature only speak to how things go after we get nature into existence, remaining silent on how the initial conditions themselves arise. Certainly scientific inquiry often proceeds on just such assumptions. If that is right, then neither of these universes will be more or less regular or irregular than the other, since the laws of nature could not make any pronouncements on the regularity or irregularity of initial states. Since they are not subject to laws of nature, there is nothing that could render them regular or irregular, except by analogy.

In addition, notice, first, that the *instrumentally* good nature of nomic regularity would not likely be compromised on the young-universe-creation scenario. Whatever goods were to be secured by nomic regularity would still be realized even if there were a fully-formed initial state created by God, since those goods presumably all arise in the course of the operation of the universe itself. If that course remains fully nomically regular, the goods derived from nomic regularity would still be in place. Second, if nomic regularity is *intrinsically* good, the degree of compromise required to get an initially complex state seems small indeed compared to the cost incurred by the pain and suffering of animals in prehuman evolutionary history. As a result, it seems that avoiding the evil of massive irregularity in the universe is not, after all, worth the evolutionary pain and suffering that it costs.

5.3.2 Knowledge and animal suffering

Richard Swinburne has developed a line of argument which might serve to amend the nomic-regularity CD in a way that speaks directly to the troubling objections we have been considering. Swinburne agrees that the created order must be configured in such a way as to allow morally significant creatures the opportunity to exercise their freedom in morally significant ways, as we saw in Chapter 4. In order for this to be the case, the created order must have the following crucial features. First, following the line of argument developed above, the universe must be nomically regular. Such nomic regularity provides us with the knowledge necessary to connect bodily motions with subsequent chains of events in the world that spring from those bodily motions. This in turn allows us to form intentions about acting so as to cause certain states of affairs in the world beyond simply moving our bodies this way or that.

Second, the environment in which these creatures live must provide genuine opportunities to choose between good and evil courses of action. This requires, for example, that our moral environment provide us with incentives for choosing both actions that are good and actions that are evil. In addition, it must be the case that our moral environment is not configured in such a way that it otherwise thwarts our choosing to do good or evil. A configuration of this sort requires, among other things, that God be hidden to some extent. Were God's existence and nature to become fully evident to me, I could no more freely and rationally choose to act on the evil incentives presented to me in my environment than I would be able to refrain from giving my wallet to the mugger who sticks a pistol in my back.

How could we acquire the beliefs that we rely upon in action? That is, when I decide that I want to drive the nail into the wood, or help someone change a tire, or cause someone harm, how am I supposed to know *how* to do those things? The answer is, of course, from experience. In the past I have noted that when I hit things with the hammer it makes them move. So I hit the nail with the hammer. In the past I have seen that when you take the metal wrench with the hexagonal hole at the end, place it on the lug nut, and turn hard, the car wheel comes off. And in the past I have seen that when I kick someone hard in the shins they scream in pain.

Since the world must be constituted in such a way that it gives me opportunities to choose between good and evil courses of action, it must be the case that my environment provides me with opportunities to learn how to help and to harm those around me. This means that I must sometimes see that when the thirsty person receives water his thirst is relieved and he is in turn pleased. And it means that I must see cases in which someone hits their shin on a rock, or is kicked in the shin, so that I can learn that events of this sort are occasions where that person is harmed.

If a belief that my action will have a certain effect is to be as well justified as possible, it will need to be backed up by beliefs that in the past actions of just that type have had that kind of effect; or that the immediate result which the action consists in bringing about has had that kind of effect in the past. What I mean by the latter is this. Every human action done by means of the body consists in bringing about some bodily movement or immediate effect in the environment, which in time has more distant effects . . . My belief that if I light hydrogen it will explode will for its strongest justification depend on beliefs that in the past when I (or others) have lit hydrogen it has exploded . . . So if my beliefs about some contemplated bad action having a bad effect are to be as well justified as possible, this will in general require there having been similar actions, of events not produced intentionally, producing similar bad effects in the past, which I can observe (or others can tell me about and I can take account of).[34]

In order to get well-justified knowledge of this sort, there must be natural evils in the world. I simply could not learn about the ways in which individuals can be helped or harmed unless I either see them experiencing want of a sort which is later relieved, or I see them harmed.

---

[34] Swinburne, *Providence and the Problem of Evil*, 181.

But isn't there some other way to secure such knowledge, without pain and suffering? Swinburne considers an alternative picture according to which God prevents all of those evils supposedly necessary for informing us about the potentially bad effects of our actions by simply implanting the needed beliefs directly in our minds. So when I decide I want to drive in the nail, God implants in my mind the belief that hitting with the hammer will do the trick. Or, when I desire to cause you harm, God implants in my mind the belief that kicking your shins would be an advisable course of action.

Swinburne argues that this more benign alternative is overall less preferable for at least three reasons. First, if this is the way we are to learn the consequences of our actions:

We could not choose to seek new knowledge by thinking, searching, and asking— knowledge of what we can do and can bring about by our actions, as well as theoretical knowledge about the world.[35]

Were our only access to these beliefs to come through direct divine activity on our minds, we would lose out on the goods of intellectual inquiry we enjoy in the actual world. Here Swinburne appeals to the same class of goods appealed to by Wright above.

Second, insofar as we acquire beliefs in this way, the beliefs we have are more akin to intuitions or hunches. That is, such beliefs would be quite unlike the beliefs that we actually have about the consequences of our actions; that is, beliefs which depend on past experience and a grasp of the causal interrelationships that obtain in the world. But insofar as our beliefs are uncertain in this way, our moral responsibility for what we do is diminished.

The less certain the effects, the less serious the choice. If there is a doubt about whether smoking causes cancer, it is less evidently a bad thing to smoke. To be well justified our beliefs need to be backed up by experience.[36]

Third, were God to attenuate the force of these two disadvantages by perhaps giving me a measure of confidence in the beliefs that exceeds the evidential support I have for them, then I would have to regard those beliefs as coming directly from God himself. That is, if I were to consider, 'How can I kill John?', and immediately I hear a voice inside my head saying 'If you shoot John, he will die', or if I wonder, 'How can I satisfy my thirst?', and a voice in my head says, 'Drinking the water will do the trick', I will, if these predictions are infallibly correct, regard the source of this knowledge as both omniscient and in full control of the universe. In that case, Swinburne claims, I would be led to see myself as 'overseen by an all-knowing and perfectly good being, i.e., a God. . . . That . . . would make the choice between good and bad impossible, given that we have certain good desires'.[37]

[35] Swinburne, *Providence and the Problem of Evil*, 182.   [36] Ibid.   [37] Ibid. 185.

As a result, creatures with morally significant freedom like ourselves must be situated in a nomically regular environment which occasionally allows for the occurrence of natural evils as a way of providing us with the knowledge necessary to do good and evil intentionally.

How is animal suffering relevant here? Swinburne claims:

A great deal of our knowledge of the disasters for humans which would follow from actions comes from the study of the actual disasters which have befallen animals. The bad states which have naturally befallen animals provide a huge reservoir of information from which we have often tapped: seeing the fate of sheep, humans have learnt of the presence of dangerous tigers; seeing the cows sink into the bog, they have learnt not to cross that bog, and so on.[38]

In assessing Swinburne's position, we must keep in mind that our focus has been on trying to find a solution to the Prehuman Suffering Problem—a solution that relies on the CD grounded in nomic regularity and its importance for free and effective choice. Nothing we have seen to this point explains that. That is, it may be that animal suffering can provide human beings with beliefs concerning the good and bad consequences of their actions that are very well justified by experience. But none of that explains why God would permit the sort of prehuman-animal suffering found in evolutionary history.

Recognizing this, Swinburne extends the analysis given above in a way aimed at addressing this very problem. Human history is too short, he claims, to give us knowledge concerning the 'very long-term consequences' of our actions. Since God has set up a world with free and effective choice, our choices will have both short- and long-term effects in the world. Only by way of the long organic history preceding human beings can we have any grasp of just how our actions might impact long-term features of the environment such as the constitution of the atmosphere, the balance of species in nature, climatic change, and so on. Thus, by considering the fate of animals in evolutionary history we learn that our actions can have long-term, morally significant consequences for our world. Swinburne continues:

The story of evolution tells us that the causation or prevention of long-term suffering is indeed within our power; such suffering can happen because it has happened. The story of prehuman evolution reveals to humans just how much the subsequent fate of animals and humans is in our hands—for it will depend on the environment which we form for them, and their genes, which we may cause to mutate.[39]

As a result, the moral-goods CD, emended in this way, explains not only why animal suffering is a valuable concomitant of human existence, but also why prehuman-animal suffering might be valuable as well.

However, Swinburne's proposal takes us only halfway there. It seems highly doubtful, at best, that the relative value of the knowledge gained by our

---

[38] Ibid. 190.   [39] Ibid. 191–2.

consideration of evolutionary history outweighs the colossal amount of suffering contained in that history. But the proposal is objectionable in a much more fundamental way. As we saw earlier, nomic-regularity CDs face two critical difficulties when it comes to explaining animal suffering in particular. They must account, first, for the Prehuman Suffering Problem, and second they must account for the Nature of Animal Mentality Problem. On this view, the harm caused to animals, both present and past, can be explained, at least in part, because it provides us with knowledge about the consequences of our behavior. But notice that nothing in this view requires that animals actually *feel pain*. We could learn everything we need to learn about the consequences of our actions by observing animals and natural history, without those animals actually having to feel anything. If seeing the cat fall from the tree and shriek is all that is necessary for us to learn about the dangers of tree climbing, creating the cat in such a way that it *actually* feels the pain as well would, it seems, be gratuitous.[40]

5.4 THE FAILURE OF NOMIC-REGULARITY CDS

Through most of this chapter we have been looking for a way of developing the nomic-regularity CD and applying it specifically to the case of animal pain and suffering. The first step in the process was to consider the various sorts of goods that nomic regularity was taken to support: free and effective choice, intellectual satisfaction, created-order goodness, and the goodness of nomic regularity itself. I have argued that a defense of this CD would require invoking one or more of the first three (instrumental) goods nomic regularity is supposed to secure. However, when we apply this CD to the specific case of animal pain and suffering, these sorts of goods do not seem to be connected with animal pain and suffering in the right way. That is, when we consider the sort of animal pain and suffering the actual world contains, it does not seem that this sort of evil (including as it does a long prehuman history and animals capable of conscious awareness of pain) is in any way necessarily connected to securing these potentially outweighing goods.

In the final section I have considered two ways of amending the nomic-regularity CD to deal with this problem. Both have failed. Thus, at this point we can only conclude that while the theist has good reason to believe that nomic regularity is a highly desirable feature of creation and has further good reason

---

[40] In fairness to Swinburne, he has a two-pronged reply to such a concern. First, he would surely argue that a world constructed in such a way that animals appear to experience pain but in fact do not violates the Principle of Honesty, discussed below. Second, he claims, as we saw in the last chapter, that the reality of animal pain and suffering is a necessary condition for certain animal behaviors having the goodness and nobility that they have. Below I explain why I find the first consideration insufficient. The second claim was discussed in Chapter 4.

to believe that nomic regularity is likely to explain a variety of types of natural evil, the theist does not have reason to think animal suffering will be among the types of natural evil explained. For such an explanation, the theist will have to invoke an additional set of considerations, to which we turn in the next chapter.

6

Chaos, Order, and Evolution

Again: the usual argument for design in organized structures is, that the various adjustments point to the designed end of life and enjoyment to which they are subservient; but it is an obvious objection that these ends in numberless cases are not attained; there is malformation and suffering, disorganization and disease; and, finally, the whole design is always defeated and put an end to by death. It is hence manifest that to take a satisfactory view of the case, we must not rely on the mere consideration of an end answered, but must recur to a higher principle—that of symmetry, order, unity of plan, and composition of organized frames: and this too, as only one branch of the yet wider scheme of universal order.

Baden Powell[1]

6.1 NOMIC REGULARITY AND CHAOS TO ORDER

CDs of the sort we have been examining in Chapter 5, that is those grounded in the goodness of nomic regularity, have failed due to their inability to respond to the Problem of Prehuman Suffering and of the Nature of Animal Mentality. Is there any way of salvaging a CD for animal suffering of this sort? There is. And we can see how such a CD can go by returning to van Inwagen's proposal concerning massive irregularity discussed in Section 5.3.1 of Chapter 5. Van Inwagen argued that massive irregularity is (arguably) a bad feature of a world. But this alone is sufficient only to show us that it is good for the cosmos, once it comes to be, to proceed in nomically regular fashion. It doesn't tell us anything about what that initial configuration of the world ought to look like. This led us to ask why the goods at which nomic regularity aims cannot all be had without any animal pain and suffering (i.e. why animals were not created by God in the way supposed by the neo-Cartesians), or with vastly less pain and suffering (i.e. why God allowed all of the prehuman pain and suffering which evolutionary history in fact includes). What this account fails to give us is an explanation of why the good(s) at which nomic regularity aim(s) (the possibility of morally significant action, intellectual goods, the manifestation of the divine

---

[1] Baden Powell, *Essays in the Spirit of the Inductive Philosophy, the Unity of Worlds, and the Philosophy of Creation* (London: Longman, Brown, Green, and Longmans, 1855), 136.

nature through created-order goods, etc.) is (are) better realized in a universe *which proceeds from chaos to order* by nomically regular means. Let's call this feature of moving from initial chaos to (pockets of) subsequent order 'chaos to order', or 'CTO' for short. In this chapter I will argue that CTO is a good feature of creation which, combined with nomic regularity, serves to provide another CD for animal pain and suffering.

Before we can defend the notion that CTO is a good feature of a created world it is important to say more precisely what it is. At the level of description at work in this argument, the universe can be said to display two types of order: synchronic and diachronic.[2] Synchronic order is order that is displayed by an array of natural entities at an instant. The arrangement of the parts of a working grandfather clock or the arrangement of the ink marks on the page you are reading are both instances of synchronic order. Diachronic order, conversely, is the order displayed by a pattern of events unfolding over time. The motions of the planets as described by Kepler's laws constitute an orderly pattern of planetary behavior across time, for example. Diachronic order is, in general, the pattern of activity of entities in the natural world that is catalogued in the language of the laws of nature.

Current science gives us reason to believe that the universe is highly diachronically ordered right from the start. The forces and laws of nature operative in the universe from very shortly after the big bang seem to be calibrated in a way that makes it possible if not probable that our universe will come to have the ingredients necessary to sustain all sorts of subsequent synchronic order, including the synchronic order necessary for life. As a result, there is no interesting sense in which the universe moves from diachronic chaos to diachronic order over time. When it comes to synchronic order, however, the opposite is true. The diachronic order in the universe in fact makes it possible for the universe to exhibit pockets of increasingly complex synchronic order. This is the sort of order we see emerging in the origins of stars, in the production of the higher elements, in the formation of planets, in the synthesis of organic molecules, in the genesis of life, and so on. And it is this sort of synchronic order that I refer to in the claim that the universe moves from chaos to order over time.

If there is good reason to create a world that is nomically regular and that *also* comes to be through a process moving from an initial state of chaos to subsequent states which include at least pockets of significant synchronic order, and in which *real* animal suffering is an unavoidable by-product, we will be able to respond to both of the objections which have plagued the various CDs proposed in Chapter 5. How might CTO deliver this result? CTO will allow us to respond to the Prehuman-Animal Suffering objection, since it will require that the sorts of organisms the world now contains, perhaps most notably human beings, come

---

[2] This way of cataloging the sorts of order in the universe is derived largely from Richard Swinburne's distinction between regularities of copresence and regularities of succession. Swinburne first sets out the distinction in his 'The Argument from Design', *Philosophy*, 43 (1968), 199–212.

to be by way of a nomically regular process. If this process began in a highly chaotic state, we can only get to the present state by means of a process which tends to allow for an overall increase in organismic complexity over time. As a result, organisms like us will require that there be precursor organisms of similar but slightly less complexity at some point in our ancestral history.[3] Because of this, we would expect to find precursor organisms which have a robust suite of mental capacities; for example, organisms with sentience, later followed by organisms with sentience plus second-order mental awareness (which organisms nonetheless lack some of the mental capacities of human beings, such as those that are characteristic of the most complex brains, those including a prefrontal cortex). As a result, we would expect to find, in our ancestral history and indeed among our contemporaries, organisms with many but not all of the mental capabilities possessed by humans. Forms of mentality, including the ability to experience pain and suffering, would thus likely be found among these precursors.

This will address the Prehuman Suffering Problem. But it should be clear now that it also provides a solution to the Nature of Animal Mentality Problem; that is, the objection that holds that there is no reason to think that nonhuman animals would have the capacity for having mental states of a morally salient sort. Given CTO, we can see that there is very good reason to think that precursor organisms are going to have to exhibit increasingly robust and complex mental states, to the point where some of them will surely be capable of sustaining nociceptive sentience with both first- and second-order awareness.

As in the case of nomic regularity, if we are going to hold that CTO is a good feature of creation, it must be either an intrinsic or an instrumental good. In what follows I will consider four attempts to argue for the goodness of CTO. On the first, CTO is an instrumental good aimed at allowing the universe to exhibit *progress*. On the second view CTO is an instrumental good aimed at allowing the universe to have a *narrative structure*. On the third view CTO is an instrumental good aimed at making moral goodness possible by *keeping God appropriately hidden*. On the fourth and final view CTO is an *intrinsic good*. I will argue that the first three views fail, while the fourth can be defended in accordance with the minimal standards for an acceptable CD.

6.1.1 Nineteenth-century progressivism

Late nineteenth-century theists dealing with the fallout from Darwinism were, as I noted earlier, struck by the problem of animal suffering the view raised. A variety of responses were proposed for explaining this evil, some of them arguing

---

[3] Of course, these need not be immediate precursors. It could be the case that we evolved from organisms with much more complex brains and minds but who, perhaps due to the high fitness costs of maintaining such minds, were not able to successfully pass on such brains to their progeny. Even in this case, however, these more complex ancestors must have themselves had precursors who, either proximately or remotely, had degrees of neural and mental complexity lesser than our own.

that the underlying explanation for animal pain and suffering was a deeper level of providential design. Pre-Darwinian Christians were struck by the design they took to be evidenced in the well-orderedness of the biological world. Arguments from design appealed to even the most absurd examples, going so far as to argue that the soft spot on the coconut was designed to make it easier for us to extract the milk.[4] Post-Darwinians found this well-orderedness a less impressive starting point for natural theology—for obvious reasons. However, some post-Darwinian theorists were rather more impressed by the fact that the processes of evolution appeared to them to be goal-directed. The fact that the nomically regular natural processes drove an evolutionary process that was *progressive* was surely a sign of the divine handiwork. Henry Ward Beecher put the point as follows in a passage we considered earlier:

If single acts [of creation] would evince design, how much more a vast universe, that by inherent laws gradually builded itself, and then created its own plants and animals, a universe so adjusted that it left by the way the poorest things, and steadily wrought toward more complex, ingenious, and beautiful results! Who designed this mighty machine, created matter, gave its laws, and impressed upon it that tendency which has brought forth the almost infinite results on the globe. And wrought them into a perfect system?[5]

Some saw a universe which 'wrought toward more complex, ingenious, and beautiful results' as fodder for an argument to replace the famous design argument of Paley. Cambridge botanist George Henslow, for example, remarked:

If the Argument from Design be not restored, that of *Adaptation* under *directivity* takes its place; and Paley's argument, readapted to Evolution, becomes as sound as before; and indeed, far strengthened as being strictly in accordance with facts.[6]

Defenders of this position were typically partisans of a Lamarckian view according to which the variations on which selection acts are not random, but are instead generated in response to adaptive need and passed along to succeeding generations. On this view, progress is both a hedge against the slow, random processes of variation envisioned by Darwin and feared by theists, as well as a clear sign of divine activity in the progress of organic history. The leading American neo-Lamarckian in this period, geologist Joseph LeConte, argued that evolutionary progress is driven by two competing forces, an external progressive force—Lamarckian use-inheritance which allowed for the introduction of adaptive change—along with an internal conservative

---

[4] An argument that was singled out for scorn by co-discoverer of evolutionary theory Alfred Russel Wallace. See John Hedley Brooke, *Science and Religion: Some Historical Perspectives* (Cambridge: Cambridge University Press, 1991), 218.

[5] Cited in James R. Moore, *The Post-Darwinian Controversies* (Cambridge: Cambridge University Press, 1979), 221.

[6] George Henslow, *Present-Day Rationalism Critically Examined* (London: Hodder & Stoughton, 1904), 53–76.

force—the law of heredity, according to which like tends to produce like. These two forces combine to preserve the existence of well-adapted species while allowing for progressive variation leading to new, typically superior, organisms.[7]

These progress theorists had some reason to be hopeful as long as Lamarckism remained a viable hypothesis. In addition, such a view seemed to fit with the spirit of an age infatuated with the notion of inevitable material, social, and spiritual progress. However, once the Lamarckian thesis fell into disfavor, the purposeless, random, directionless march of evolution sapped any hope of finding God's design in nature's *progress*.[8]

History aside, it is hard to see how the apparent progress of evolution could provide much comfort to the theist confronted with the suffering of animals in evolutionary history. First, many of these progressivists praised progress as a sign that God was leading the universe to a perfected state. But such progress only provides an explanation for the evil it involves if permitting the evil is necessary for securing the perfected state. Nothing in the progressivist view provides us with a hint as to how the sort of progress supposedly involved in evolutionary history—progress which included animal death, pain, and suffering—could be a necessary condition for that. Second, like many of the variants considered so far, this view leaves unexplained why nonhuman organisms must have the sort of mental capacities capable of permitting pain and suffering in the first place. As we have seen, many adaptive behaviors can apparently be secured without the mental states that accompany those behaviors in humans. Thus, this defense of the notion that the movement from chaos to order represents a good means of creation seems simply question begging.

6.1.2 Narrative structure

A second and more recent attempt to defend the goodness of CTO has been offered in a series of works by theologian John Haught. Haught describes the problems raised for the theist by evolution as follows:

What is so theologically challenging . . . about the [Darwinian] account of life? . . . First, as we have already seen, the variations that lead to differentiation of species are said to be purely *random*, in the sense of being 'undirected'. . . . In the second place, the fact that individuals have to struggle for survival, and that most of them suffer and lose out in the contest, points to the underlying *indifference* of natural selection, the mechanism that so mercilessly eliminates the weaker organisms. Finally, as a third ingredient in the recipe

---

[7] LeConte defends this view at length in his *Evolution: Its Nature, its Evidences, and its Relation to Religious Thought* (New York: Appleton, 1891).

[8] There has been one recent attempt to revive a neo-Lamarckian progress thesis for theodicean purposes, in Michael Corey's *Evolution and the Problem of Natural Evil* (Lanham, Md.: University Press of America, 2000), esp. ch. 2. However, Corey's case depends on a host of dubious biological claims.

of evolution, life's experiments have required an almost unimaginably extensive amount of *time* for the diversity of species to come about. That the origin of life would take so many billions of years to bring about intelligent beings seems . . . to be clear evidence that neither life nor mind is the consequence of an intelligent divine plan for the universe. We humans . . . could have done a much quicker and more competent job of it.[9]

Appearances notwithstanding, Haught argues that those features of the natural world which make it appear to be an endless, random, indifferent cascade of events are instead conditions that are necessary for creating a world capable of fully manifesting divine glory and grace. Haught claims that a universe which moves from chaos to order by nomically regular means is necessary for securing a world that is (1) truly distinct from God, (2) capable of supporting a 'narrative structure', and (3) filled with *promise*. Let's consider each of these in turn.

In order for the creation to give genuine expression to divine goodness and love, it must be *distinct* from the being of God and have a sufficient degree of *independence* from God:

As we know even from our limited human interpersonal experience, genuine love never forces or compels. Love allows others sufficient scope to become themselves. So if there is truth in the biblical conviction that God really cares for this world as something other than God, then the universe must always have had some degree of autonomy, even during its long prehuman evolution. Otherwise, it would have been nothing more than an extension of God's own being, an appendage of deity. In that case, it could never have become genuinely other than God. There has to be room for contingency and chance in any universe held to be both distinct from and simultaneously loved by God. At the same time, the remorseless consistency of the laws of nature, including that of natural selection, is also essential for the relative autonomy with which the world is graciously endowed by its creator.

Moreover, if nature is truly differentiated from God, as it must be if we are to avoid pantheism, it has to have considerable temporal scope for wandering about experimentally. And once we allow that God's creative and providential activity includes a liberal posture of letting the world be, and not a manipulative controlling of it, we can hardly be surprised that the world's creation does not take place in one magical instant, or that every adaptation in evolution will be perfect. . . .

However a coherent theology may argue that God could not truly care for the universe unless the universe is allowed in some sense to be self-actualizing, though self-actualizing in a way that occurs within the boundary of relevant possibilities proposed to it by its creator. The enormous epochs of gradual evolutionary emergence, and the autonomous evolution of life by random variation and natural selection, are consistent with the idea of a God who loves the world enough to allow it to become distinct from its creative ground.[10]

---

[9] J. F. Haught, *Deeper than Darwin: The Prospect for Religion in the Age of Evolution* (Boulder, Col.: Westview, 2003), 70.
[10] Ibid. 78.

The 'autonomy' necessary for the creation to be 'something other than God' precludes the possibility that God might bring about the creation in the fully-formed way envisioned by the young-universe creationist:

For God's love of creation to be actualized, the beloved world must be truly 'other' than God. And an instantaneously finished universe, one from which our present condition of historical becoming and existential ambiguity could be envisaged as a subsequent estrangement, would in principle have been only an emanation or appendage of deity and not something truly other than God. A world that is not clearly distinct from God could not be the recipient of divine love. And an instantaneously completed world could never have established an independent existence vis-à-vis its creator. The idea of a world perfectly constituted *ab initio* would, in other words, be logically incompatible with any idea of divine creation emerging from the depths of selfless love.[11]

Not only is CTO via nomic regularity required for a world to be distinct and sufficiently independent, it is also necessary for a world to be capable of supporting a narrative structure and ultimate promise. It is these two features which allow the creation to be the recipient of both divine love and grace. Thus, God's aim for the universe is to secure not a static, fixed, and perfect world, but one capable of developing and exhibiting the sort of freedom and independence characteristic of a narratively structured existence. In fact, Haught goes so far as to say that 'At its very foundations, the universe appears to have been shaped by what I would like to call the "narrative cosmological principle"'.[12]

This narrative capacity requires three features: contingency, nomicity, and sufficient time:

It is through portals of *contingency* that what is truly new enters into the universe, and life acquires a historical status. Events that we confusedly refer to as random, and accidental, undirected or indeterminate are essential to evolution's recipe.

Second, nature must also possess a set of invariant and inviolable physical constraints, namely, the laws of physics and chemistry. . . .

Third, and finally, Darwinian processes require a vast amount of time to lock into replicative consistency the new possibilities that emerge contingently in the life-story.

Contingency, as we have just seen, renders nature open to *novelty*, an essential element in evolution. The consistency embedded in physical laws and natural selection endows the evolutionary process with a *coherence* that gives organizational unity and continuity to life across time. And nature's irreversible temporality, in conjunction with the elements of contingency and consistency, marks the universe with sharp *historicity*. After Darwin—and even more so after Einstein—nature has revealed itself, beneath previous impressions of it, as being an immense story. And the significance of the three features we have just isolated is that they make it possible for a universe to have a narrative disposition.[13]

---

[11] Haught, *Deeper than Darwin*, 168.   [12] Ibid. 60.   [13] Ibid. 58–60.

Finally, Haught claims that contingency, nomicity, and time are required for the universe to be a place of *promise*. The contingency is required in order to make real the possibility that things might go astray. Nomicity provides a way for God to insure that there are limits on how far nature can wander. Time is required in order to give the universe and its inhabitants the ability to bring the potential of the universe to fruition. Evolutionary cosmology, in other words, 'invites us to complete the biblical vision of life based on hope for surprise rather than allowing us to wax nostalgic for what we imagine once was'.[14]

Achieving these three goods requires that the door be left open for the possibility of moral and natural evil in the creation. This, Haught claims, is just what one would expect when a divinely created universe is allowed this sort of distinctness and contingency over time:

Evolution . . . means that the world is unfinished. But if it is unfinished, then we cannot justifiably expect it to be perfect. It *inevitably* has a dark side. Redemption . . . must mean . . . the healing of *tragedy* . . . that accompanies a universe *in via*. . . . It would be callous indeed on the part of theologians to perpetuate the one-sidedly anthropocentric and retributive notions of pain and redemption that used to fit so comfortably into pre-evolutionary pictures of the world.[15]

It is important to see that in defending this picture Haught is taking head-on the formidable challenge raised by the problem of animal pain and suffering in prehuman natural history. However, the positions Haught presents are woefully underdefended. He first argues that a universe that is not appropriately 'self-actualizing' cannot possibly be *distinct* from God. This is why, for example, he thinks that young-earth creationism would entail something on the order of pantheism. Haught claims that such a world would be a 'mere appendage' of the deity. But the underlying claim here is false. Why must we think that if an agent directly actualizes a state of affairs then that state of affairs is not distinct from the agent? In fact, how could we think such a thing? Certainly our paintings and sculptures are not parts of us even though they are non-self-actualizing.[16] Furthermore, even if it is correct that a universe created fully formed could not be independent of God, how could we conclude that a universe created as a chaotic initial singularity secures such independence? If one is a divine appendage, surely

---

[14] Ibid. 173–4.   [15] Ibid. 169.

[16] One referee has objected that perhaps the painting analogy is not apt. The painting is clearly distinct from us if for no other reason than that we did not produce the canvas, the paint, and so on. Would we think that some product was independent of us if it rather grew out of our bodies organically? And isn't that a closer analogue to creation than the painter analogy? Perhaps the organic-growth analogy is more similar. But it doesn't help Haught's cause. The reasons for this are twofold. First, theologians have traditionally rejected the notion that the creation springs directly from the substance of God and thus the analogy is inapt for other reasons. Second, even if we allow the analogy to stand, it is hard to see what metaphysic of substance would require that the 'outgrowth' engage in self-determination over long spans of time after its origin in order to count as a distinct substance.

the other will be as well. And if that is right, how could any of the subsequent stages of the universe be any more distinct from the divine being?

Second, the conditions Haught proposes as necessary for narrative capacity are misplaced. For Haught, presenting the universe fully formed in the way described in Genesis precludes the possibility that it can come to have its own narrative structure.[17] Thus, if the story of the garden of Eden were to have been literally true, we would be forced to say that Adam and Eve would have been unable to secure narrative structure within their universe by, say, tending the garden and exercising dominion over the earth. Why should we think that plausible? It might well be the case that the universe must move forward in time in order to cultivate the narrative of creation. But why would a fully-formed universe lack the capacity to develop a forward-directed narrative for this reason? Without an answer, it is hard to see how this consideration could be relevant to a defense of CTO.

Perhaps Haught would argue that we have missed the point. My criticism makes the assumption that the narrative capacity applies only to Adam and Eve, or perhaps to human beings more generally. Perhaps *they* can impose narrative structure on their corner of the universe, even a fully-formed universe. Perhaps our focus should be on something more all-encompassing or global. That is, Haught may be proposing that the narrative capacity in question applies to the universal natural drama as a whole. Can the goods of an independent, contingent, narrative-supporting natural world outweigh the natural evil we find in it, including animal suffering?

If we think so, it is only because we have allowed ourselves to apply something like a free-will CD to the universe as a whole. In Chapter 4 we looked at Swinburne's claim that there is something intrinsically good and noble about the behavior of animals when they seek to rescue their young from peril or pursue a mate in the face of danger. There we saw that this sort of anthropomorphism is misplaced. These activities can only be counted as genuinely good when they result from actual intentional behavior (free or not). We can see this (again) by focusing our attention on the behaviors of certain kinds of purely mechanical devices. There is nothing meritorious or valuable about the behavior of the tow truck that revs its engine while straining to winch a car from the ditch. Of course it is sacrificing its own (mechanical) energy and integrity for the sake of the other (car). Perhaps it even puts 'itself' at risk of falling into the ditch. But it seems odd to regard its action as *good*, except insofar as the results serve the ends of the beings who made the mechanisms in the first place. With Haught's CD we are tempted to fall prey to a new variety of anthropomorphism, attributing to the universe as a whole the capacity for producing good and meaningful outcomes in light of nature's own independence and contingency. But this sort

---

[17] I here use fully formed in the sense that it is used by Haught, a sense which parallels the sense used in describing the 'omphalic' worlds of Chapter 5. A fully-formed universe is thus not one that is static. Rather, it is one that displays the full range of 'types' of substances from the beginning.

of anthropomorphism is no better than the variety criticized earlier. Once again we are being tempted to attribute characteristics to entities that cannot possess them.

The position that Haught defends is not novel, having been tried out by some nineteenth-century theologians as well. But, for reasons similar to those I just described, the view was consistently rejected. The nineteenth-century philosopher Borden Bowne explains the grounds for the rejection in the following passage, also mentioned earlier:

> The fact that evolution in any way diminishes the Creator's responsibility for evil is really somewhat infantile. It rests on the assumption that there is some element of . . . self-determination in the system whereby it is able to make new departures on its own account. But in a mechanical system there is no such element, and the founder is responsible for the outcome.[18]

For Bowne, the universe lacks the sort of independence necessary to diminish divine responsibility for natural evil, because the universe is not free or 'self-determining'.

Finally, couldn't it be the case there was sufficient contingency, nomicity, and time, even on the fully-formed-creation scenario, to allow for ultimate promise in the universe? After all, it appears that Adam and Eve faced the prospect of achieving ultimate fulfillment through communion with God and dominion over the order of nature if they remained pure; and yet there was still sufficient contingency to allow them, ultimately, to fail in this endeavor.

Leaving these philosophical concerns behind, there is a second perhaps more serious worry here. Haught's conditions for a universe that is a suitable object of divine creation seems so unabashedly ad hoc. Haught gives the illusion of specifying the characteristics that a divinely created world would have, and then explaining how the actual world fits the specifications. But it is hard to avoid the impression that he has rather looked at the apparently bumbling, random, indifferent course of natural history as specified by contemporary evolutionary cosmology and concocted a story that keeps reality from slipping from the theist's grasp. One gets a sense that theists like Haught could retrodict the existence of almost any world, no matter how bleak.

Unfortunately, neither the approach of the nineteenth-century progressivists nor that of Haught seems capable of filling the gap in the CDs grounded in CTO.

6.1.3 Divine hiddenness

In his recent book *Finding Darwin's God* biologist Kenneth Miller defends CTO as follows:

> If he so chose, the God whose presence is taught by most Western religions could have fashioned anything, ourselves included, *ex nihilo*, from his wish alone . . . [But] if the

---

[18] Borden Bowne, *Philosophy of Theism* (New York: Harper, 1887), 227.

persistence of life were beyond the capabilities of matter, if a string of constant miracles were needed for each turn of the cell's cycle or each flicker of a cilium, the hand of God would be written directly into every living thing—His presence at the edge of the human sandbox would be unmistakable. Such findings might confirm our faith, but they would also undermine our independence. How could we fairly choose between God and man when the presence and the power of the divine so obviously and so literally controlled our every breath? Our freedom as His creatures requires a little space, some integrity, a consistency and self-sufficiency to the material world.[19]

In similar fashion, Michael Corey argues:

There is an even more compelling reason why God would have wanted to influence the evolution of life here so indirectly: because He would have wanted to preserve the necessary epistemic distance between Himself and the human race at all cost, so as to ensure the integrity of our essential freedom over against Himself. Had God opted to create life here in a significantly more direct and obvious manner, it would have quickly become self-evident to virtually everyone that an Infinite Creative Power had been responsible for generating life on this planet, and it is this unmitigated awareness of God's existence and great glory that would have subsequently compromised our free will to an unacceptable extent. . . . Naturalistic evolution is the preferred mode of creation in such a world because it makes life's origin ambiguous, which is precisely what is required if humans are to be capable of maintaining a modicum of free will over against their maker.[20]

The argument here is compressed and deserves a bit of unpacking. Above we considered the view according to which free and effective creaturely freedom requires that certain antecedent conditions be in place. For example, we saw that nomic regularity is required in order for creatures to be able to act intentionally. Some, myself included, have also argued that another condition required for morally significant freedom is a measure of *divine hiddenness*. In brief, the position is that were God to make his existence and perfect nature fully obvious to us, we would be coerced into choosing to refrain from evildoing in all cases, effectively thwarting our ability to choose freely between good and evil alternatives. As we saw earlier, it is this sort of freedom that is distinctively valuable for creatures in the earthly life engaged in soul-making.

Is it plausible to think that God must be 'epistemically distant' from us in order to preserve this sort of freedom? Perhaps there are other ways in which God could mitigate the potentially coercive force of his existence and nature, without making himself hidden in this way. In order to know what to say on this matter, we need to consider how our ability to make free and morally significant choices would be affected were God to make his existence and nature known to us in evident ways. It is reasonable to think that our behavior would be profoundly affected were we to be made aware of the existence of a perfectly good creator

---

[19] Kenneth Miller, *Finding Darwin's God* (New York: HarperCollins, 1999), 290.
[20] Corey, *Evolution*, 120.

God who, among other things, insures that those who love and pursue him are ultimately rewarded for eternity, and that those who pursue evil and wickedness are ultimately punished for these pursuits for eternity. Indeed, we can imagine a number of quite mundane examples which make such consequences seem likely. Drivers do not feel at liberty to exceed the speed limit or to fail to stop fully at a stop sign when a police officer is behind them. Being forcefully aware of the officer's presence provides me with overwhelmingly strong incentives to act in a law-abiding way. The same, of course, seems true of our liberty to do evil were we to take ourselves to be under the watchful eye of God himself. How could the coercive force of the divine presence be mitigated so as to protect creaturely freedom?

To answer this question we must consider exactly how the challenges to freedom raised by these threats of disutile consequences work.[21] There are three primary factors relevant to assessing the coerciveness of such consequences: *threat strength*, *threat imminence*, and *threat indifference*. Threat strength is the subjective disutility of the consequences that will result if the threat is not heeded. The greater the threat strength, the more coercive the threat will be. Threat imminence is the extent to which the threatener believes or feels that the disutile consequences will be certainly and immediately carried out if the terms of the threat are not met. The more imminent the threat, the more coercive force the threat carries. Finally, threat indifference is the extent to which the threatened is concerned about the promised consequences if the terms of the threat are not met. The more threat-indifferent one is, the less coerced one will be by a threat.

As I noted, threat imminence is multifaceted. Three facets are particularly relevant here. I will call them 'probabilistic imminence', 'temporal imminence', and 'epistemic imminence'. Probabilistic imminence is the extent to which the threatened believes that the consequences of the threat can be successfully carried out. If I am threatened with being shot by a mugger shoving a gun in my back, I will feel at greater risk than were I to receive a similar threat by cellphone from a marksman with a rifle pointed at me from a hill two miles away. The fact that I think the marksman will more likely miss mitigates the force of the threat to some extent. Likewise, temporal imminence represents how quickly the threatened consequences will be carried out if one fails to meet the terms of the threat. Thus, one will feel greater coercive pressure when threatened with immediate death by gunshot than one would when being threatened with a slow-acting poison which will kill one slowly but certainly after ten years. Finally, epistemic imminence is the extent to which one is forcefully aware of

---

[21] I have discussed these issues and their connection to divine hiddenness in 'Coercion and the Hiddenness of God', *American Philosophical Quarterly*, 30 (1993), 27–38, and 'Deus Absconditus', in Daniel Howard-Snyder and Paul Moser (eds.), *Divine Hiddenness and Human Reason* (Cambridge: Cambridge University Press, 2001), 62–82.

the threatened consequences. This is the most difficult condition to characterize with any precision, but it is the characteristic which explains why we think, for example, that advertisements describing the consequences of drinking and driving are effective. Showing graphic accident scenes caused by drunk driving does not provide people with new information. No one thinks that viewers of these ads come to their first realization that something bad might happen as a result of driving drunk. Rather, the aim is to provide viewers with an epistemically forceful presentation of those negative consequences. This epistemic force is the feature meant to be captured with epistemic imminence. The more epistemically imminent a threat, the more coercive force the threat has.

On this analysis there are five potential ways of mitigating the coercive force of threats; namely, by mitigating one of the following: threat strength, probabilisitic imminence, temporal imminence, epistemic imminence, or threat indifference. However, when it comes to divine hiddenness it is clear that many of these cannot be mitigated after all, especially on a Christian conception of these matters. For example, might God do something to diminish threat strength? Perhaps he might not tell us exactly what the temporal and eternal consequences would be for a continuing life of enslavement to our base desires rather than loving and serving the creator. Yet God would be doing us no favor by telling us that the consequences of living such a life are less serious than they in fact are. To do so would not only be deceptive, but it might further tempt us to wrongdoing which would then carry far worse consequences than we could have believed.

Similarly, since at least some of the negative consequences here are ones that are brought about directly by God, there would be no doubt that those consequences would occur, and thus no room for mitigating probabilistic imminence. Let's skip consideration of temporal and epistemic imminence for a moment and consider threat indifference. The extent to which one is threat-indifferent appears to be determined in large measure by the choices one freely makes. If I have done things which have cultivated reckless bravado in myself, I am unlikely to be moved by the threats of others. On the other hand if I have cultivated in myself an inordinate measure of cowardice, I am likely to be cowed into submission by the slightest threat. To change my threat indifference would require interfering with the process of soul-making that I have undertaken. As a result, God could not mitigate this factor without improperly interfering with human freedom and autonomy. More specifically, interfering in this way would serve to undermine (what I called in the last chapter) the 'effectiveness' of choice. As a result, mitigation will have to come either from temporal or epistemic imminence.

Mitigating temporal imminence will not have the needed effect in this case. Since the threatened consequence is one of maximal severity, it is hard to see how delaying the start of consequences can mitigate its coercive force. As a result, the only way to have an environment which is conducive to genuine free choice and soul-making is for the world to be such that divine existence is, to some extent, hidden.

Of course, none of this requires that God's existence be utterly opaque. It merely must be the case that we are not so powerfully aware of it that the coercive force of the threat undercuts our freedom. Thus, this view is certainly compatible with the idea that there are, for example, arguments for the existence of God that we can know to be sound. Sound arguments alone would not make for heightened epistemic imminence. This should be clear to anyone who has taught the ontological argument. Many who find the argument valid and who accept the premises do not find themselves at all moved to accept the conclusion. On the other hand highly obvious, evident, rationally irresistible or undeniable arguments would, on this view, serve to undercut freedom. If the existence of God were to be as evidently true as the validity of *modus ponens*, this would indeed be problematic.

What Miller and Corey are arguing for then is the claim that were God to create the universe in fully-formed fashion, perhaps six to ten thousand years ago, this fact would make the existence of God so evident and obvious that it would undermine the requisite divine hiddenness, thus preventing creatures from being able to exercise morally significant freedom. As a result, God elects to bring about the sorts of complexity we have in our universe through largely or entirely nomically regular means, moving from chaos to order. In this way the need for divine hiddenness provides an argument for the need for CTO. Insofar as we have an argument for hiddenness, we have an argument that God has good reason to bring about the existence of human beings through a gradual and nomically regular process which requires organisms with increasingly robust mental capacities. Some of these intermediate organisms will have the capacities for, among other things, sentience and nociception. Characteristics such as these will be necessary evolutionary precursors to human beings or other organisms like us (that is, having the capacities for free and effective choice and rational inquiry).

There are two serious objections that this view faces. First, it might seem doubtful that God wouldn't be sufficiently hidden if he were to create a fully-formed and recent creation with all the signs of apparent old age built into it. Above we considered the possibility that God could create the world in this way but introduce deceptive evidence which leads us to infer that it is in fact much older, and developing complexity through nomically regular means. As we saw, one might argue that this would be objectionable because it would constitute a violation of God's obligation not to deceive. Yet in that earlier discussion we also noted that it seems hard to defend these sorts of principles when failing to deceive comes at such a high cost. Is the suffering of animals through evolutionary history worth it, simply to prevent some geologists from being misled about the age of fossils? It is hard to believe that it is.

Second, this position invites one to consider just how much divine hiddenness is required in order to secure an environment suitable for morally significant freedom. Would the presence of a creator who evidently creates a fully-formed universe within the last ten thousand years improperly overwhelm creaturely freedom? It is hard to make this argument plausible when we take note of the fact that vast numbers of people over the last two millennia have believed in just such arguments. That is, prior to 1859, many if not most in the West fully accepted that the data—theological, philosophical, and empirical—resoundingly implied the existence of just such a being. As a result, for this claim to be plausible we would have to believe that the free and effective choice of all of those who accepted such arguments during this period was disabled. Needless to say, this is unbelievable.

6.2 A DEFENSE OF CTO

A successful CD for animal suffering grounded in nomic regularity will require a defense of two key theses. First, it is good that the universe be nomically regular; second, it is good that the universe proceed to a state of order from an initial state of chaos. Our first three attempts to argue for CTO have treated it as an instrumental good. That is, these views cast CTO as a good aimed at the further goods of progress, universal narrative structure, and divine hiddenness. All three seem to have fatal difficulties. Does CTO fare better when regarded rather as an intrinsic good?

Just as some have argued for the intrinsic goodness of nomic regularity, as we saw in Chapter 5, a number of theists have argued for the intrinsic goodness of CTO. It is interesting to note as well that some of these defenses precede the publication of Darwin's *Origin* by centuries. This is important (if these defenses are to be taken seriously) because it gives evidence that these are not merely attempts to construct ad hoc accommodations of what appears to be a troublesome 'anomaly' for theism.

Augustine endorsed a view of creation which seems to have drawn on a developmental view proposed by Gregory of Nyssa (*c.*335–95). On this developmental picture, Gregory writes, 'The sources, causes, and potencies of all things were collectively set forth in an instant.... Then there followed a certain necessary series, according to a certain order, as the nature of the Maker required, appearing not by chance but because the necessary arrangements of nature required succession and the things that would come to be'.[22]

Augustine combined this developmental picture with a stoic view of creation by means of 'seminal principles' according to which the initial creation includes

---

[22] Cited in Ernan McMullin, 'The Origin of Natural Kinds: Early Christian Alternatives'. (Originally from *Apologetic Treatise on the Hexaemeron*, in *Patrologia Graeca*, ed. J. P. Migne, vol. 44, col. 72.)

'seeds' that lie dormant until subsequent conditions cause those seeds to bring forth organisms of various sorts. For Augustine, seeds of all species existed from the beginning of creation, but tokens of each species emerged progressively through natural history as appropriate conditions for their existence also emerged. 'We must picture the world, when God made all things together, as having had all things which were made in it, and with it when they were made. This includes not only the heavens, the sun, the moon, and the stars, but also the beings which water and earth produced in potency and in their causes before they came forth in the course of time.'[23]

Less well known is that certain figures in the modern period also endorsed models according to which it is good for God to create by bringing chaos from order. In the *Principles of Philosophy* Descartes developed an evolutionary picture of the physical universe according to which planets were formed by settled ash in the solar vortex. Although Descartes does not attempt to make any theological connections with the view, the overall Cartesian picture favors the notion of a universe which goes from initially chaotic states to states of order by means of the nomically regular processes which God establishes in creation. The Cartesian proposal inspired others to develop evolutionary pictures of the universe in greater scientific detail. The earliest and most complete evolutionary accounts are found in Thomas Burnet's *Sacred Theory of the Earth* in 1681 and William Whiston's *A New Theory of the Earth* in 1696. Burnet and Whiston both appealed to biblical and philosophical considerations in favor of their evolutionary conception of creation. Both argued that since God's ordinary course of providence in the universe consists in bringing about complex states of affairs via nomically regular means, we should insist on miraculous explanations for states of the natural world only when absolutely necessary. Thus, when considering the question of order in the cosmos, Whiston writes:

for if a miraculous power be allow'd in a needless case, we shall be ever at a loss how far to extend it, and where mechanical causes ought to take place. On which considerations I take extraordinary acceleration of natural causes to be, tho' not impossible... nor improbable neither, yet in the present case, groundless, unnecessary, perplexing of the cause and by no means a solution of the present Affair.[24]

Similarly, Burnet:

And as in matters of Religion, we are to follow the known and revealed will of God, and not to trust in every impulse or motion of Enthusiasm, as coming from the Divine Spirit, unless there be evident marks that it is Supernatural and cannot come from our own; So neither are we, without necessity, to quit the known and ordinary Will and Power of God establisht in the course of Nature, and fly to Supernatural Causes, or his extraordinary Will; for this is a kind of Enthusiasm or Fanatacism, as well as the

---

[23] Augustine, *De Genesi ad Litteram*, 5. 23. 45.
[24] William Whiston, *A New Theory of the Earth* (London: Tooke, 1696), 52–3.

other: And no doubt that the great prodigality and waste of Miracles which some make, is no way to the honour of God or Religion.[25]

Neither Burnet nor Whiston was motivated by any sort of thoroughgoing naturalistic spirit here. In fact, Whiston, a protégé of Newton, agreed with his master, who famously invoked the necessity of regular divine intervention to keep the planets from collapsing out of their orbits. The issue is rather that nomic regularity and CTO are good modes of creation, and God will abide by them all other things being equal.

Burnet explains the motivation for his picture by noting that we no more need appeal to direct supernatural intervention to explain the development of the physical universe from initial chaos to ordered complexity, than we do when explaining the development of the human organism in the womb:

David admires the Wisdom of God in the Origin and formation of his Body; *My Body*, he says, *was not hid from thee, when I was made in secret, curiously wrought in the lower parts of the Earth; Thine eyes did see my substance being yet unperfect, and in thy Book all my members were written* . . . According to these examples we must likewise consider the Greater Bodies of Nature, The Earth, and the Sublunary World; we must go to the origin of them, the Seminal Mass, the Chaos out of which they rise; Look upon the World first as an Embryo-world, without shape or form, and then consider how its Members were fashion'd.[26]

Burnet and Whiston are instead motivated by the thought that there is something rather in keeping with the general pattern of natural providence to be found in a universe in which order emerges out of chaos via nomically regular means. In part they find the view attractive because it is evident that other complex states in the universe are wrought by nomically regular means (embryonic development, for example). In addition, they note that we must think nomic regularity to be a feature of the universe that is important to God since it is pervasive and yet comes at a cost: the cost of natural evils.

The CTO thesis is further defended by late nineteenth-century figures. This defense is partly in reaction to the expressed views of those critics who saw that nomic regularity was not, as we saw in Chapter 5, sufficient to account for the substantial quantity of pain and suffering required by the evolutionary view. One critic of the sorts of views we looked at there, the disciple of Herbert Spencer, John Fiske, argued as follows:

I will add that it is impossible to call that Being good who, existing prior to the phenomenal universe, and creating it out of the plenitude of infinite power and foreknowledge, endowed it with such properties that its material and moral development must inevitably be attended by the misery of untold millions of sentient creatures for

[25] Thomas Burnet, *Sacred Theory of the Earth* (1684; repr. Carbondale, Ill.: Southern Illinois University Press, 1965), 221.
[26] Ibid. 223.

whose existence their creator is ultimately alone responsible. . . . As soon as we seem to go beyond the process of evolution disclosed by science, and posit an external Agency which is in the slightest degree anthropomorphic, we are obliged either to supplement and limit this Agency by a second one that is diabolic, or else to include elements of diabolism in the character of the first Agency itself.[27]

In response, figures like Beecher claimed, as we have seen, that a universe that exhibits CTO and is thereby designed as a machine-making machine is a greater reflection of divine majesty than is the creation of the finished product. Beecher illustrates the point by imagining a modified case of Paley's example in which one infers the existence of the watchmaker from the existence of the watch:

> Suppose, then, that someone should take [a man] to Waltham and introduce him into that vast watch-factory, where watches are created in hundreds and thousands by machinery; and suppose the question be put to him: 'What then do you think about the man who created this machinery, which of itself goes on cutting out wheels, springs, and pinions, and everything that belongs to making a watch?'. . . If it be evidence of design in creation that God adapted one single flower to its place and functions, is it not greater evidence if there is a system of such adaptations going on from eternity to eternity?[28]

Earlier I referred to the remarks in this sermon by Beecher as an attempt to defend the goodness of nomic regularity. Those remarks do indeed contain such an argument. But it should now be clear that they are something more than that as well. What Beecher finds remarkable about creation is both nomic regularity *and* CTO.

More recently, Howard Van Till has mounted a sustained defense of a view he takes to be continuous with those of Augustine and the others we have examined above on this matter. According to Van Till, the development of the world from chaos to order via nomically regular means is a sign of divine blessing:

> I find a substantial basis for articulating a 'doctrine of Creation's functional integrity' that envisions a world that was brought into being (and is continuously sustained in being) only by the effective will of God, a world radically dependent upon God for every one of its capacities for creaturely action, a world gifted by God from the outset with all of the form-producing capacities necessary for the actualization of the multitude of physical structures and life forms that have appeared in the course of Creation's formative history, and a world whose formational fecundity can be understood only as a manifestation of the Creator's continuous blessing for fruitfulness.[29]

From Augustine to Van Till there is a substantial thread of thought in the Christian-theistic tradition arguing for the importance not only of nomic regularity but also of CTO. Were this line of thought to emerge only after 1859,

---

[27] John Fiske, *Miscellaneous Writings, iv. Outline of Cosmic Philosophy* (New York: Houghton, Mifflin, 1902), 225.

[28] H. W. Beecher, *Evolution and Religion* (New York: Fords, Howard, and Hurlbert, 1885), 116. Beecher then goes on to compare the relative 'magnificence' of an Oriental rug and of an Oriental rug-making machine.

[29] H. J. Van Till, 'Basil, Augustine, and the Doctrine of Creation's Functional Integrity', *Science and Christian Belief*, 8 (1996), 22.

one might find the defense of CTO merely ad hoc. It did not. The fundamental claim defended by all of these figures is simply that a universe which acts as a machine-making machine, producing substantial amounts of aesthetic, moral, and religious value over time, is of greater value than creation of the finished project by divine fiat.

Adopting this position opens the door to a CD of animal suffering according to which that suffering is a necessary condition for securing outweighing goods; namely, the emergence of organisms capable of imaging God in the way Christians think human beings do. That is, on this view, the emergence of beings like us in a universe in which CTO and nomic regularity obtain is going to require a spectrum of precursor organisms with increasingly more complex mental capacities. In order to have organisms which, like us, are capable of intellectual reflection, deliberation, agency, morally significant action, etc., there must first be less complex organisms which have only more primitive capacities such as the ability to experience pleasure and pain, or sentience.

This view faces a few serious objections. First, it must be the case that one finds CTO to be a valuable feature of the created order. Second, one must find that the good of a universe which exemplifies CTO outweighs the pain and suffering endemic to the evolutionary picture. Unfortunately, neither of these claims easily commends itself. If one finds it plausible that the machine-making-machine universe is intrinsically more valuable than creation of the fully-formed product, then one will find the first claim attractive. It is hard to know how to argue for the position beyond offering various thought experiments. For example, we might appeal to examples of the sort raised by Henry Beecher. Above we saw him making the argument based on our impressions of the greatness of a machine capable of producing watches. In a sermon of 1885, quoted above, in the Introduction, Beecher similarly remarked that when we encounter an Oriental rug we immediately see its wonder, beauty, and design:

Well, that is a beautiful design, and these are skilful women that made it, there can be no question about that. But now behold the power-loom, where not simply a rug with long, drudging work by hand is being created, but where the machine is creating carpet in endless lengths . . . Now the question is this: Is it an evidence of design in these women that they turn out such work, and is it not evidence of a higher design in the man who turned out that machine . . . which could carry on this work a thousand-fold more magnificently than human fingers did?[30]

With this analogy, Beecher aimed to liken the universe to the power-loom, a machine-making machine which evinces the wisdom and power of its creator even more evidently than the rug it produces because of its ability to turn chaos into beautiful order. As Beecher summed up the underlying sentiment, 'design by wholesale is grander that design by retail'.[31]

---

[30] Beecher, *Evolution*, 116.   [31] Ibid. 115.

Could one regard this good as sufficient to outweigh the pain and suffering it spawns? The question is difficult in part because we cannot subject the intuitions that might underlie either answer to the sorts of thought experiments that were employed when considering Wright's 'intellectual-pleasures' defense of nomic regularity.[32] It is helpful to recall here that the standard for a successful CD requires that our explanation for evil be one that we are not warranted in rejecting given our justified acceptances. Can this CD survive that standard in the face of this objection? If you think not, then presumably you do so either because you think CTO is not an intrinsic good at all, or you think it is a good that cannot outweigh the animal suffering it spawns. For those who think it is not an intrinsic good at all it is hard to know what to say, except to point out that there are many other thinkers who disagree. It is hard to know how to resolve this dispute, since it is one over whether or not CTO is an intrinsically good feature of a creation. We cannot resolve the dispute by asking whether or not CTO brings about some other good or whether that other good could be secured without CTO. So it appears we have a mere clash of intuitions. And it is unreasonable to think that we are warranted in rejecting the claim that CTO is a good in the face of an unresolveable clash of this sort. At least the one inclined to accept the intrinsic goodness of CTO seems to be under no obligation to reject such a claim in light of this disagreement.

The other alternative is to claim that CTO might well be a good, but that it is surely not a good worth having at the expense of the animal suffering it requires. It is hard to see how one could have a great deal of confidence in such judgments either. Making this sort of comparison would require, first, that the purported goods are indeed comparable or commensurable. Second, it would require that we be able to make a confident judgment about the relative goodness of the good and badness of the evils. If these purported goods and evils are not comparable, then there is no way to sustain the claim that the goodness of one outweighs the badness of the other, or vice versa. If they are comparable—and again, it is hard to see just how we could come to have any confidence that they are—we must ask ourselves what grounds our judgment that they are.

Some might claim that the judgment that the cost of animal suffering is too high is simply an ungrounded moral intuition. In this case I cannot argue, as I did above, that we cannot take such an intuition seriously simply because a variety of thinkers have intuited otherwise. Indeed, I am not sure any other

[32] As discussed above, Peter van Inwagen has argued, in 'The Problem of Evil', 82–4, that the sort of animal suffering we find in evolutionary natural history is required in a world that has as much good as our world and which is not massively irregular. Defending this claim requires defending the further claim that we have no good reason to think that the totality of animal suffering in the actual world is a greater defect than massive irregularity would be. In what follows I will be setting out an argument concerning the relative defectiveness of the totality of animal suffering in the actual world and the absence of CTO that closely parallels van Inwagen's argument.

thinkers have had occasion to form intuitions about the relative goodness of the totality of animal pain and suffering and the goodness of CTO. Once we reflect on the matter, what should we think about the intuitions we might form, if any, concerning relative goodness in this case? Perhaps we should think that there is no reason to trust such intuitions at all. As Peter van Inwagen has noted, such intuitions are either 'a gift from God, a product of evolution, or socially inculcated or stem from some combination of these sources. Why should we suppose that any of these sources would provide us with the means to make correct value-judgments in areas that have nothing to do with the practical concerns of everyday life?'.[33]

It may not be necessary to make appeal to this sort of skepticism concerning value judgments that do not concern ordinary affairs if it turns out that one doesn't find it evident that CTO is not a good sufficient to outweigh the totality of animal suffering. I for one don't find myself stricken with powerful moral intuitions either way on this question. No doubt I might be anomalous in that regard. But even if one's intuitions are more firm, there is good reason to be doubtful about the veracity of those opinions. Indeed, I think the degree of doubt makes it unreasonable to think that we are warranted in rejecting this CD.

6.3 A FINAL OBJECTION TO THE CD FROM NOMIC REGULARITY AND CTO

The CD set forth here faces one final, and potentially rather formidable, objection. Let's assume that one finds it plausible that some collection of proposed goods arising from nomic regularity and CTO are sufficient to outweigh the evil they spawn. One might object here that even if this is the case, this CD is fatally flawed. In Chapter 1 we noted that three conditions are necessary for an evil to be morally permissible. The third condition was that the evil must be within the rights of the permitter, in this case God, to permit. This is important, since even in cases where an evil serves to secure a genuinely *outweighing* good it might be the case that it would be impermissible nonetheless. This is obvious from consideration of the standard objections to simple forms of utilitarianism. It might in fact be true that if the sheriff allows the lynch mob to kill a falsely accused man this will avert a calamitous riot. Yet even if this is the only way to prevent the riot, the sheriff cannot allow the falsely accused man to be lynched. The prospect of future greater good, no matter how much greater it might be, could not on its own morally justify such permission. The reason for this is that persons have a right to be treated as ends, and thus their mistreatment cannot be justified by pointing to greater goods that might arise

---

[33] van Inwagen, 'The Problem of Evil', 83.

from mistreating them, especially when those greater goods are of no benefit to the victim.

Closely related to this is a recent general objection raised by Marilyn Adams to the project of theodicy as it has been undertaken by many contemporary analytic philosophers. Adams complains that contemporary reflection on the problem of evil has led philosophers to search for potentially outweighing goods which, on some global scale, serve to 'balance off' the world's evils. There is nothing wrong with this on its own. But Adams argues that while divine goodness might require that the universe contain such outweighing goods, this alone is insufficient to vindicate that divine goodness. The reason for this, in part, springs from the considerations raised above. If the good in question requires the evil of treating someone as a means, then no one has the right to permit that person to be treated in this way, regardless of the supposed greater good it will bring about.

In addition, Adams argues, the evils experienced by created persons must be (a) such that the person suffering the evil is the recipient of outweighing good themselves, and (b) such that no person be subjected to evils which on the whole make their lives on balance not worth living. For Adams, a God who loves his creation must be concerned about the good of the individuals in it and not merely about global scales of goodness and evil. As a result, successful explanations for evil, that is successful CDs, must explain how individuals can be compensated for the evils they suffer, and how no evil can serve to make one's life on balance not worth living.

The relevance to the CD presently under discussion should be clear. One could argue that the same line of reasoning pressed by Adams could also be used to show that the CDs of the sort we have been considering must be rejected. In all of the CDs developed in this chapter and the last the suffering of animals supports certain goods which do not benefit the animals themselves. Is there something fundamentally unjust or unloving about a creation which requires animals to experience substantial amounts of pain and suffering from which, at least in many cases, they receive no benefit at all, and which might, in a number of cases, make the life the animal has not worth living?

Before we turn to this question, note that considerations of this sort could be used to generate a nonevidential argument for evil that differs from the evidential sort we considered in Chapter 1 and which has been in the background since. On that argument the atheist insists that some evils are gratuitous, since it is obvious, or probable, or reasonable to believe that those evils fail to bring about any outweighing good at all. But if we can identify cases in which future goods are simply irrelevant, that is cases where no amount of future good could render an evil morally permissible, and such evils are actual, then it appears we have discovered evils that we can know are not morally permissible by God. This is important, because such an argument would not run the risk of relying on any suspicious sort of noseeum inferences. These evils create difficulties not simply because we cannot see any outweighing goods that they serve to bring about, but rather because we *can* see, right from the very start, that there are no goods which would serve to make the evils from which they are derived morally permissible. As a result, an argument from evil developed in this way would not merely seek to show that it is very probable that—or, for all we know,—this or that evil is not outweighed. Rather, it would argue that outweighing goods simply have no place in the discussion.

Let's call such evils, if any there be, undefeatable evils (UEs) since the impermissibility of the evil is independent of its role in securing outweighing goods. There are two important species of UE. First, there are UEs which are not morally permissible under any circumstance. Second, there are UEs which are permissible because (a) their permission (or the permission of some worse UE) is necessary for securing some outweighing good AND (b) the victim of the evil is compensated appropriately for their victimization. In these cases it is not that the compensation adds to the utility of the greater good and thereby suffices for outweighing the evil. Rather, it is that compensation to the victim *justifies* the evil, while the greater good serves to *outweigh* the evil. Adams describes such cases as those in which the evils are not *defeated* by the corresponding goods, but are rather *engulfed* by them. Let's call these two sorts of cases *pure* and *impure* UEs respectively.

These considerations are especially relevant in this context, since on the views described here animals are made victims in order to secure greater goods where those greater goods do not primarily or substantially benefit the animals. As a result, we might think that this CD cannot possibly succeed, since the goods cited cannot outweigh the suffering of those animals, at least insofar as that suffering counts as UE.

To address this worry we will need first to consider whether or not the types of evil under discussion here, that is evils experienced in the service of bringing about some greater good without serving to directly enhance the well-being of the suffering individual, plausibly count as UEs in the first place. If so, we will need to consider whether or not animals can be the subjects of UE. Finally, if so, we will have to consider whether or not animal suffering is pure or impure, and whether or not this CD can reasonably explain how animal pain and suffering might be *engulfed*. Let's consider these in turn.

Although many Christian philosophers are inclined to regard evils experienced by persons which serve only to enhance the global goodness of the world as UEs, the underlying arguments for this claim are far from clear. In a brief critique of such arguments Peter van Inwagen argues that one principle necessary for making such arguments work is the following:

It is wrong to allow something bad to happen to X—without X's permission—in order to secure some benefit for others (and no benefit for X).[34]

---

[34] van Inwagen, 'The Problem of Evil', 121.

Van Inwagen raises serious worries about the universal applicability of such a moral principle. We might take this principle as an instance of the more general, and fairly uncontroversial, principle that persons are to be treated as ends and never as means only. But, *pace* Kant, even this more general principle seems suspect in certain cases. Van Inwagen notes that the principle he cites, and presumably the more general Kantian principle as well, seems especially suspect in cases in which (a) the permitter of the evil is in a position of lawful authority over X and the 'others', (b) the permitter is responsible for the welfare of all of them, (c) the good to be gained substantially outweighs the evil experienced by X, and (d) there is no other way to obtain the goods for the others without permitting an overall balance of goods and evils that is worse. He cites cases such as those in which a government agency forcibly quarantines patients ill with a communicable disease. We might even imagine a case in which the disease in question is so contagious and fatal that the quarantined patient is not even allowed access to medical personnel.

Yet even if finite creatures might be forced to violate these categorical imperatives, one might think that an omnipotent and omniscient creator would never be. For if God were to foresee that a universe would have these (always impermissible) UEs, he would choose not to create it at all. And if all actualizable universes had some such evils, then God would refrain from creating altogether.

This sort of reasoning simply begs the question. Let's consider the following epistemic possibility. Among all the worlds available for God to create, every one with morally significant beings also has at least one evil that fails to benefit the sufferer. Further, one world among the infinite range of possibilities contains the greatest balance of global good over evil, and that one world is such that the balance of good over evil is very great indeed. Finally, assume that this world has only one evil which contributes substantially towards some greater good and for which the sufferer is not benefited. Under these conditions God would be under no obligation to choose to refrain from creating altogether. In fact, one might imagine that were we to be able to consult with the morally significant agents who would inhabit this world were it to be created, they themselves would readily consent to being created in such a world.

Some might find the arguments, or ruminations, offered here utterly unconvincing. That is, they might find that the categorical imperatives described above still seem quite true and thus weigh in favor of the claim that God would always refrain from creating worlds containing evils that run afoul of these principles. But for those who are uncertain on this point, that is for those who think that their justified acceptances do not require them to accept these categorical imperatives of creation, this objection will lack force against the CDs raised in this chapter.

However, and we now turn to our second question, even if one does think that these sorts of principles must be accepted, one can still think that the scope of the principle is restricted to *persons* and that since nonhuman animals do not count as persons, it is not applicable to them, and thus does not provide grounds for rejecting the CDs defended in this chapter. The reader might be disappointed to discover at this point that I have no intention of providing a full-fledged defense of a position concerning the personhood of nonhuman animals in this book. However, a few reflections are in order. First, western theistic traditions have almost univocally accepted the position that personhood is restricted to God and those things made in the divine image. Among terrestrial organisms, human beings exhaust this category. As a result, these theists would by and large resist applying the categorical principles above to nonhuman animals. For such theists at least, we haven't identified any warranted acceptances that would justify their rejecting this CD on these grounds.

One might think that adopting this sort of position invites these theists to describe a criterion of personhood, or perhaps to provide an explanation of exactly what it means to be created in the divine image. But it is not clear why these theists are obliged to do this. The fact that human beings have this sort of privileged status can, for these theists, be something reasonably believed on the basis of divine revelation. And it is worth noting that even if the theist cannot provide necessary and sufficient conditions for personhood, we are certainly entitled to the claims that the differences between human and nonhuman animals are radical and evident. Those who are skeptical about this are invited to pause and spend a few moments reflecting on the following: personal computers, Beethoven's Ninth Symphony, *The Adventures of Tom Sawyer*, the paintings in the Sistine Chapel, Gary Kasparov, 747s, *Les Miserables*, and the Super Bowl. No such achievements, nor anything remotely like or analogous to them, are found in the nonhuman-animal world.

To some this may appear to accord creation less respect than it is due. If we fail to regard the organisms in creation as meriting personal respect, the creation will simply be a tool for our own use and pleasure. The argument in the final section of Chapter 2 was meant to show that this charge is mistaken. Christians can regard creation in general, and nonhuman animals in particular, as worthy of intrinsic moral respect. And yet this stance is fully compatible with holding that such animals can, under certain circumstances, permissibly be treated as means. As a result, even if one finds the categorical imperatives above plausible, one need not think they plausibly apply to nonhuman animals.

What about those who are still convinced that these imperatives both are true and apply to nonhuman animals? For such individuals we must turn to our third question and consider whether or not allowing animals to experience pain and suffering constitutes a pure or an impure UE. Recall that in this chapter we are considering CDs which account for animal suffering in terms of greater goods which do not involve goods for the animals themselves. Thus, if we accept the truth of the categorical imperatives, and if we think nonhuman animals fall within the scope of those imperatives, then there must be some compensation provided for animals which serves to defeat the pain and suffering they experience and which is such that it makes their lives on balance worth living. In cases of pure UEs, the evils, from which the sufferer does not benefit, are merely outweighed by a sufficient quantity and duration of goods experienced by the individual. In the case of impure UEs the evils, from which the sufferer does not benefit, are integrated into a whole life in such a way that the individual ultimately is enriched by it.

It is worth noting here that Marilyn Adams does not apply this sort of reasoning to nonhuman animals herself.[35] However, those who are convinced that some nonhuman animals should be regarded as persons will likely apply such reasoning in these cases. And yet even here it seems that the defender of the CD grounded in CTO can argue that God grants a blissful immortal existence to animals as a way of compensating them for their suffering. In Chaper 4 we looked at the arguments of those who aimed to use animal immortality as some sort of explanation for animal suffering. There I noted that we can appeal to animal immortality as a way of softening the problem of animal suffering only if we first have some explanation of why animal suffering was necessary in the first place. This chapter provides the very thing that is needed. Animal suffering is necessary since, in a world that is governed by nomic regularity and CTO, a spectrum of organisms with increasingly complex cognitive capacities is necessary in order to secure the emergence of beings capable of morally significant freedom. Robert Wennberg argues that this would, perhaps, be enough, though offering a cautionary hope that perhaps something more might ultimately be available:

Would the fact that God guarantees that a creature's life, despite its considerable pain and suffering, is good on the whole thereby render unproblematic a good and compassionate God's permitting that pain and suffering *solely* for ends that do not benefit the one who suffers? . . . [In the case of nonhuman animals] this pain and suffering, then, would be permitted by God for the sake of various goods associated with human advantage . . . but not for the sake of the sufferer, in this case the individual animal. Would a compassionate and all-powerful God, we may wonder, use sentient creatures in this way? One can at least begin to imagine, in the context of postmortem possibilities, how God might render good on the whole of the life of a zebra eaten alive by spotted hyenas on the plains of the Serengeti.[36]

If, however, one takes animal pain and suffering to constitute a pure UE, this CD will have failed. It is unclear, however, why we should think that the pain and suffering of animals couldn't possibly be, in Adams's terminology, engulfed.

---

[35] Marilyn Adams, *Horrendous Evils and the Goodness of God* (Ithaca, NY: Cornell University Press, 2000), 28. Adams says specifically that most animals lack the cognitive and affective capacities required to have lives capable of meaning. Even those that can suffer pain, she argues, lack the 'self-consciousness and the sort of transtemporal psychic unity required to participate in horrors'.

[36] R. Wennberg, *God, Humans, and Animals* (Grand Rapids, Mich.: Eerdmans, 2002), 338–9.

6.4 CONCLUSION

In Chapter 5 we saw that attempts to explain the reality of animal pain and suffering in terms of CDs grounded in nomic regularity alone fail. What is required is a CD which explains why it is good that the universe be nomically regular and good that it develop over time from chaos to order. However, defenses of the goodness of CTO offered in the service of developing a CD of animal suffering will have to rely on CTO's intrinsic goodness. Such a view has been widely defended in the Christian tradition from at least the fourth century through the present. If the intrinsic goodness of CTO and the outweighing goodness of CTO and nomic regularity are not claims we are warranted in rejecting given our acceptances, we will have our final CD for animal pain and suffering. This CD clears that hurdle.

7

Combining CDs

In Chapters 2 through 6 we have examined a variety of approaches to explaining animal pain and suffering. In each case we have considered whether or not each explanation type meets the requirements for a successful set out in Chapter 1. With the project conceived this way, the CDs developed in Chapters 2, 3, 4, and 6 can, depending on one's warranted acceptances, succeed. However, in Chapters 3, 4, and 6 we considered a way in which a critic might dissent from the CDs developed therein which runs along the following lines: 'While it may be the case that G (an outweighing good cited in the CD) is a good, and that G might require or have as a consequence animal suffering, G simply is not a weighty enough good to offset the massive quantities of such animal suffering that we find in the actual world'. For this critic the vast quantity of animal suffering is simply too great.

We should not find this sort of objection decisive for two reasons. The first reason for this is that our judgments about the relative weights of the goods and evils in view here must be tempered, first, by the sort of moral skepticism I urged is warranted (in Chapter 6), and second by the recognition of the fact that animal pain and suffering, while both real and bad, is, we have reason to believe, not as bad as pain and suffering in humans. How bad is it? It is not clear how to go about answering this question, since this is not merely a matter of adding up instances of injury or units of pain. As we saw in Chapter 2, it is not at all clear how to think about the qualitative nature of animal experiences of pain and suffering. Even if animals have second-order awareness of their first-order nociceptive states, and even if those states are an object of concern for the animal sufficient to play a role in motivating action, it is hard to know how 'bad' those states are.

Two further things should be said about this last point. First, although there has been life on the earth for over three billion years, the span of time during which there have existed animals capable of experiencing pain has been vastly shorter. And this is a fact that must be acknowledged even by those who utterly reject the neo-Cartesian CDs in Chapter 2. Although details concerning these matters are vague, we do know that there are no organisms with even a rudimentary nervous system until the Paleozoic period, roughly five hundred million years ago. Yet in these very early cases organisms lack the centralized and compartmentalized nervous systems required for basic sentience. Organisms of that sort appear first roughly three hundred million years ago. And even in these cases attributing mental states with rich qualitative character is not warranted even by a generous reading of the neurological evidence.

Once creatures capable of sentience with a rich qualitative character emerge, sometime within the last 300 million years, the capacity for experiencing and appreciating pain is real, though still vastly diminished. There is no reason, for example, to think that these creatures are capable of consciously remembering or anticipating pain—thereby giving their pain at most an instantaneous character—at least until we are able to attribute beliefs to animals, something that is highly implausible until the emergence of a developed cerebral cortex. While such development may be present in some reptile brains, it is likely that the required specialization does not arise until the appearance of the mammalian neocortex, roughly 190 million years ago.[1] The first humanoid primates don't appear until roughly 180 million years later. No doubt, this 180-million-year span is significant. But even during this time period it is only those sentient organisms with the most highly developed nervous systems that are capable of experiencing pain in such a way that it can have any severity, and any sort of moral relevance.

Second, it is worth remembering that insofar as organisms come to have the neural capacities required to experience pain and suffering in a more profound way, they will correspondingly enjoy pleasure in a more profound way. The reason for this is simply that the capacities which serve to make pain morally salient would serve to make pleasure morally salient, and potentially counterbalancing. What are those capacities? As we saw in Chapter 2, they are, for example, capacities for having second-order awareness of first-order mental states, the capacity to be concerned about those second-order awarenesses, the capacity to have those awarenesses play a role in mediating action, etc. If there is good reason for organisms to be capable of nociception in the first place, and it is good for organisms to have these sorts of capacities, they will be able to have morally relevant pain and suffering, but will also be able to have morally relevant pleasure. Again this will not serve fully to counterbalance the badness of the experience of pain, but it mitigates its severity to some degree.

However, what of the person who is willing to acknowledge that we must be somewhat skeptical about our own judgments concerning the relative weights of various types of goods and evils, and who admits that we may have a very poor grip on just how bad animal pain and suffering is, and yet is *still* convinced that the goods cited in any of the CDs described here are not worth the cost of the actual quantity of animal pain and suffering? This person needs to consider the

---

[1] On the structure of the reptilian brain see H. J. Karten and T. Shimuzu, 'The Origins of Neocortex: Connections and Lamination as Distinct Events in Evolution', *Journal of Cognitive Neuroscience*, 1 (1989), 291–301. For a discussion of the origin of the mammalian brain and its significance see T. W. Deacon, 'Rethinking Mammalian Brain Evolution', *American Zoologist*, 30 (1990), 629–705.

second reason that we should resist this conclusion; namely, that the one aiming to explain animal suffering is not limited to the explanatory power of each of the CDs taken severally. In Chapters 5 and 6, for example, we looked at a number of ways of developing CDs built around the claim that animal suffering serves to secure some outweighing good, where the good in question is not enjoyed by the suffering animals themselves. Most of these were variants of 'natural-law' CDs on which the goods of nomic regularity and/or CTO both require and outweigh the animal suffering that results from their obtaining. Taken severally, I argued, only one of these CDs measures up even to the minimal standard laid out in Chapter 1. However, there is no reason that the CD from nomic regularity and CTO cannot be accepted in conjunction with other CDs, even those which could not be thought to provide an explanation for the entirety of animal pain and suffering on their own. In Chapter 6, for example, we considered Wright's claim that the intellectual pleasures of scientific discovery in the fields of paleontology, for example, might be sufficient to outweigh the totality of animal suffering in evolutionary history. I argued that the 'dog-torturing-scientist' example gives us good reason to think that Wright is mistaken about that. It might nonetheless be true that the good of intellectual pleasure is *one part* of the reason that God allowed the mechanism of creation to include evolution and natural selection. Nothing in my counterexample undermines *that* claim.

What is true in the case of intellectual pleasures might be true of some of our other goods as well. If we consider all of the proposed intrinsic and instrumental goods thought to come from nomic regularity and CTO, for example, perhaps the overall quantity of good would serve to outweigh the pain and suffering we find in evolutionary natural history. Perhaps massive irregularity is not so bad as to explain the totality of animal pain; perhaps the intellectual pleasure of the discovery of organic natural history cannot outweigh animal pain; perhaps maintaining the Permissibility of Deception Principle is not worth the price of animal pain, and so on. But is it obvious that all of these together cannot outweigh the totality of animal suffering?

Raising this question here shows that, to a certain extent, the structure of the argument in this book has been artificial. In one sense, when looking for explanations of extant evils in terms of greater goods it is much more natural to think to look for the totality of greater goods for which the evils in question might be necessary conditions. Indeed, it seems quite implausible to think that an evil as widespread as the evil in question here, animal pain and suffering, could or would be explained only by appeal to one narrow range of goods. It seems far more likely that there would be a whole host of goods that God aims to bring about through creation, and that certain types of permitted evil are aimed at securing more than one of these goods. So why take such explanations seriatim? One reason is that some of these explanations are simply inconsistent with each other. Were one to favor neo-Cartesian explanations, then one simply could not endorse any of the explanations described in Chapter 4, for example. As a result, there is some value in seeing whether or not any explanation taken singly is sufficient. A second reason is that if some of these explanations are sufficient taken alone, we could combine those that are consistent with one another to form an even stronger overall explanation, one that will be immune from defeat simply by arguments which show the failure of one component or another. In these closing remarks I want to consider how such a stronger combinatory case might be made.

How might we attempt to forge together some of the CDs developed in earlier chapters? In Chapter 3 we considered CDs grounded in the Fall. It might be thought that such CDs cannot easily be conjoined with others, since they make central the claim that the reality of pain and suffering in animals is a distortion or disruption of creation introduced by moral wrongdoing. Further, this disruption will ultimately be purged from creation by God either in the life to come or in the new heaven and new earth. Here permitting animal pain and suffering does not provide some necessary conditions or a backdrop for securing certain outweighing goods. Their obtaining, even their very possibility, is the result of malevolence. Yet these different styles of explanation are not as orthogonal as they initially seem. Perhaps the reality of animal pain and suffering is, as I proposed at the end of Chapter 3, the result of the misuse of freedom by preternatural beings. If that misuse resulted in the existence of animals which were liable to bodily injury, then it was better for God to make pain and suffering possible for these animals for reasons outlined in Chapter 4; that is, because being able to experience pain is necessary for animals to be able to preserve their organismic integrity in a world which makes them liable to damage.

Likewise, we might think that the CD outlined in Chapter 2, arguing that animal pain and suffering is not real or morally salient, could not be combined with any of the other CDs, since all of the others regard animal pain and suffering as both real and evil. Nonetheless, the considerations raised in Chapter 2 at least reinforce a measure of skepticism about how well we understand the badness of those states of animal pain and suffering we regard as evil. On initial approach to this topic it is easy to assume, quite unreflectively, that we know exactly what commodity we are dealing with when it comes to animal pain. If nothing else, the considerations raised by the neo-Cartesian shake that confidence and make us wonder just how much good is required to outweigh this sort of evil.

The CDs described in Chapters 4 through 6 are readily combinable as well. In those chapters we considered explanations for animal pain and suffering taken severally. For all we know, however, animal pain and suffering might be explained in part by each of the following:

(1) The good of a world in which there are nonhuman animals capable of good, spontaneous, and intentional actions (Sect. 4.1).
(2) The good of preserving organismic integrity in a world where animals are liable to physical harm (Sect. 4.2).

(3) The good of an eternal existence where animals can enjoy, in limited respects, the goodness of the presence of God (Sect. 4.3).

(4) The good of a nomically regular world which supports free and effective choice, intellectual inquiry, and a good and diverse created order (Ch. 5).

(5) The good of a universe which moves from chaos to order (Ch. 6).

In this way the resources of Chapters 2 through 6 provide us with far more by way of explanation than one gets from taking each of the CDs severally.

And yet . . . one might nonetheless persist in the thought that there is something about the CDs described here, even taken in combination, which leaves them short of a satisfactory explanation. Let's consider our final version of this worry. Back in Chapter 1 I argued that the only burden borne by the critic of the evidential argument based on animal pain and suffering is to help the person vexed by evil to see that they are not warranted in rejecting certain explanations for the existence of evil which are such that, if those explanations are true, they would be good explanations. What would it take for an explanation to be such that it is good if true? In Chapter 1 I argued that a good explanation would have to show how it could be permissible for God to allow conditions to obtain which are necessary for securing an outweighing good and which make possible the permission of evil we find in our world. That is the standard on which we have been operating throughout the book.

One could raise the question, however, of whether or not in fact we have met even this minimal standard. Have we really been able to see, given these CDs taken severally or collectively, that the explanations that have been offered are indeed *good*? That is, have these CDs shown us that, if they are true, God is justified in permitting animal suffering in the amounts and types that in fact occur? Daniel Howard-Snyder has argued that the explanations for evil available to us, whether they concern animal pain and suffering or evil taken more generally, do not license us to claim that we have been able to see this. Howard-Snyder puts the point this way:

Suppose we lump together all the different reasons [for evil] . . . Let's call the result *The Reason*. And let's focus on the enormous quantity of evil in the world rather than some particular horror or the suffering of isolated nonhuman animals. The question, then, is this: would The Reason justify God in permitting *so much* evil rather than *a lot* less? . . . for my own part, on careful reflection I can't see how [any of the goods cited in The Reason] would have been lost or significantly diminished if God had systematically prevented [some substantial type of evil]. Thus, I can't see how The Reason *requires* God to permit so much evil rather than a lot less. That's why I can't see how The Reason would *justify* God in permitting so much evil. We can't see how any reason we know of, or the whole lot of them combined, would justify God in permitting so much horrific evil or any particular horror. We need to own up to that fact.[2]

---

[2] F. Howard-Snyder, 'Christianity and Ethics', in Michael Murray (ed.), *Reason for the Hope Within* (Grand Rapids, Mich.: Eerdmans, 1999), 100–1.

Were we to apply such reasoning to our current case, we should conclude that Howard-Snyder is right in claiming that the various CDs developed here do not, when taken together, provide us with an explanation for evil which makes it clear to us that animal suffering of the sorts and amount we find in the actual world is permissible. Is this a cause for concern? Does this fact show us that we have not met even the minimal standards we have set for ourselves for a satisfactory explanation?

No. To see why, let's return to the various CDs we have considered, taken in combination in whatever way the reader finds most compelling. Let's call this conjunction of CDs *The Reason*. Does The Reason explain why God permits so much animal pain and suffering rather than a lot less? Let's call this question *The Question*. It is hard to answer The Question in part because it is hard to know what it is asking. One thing The Question might be asking is this: When we consider The Reason, is it evident to us that the goods referred to in it could not be had without allowing just as much animal suffering as the actual world contains and not a lot less? The answer to this question is surely no. How could it be otherwise? How could we even expect to know how much deviation from nomic regularity, for example, is permissible before the world becomes an unsuitable environment for free and effective choice? Perhaps we think that eliminating miraculously intervention to prevent all animal pain and suffering due to viral infection would greatly reduce the overall quantity of evil in the world and that *surely* eliminating this category of evil by miraculous intervention could not eliminate the possibility of free and effective action. But how could we have confidence in such a thing? If, as I argued earlier, God's justice would require that such a policy would also oblige him to prevent all suffering due to other pathogens—and who knows what other causes—how could we assess the extent to which nomic regularity would be disrupted? How would we know such a thing? How could we know such a thing? Understood this way, we can't answer The Question because our powers are simply too meager—we shouldn't have expected to be able to answer it.

Maybe we should understand The Question another way. Perhaps it is asking only this: When we consider The Reason, do we have any grounds for affirming that it *does not* explain why God permits so much animal pain and suffering rather than a lot less? I think the answer to this question is also surely no. It might be, for all we are able to discern, that The Reason does suffice to explain why there is exactly the amount of animal pain and suffering that there is. Of course, there might be types of animal pain and suffering which are such that we cannot see exactly *how* those very types are required in order to secure the sorts of outweighing goods identified in The Reason. But our being unable to see how a particular type of evil is required to secure the goods in view is simply no guarantee that it isn't required. This is exactly the same insight that the inscrutabilist rightly insists on, as we saw in Chapter 1. As a result, we are not warranted in rejecting the claim, in this case, that The Reason is indeed a good explanation for the types and quantities of animal suffering that the actual world contains.

Where does all of this leave us? It leaves many theists in the position of being able to offer a variety of successful CDs for animal pain and suffering. It may further leave some nontheists in the position of being unable to sustain a reasonable commitment to atheism on the evidence of apparent animal pain and suffering. For theists and nontheists of this sort, these CDs can be taken to provide an even more potent explanation for evil when taken in certain combinations. As we have seen, none of this should lead us to think that such explanations are capable of making the fairness or permissibility of the animal suffering of the actual world evident to us. This is something of which our human powers are incapable, and it is something unnecessary for fairly resolving our concerns about the reality of evil as we find it in the realm of nonhuman animals.

Bibliography

ADAMS, M. M., *Horrendous Evils and the Goodness of God* (Ithaca, NY: Cornell University Press, 2000).

ADAMS, R. M., *Finite and Infinite Goods* (Oxford: Oxford University Press, 1999).

ALAIS, D., and BLAKE, R. (eds.), *Binocular Rivalry* (Cambridge, Mass.: MIT Press, 2005).

ALLEN, C., 'Animal pain', *Noûs*, 38 (2004), 617–43.

ALMEIDA, M., and OPPY, G., 'Sceptical Theism and Evidential Arguments from Evil', *Australasian Journal of Philosophy*, 81/3 (2003), 496–516.

ALSTON, W. P., *Perceiving God: The Epistemology of Religious Experience* (Ithaca, NY: Cornell University Press, 1991).

_____ 'Some (Temporarily) Final Thoughts on Evidential Arguments from Evil', in Daniel Howard-Snyder (1996).

The Apocrypha and Pseudepigrapha of the Old Testament, trans. R. H. Charles (Oxford: Clarendon, 1913), also online at <http://www.pseudepigrapha.com/pseudepigrapha/apcmose.htm>, accessed Nov. 2007.

AQUINAS, THOMAS, *St Thomas on Evil*, trans. J. Oesterle (Notre Dame, Ind.: University of Notre Dame Press, 1993).

_____ *Summa Contra Gentiles*, ed. V. Bourke (Notre Dame, Ind.: Notre Dame Press, 1995).

AUGUSTINE, *The Literal Meaning of Genesis*, i, trans. and annot. John Hammond Taylor (New York: Newman, 1982).

BEECHER, H. W., *Evolution and Religion* (New York: Fords, Howard and Hurlbert, 1885).

BENNETT, J., 'How is Cognitive Ethology Possible', in C. Ristau (ed.), *Cognitive Ethology: The Minds of Other Animals* (London: Erlbaum, 1991).

BERGMANN, M., 'Skeptical Theism and Rowe's New Evidential Argument from Evil', *Noûs*, 35/2 (2001), 278–96.

BERMOND, B., 'The Myth of Animal Suffering', in M. Dol, S. Kasanmoentalib, S. Lijmbach, E. Rivas, and R. van den Bos (1997) (eds.).

_____ 'Consciousness or the Art of Foul Play', *Journal of Agricultural and Environmental Ethics*, 10/3 (1998), 227–47.

_____ 'A Neuropsychological and Evolutionary Approach to Animal Consciousness and Animal Suffering', *Animal Welfare*, 10 (2001), 47–62.

BLOCK, N., 'On a Confusion About a Function of Consciousness', *Behavioral and Brain Sciences*, 18 (1995), 227–87.

BOWLER, P., *Evolution: The History of an Idea* (Berkeley, Calif.: University of California Press, 1989).

BOWNE, B., *Philosophy of Theism* (New York: Harper, 1887).

BOYD, G., *Satan and the Problem of Evil* (Downers Grove, HI: InterVarsity Press, 2001).

BOYER, P., *Religion Explained* (New York: Basic, 2001).

BROOKE, J. H., *Science and Religion: Some Historical Perspectives* (Cambridge: Cambridge University Press, 1991).

BRUNNER, E., *The Christian Doctrine of Creation and Redemption*, trans. Olive Wyon (Philadelphia, Pa.: Westminster, 1950).

BUDIANSKY, S., *The Truth About Dogs* (New York: Penguin, 2001).

BURNET, T., *Sacred Theory of the Earth* (Carbondale, Ill.: Southern Illinois University Press, 1965).

CALVIN, J., *Calvin's Commentaries: The Epistles of Paul the Apostle to the Romans and to the Thessalonians*, D. W. Torrance and T. F. Torrance ed. (Edinburgh: Oliver and Boyd, 1961).

—— *Commentary on the Epistle of Paul to the Romans*, trans. John Owen (Edinburgh: Calvin Translation Society, 1849).

CARRUTHERS, P., 'Brute Experience', *Journal of Philosophy*, 86/5 (1989), 258–69.

—— *Phenomenal Consciousness: A Naturalistic Theory* (Cambridge: Cambridge University Press, 2000).

CHALMERS, T., *The Evidence and Authority of the Christian Revelation* (Hartford, Conn.: Sheldon and Goodrich, 1816).

CHURCHLAND, P., *Brain-wise* (Cambridge, Mass.: MIT Press, 2002).

CLARK, B., and WILLIAM POWER, E. (eds.), *International Journal for the Philosophy of Religion*, 31/2–3 (1992); special issue: 'The Epistemic Status of Religious Belief.'

COREY, M., *Evolution and the Problem of Natural Evil* (Lanham, Md.: University Press of America, 2000).

DAMASIO, A., TRANEL, D., and DAMASIO, H., 'Individuals with Sociopathic Behavior Caused by Frontal Damage Fail to Respond Autonomically to Social Stimuli', *Behavioural Brain Research*, 41 (1990), 81–94.

DARWIN, C., *The Life and Letters of Charles Darwin*, ii, ed. F. Darwin (New York: Appleton, 1901).

—— *More Letters of Charles Darwin*, i, ed. F. Darwin and A. Seward (New York: Appleton, 1903).

DAVIES, P., *Mind of God* (New York: Simon & Shuster, 1993).

DAWKINS, R., *River out of Eden* (New York: HarperCollins, 1996).

DEACON, T. W., 'Rethinking Mammalian Brain Evolution', *American Zoologist*, 30 (1990), 629–705.

DEGRAZIA, D., *Taking Animals Seriously: Mental Life and Moral Status* (Cambridge: Cambridge University Press, 1996).

DENNETT, D., 'Why You Can't Make a Computer that Feels Pain', in *Brainstorms: Philosophical Essays on Mind and Psychology* (Cambridge, Mass.: MIT Press/Bradford, 1981).

DESCARTES, R., *The Philosophical Writings of Descartes*, i–iii, ed. J. Cottingham, R. Stoothoff, D. Murdoch, and A. Kenny (Cambridge: Cambridge University Press, 1985).

DOL, M., KASANMOENTALIB, S., LIJMBACH, S., RIVAS, E., and VAN DEN BOS, R. (eds.), *Animal Consciousness and Animal Ethics: Perspectives from the Netherlands* (Assen: Van Gorcum, 1997).

DRAPER, P., 'Pain and Pleasure: An Evidential Problem for Theists', *Noûs*, 23 (June 1989), 331–50.

ECCLES, S. J., *The Human Psyche* (Berlin: Springer-Verlag, 1980).

FISHER, G. P., *The Grounds of Theistic and Christian Belief* (New York: Scribner, 1919).

FISKE, J., *Miscellaneous Writings, iv. Outline of Cosmic Philosophy* (New York: Houghton, Mifflin, 1902).

GALLUP, G., 'Do Minds Exist in Species Other than Our Own?', *Neuroscience and Biobehavioral Reviews*, 9 (1985), 631–41.

GEIVETT, D., and SWEETMAN, B., *Contemporary Perspectives on Religious Epistemology* (Oxford: Oxford University Press, 1992).

GILLESPIE, N., *Charles Darwin and the Problem of Creation* (Chicago, Ill.: University of Chicago Press, 1979).

GOSSE, P., *Omphalos: An Attempt to Untie the Geological Knot* (London: Voorst, 1857; repr. Woodbridge, Conn.: Ox Bow, 1998).

GRANT, J., 'Learning and Memory without a Brain', in M. Bekoff, C. Allen, and G. Burghardt (eds.), *The Cognitive Animal: Empirical and Theoretical Perspectives on Animal Cognition* (Cambridge, Mass.: MIT Press, 2002).

GRIFFIN, D. R., *God, Power, and Evil* (Philadelphia, Pa.: Westminster, 1976).

—— *Evil Revisited: Responses and Reconsiderations* (Albany, NY: State University of New York Press, 1991).

GUTHRIE, S., *Faces in the Clouds* (Oxford: Oxford University Press, 1995).

—— 'Anthropomorphism: A Definition and Theory', in R. Mitchell, N. Thompson, and H. Miles (1997).

HARDCASTLE, V., 'When a Pain is Not', *Journal of Philosophy*, 94 (1997), 381–409.

—— *The Myth of Pain* (Cambridge, Mass.: MIT Press, 1999).

HARRISON, P., 'Theodicy and animal pain', *Philosophy*, 64 (1989), 79–92.

HARTSHORNE, C., *Omnipotence and Other Theological Mistakes* (Albany, NY: State University of New York Press, 1984).

HASKER, W., 'The Necessity of Gratuitous Evil', *Faith and Philosophy*, 9 (1992), 23–44.

—— *Providence, Evil, and the Openness of God* (New York: Routledge, 2004).

HAUGHT, J. F., *Deeper Than Darwin: The Prospect for Religion in the Age of Evolution* (Boulder, Col.: Westview, 2003).

HENSLOW, G., *Present-Day Rationalism Critically Examined* (London: Hodder & Stoughton, 1904).

HERZOG, HAROLD A., and GALVIN, SHELLEY, 'Common Sense and the Mental Lives of Animals: An Empirical Approach', in R. Mitchell, N. Thompson, and H. Miles (1997).

HIRSTEIN, W., and RAMACHANDRAN, V., 'Capgras Syndrome: A Novel Probe for Understanding the Neural Representation of the Identity and Familiarity of Persons', *Proceedings of the Royal Society B: Biological Sciences*, 264 (22 March 1997), 437–44.

HOWARD-SNYDER, D., 'The Argument from Inscrutable Evil', in Howard-Snyder (ed.), *The Evidential Argument from Evil* (Bloomington, Ind.: Indiana University Press, 1996).

—— 'God, Evil, and Suffering', in M. Murray (1999).

—— and BERGMANN, M., 'Grounds for Belief in God Aside, Does Evil Make Atheism More Reasonable than Theism?', in M. Peterson and M. van Arragon (eds.), *Contemporary Debates in Philosophy of Religion* (Malden, Mass.: Blackwell, 2003).

—— and HOWARD-SNYDER, F., 'How an Unsurpassable Being Can Create a Surpassable World', *Faith and Philosophy*, 11 (1994), 260–8.

—— and O'LEARY-HAWTHORNE, J., 'Transworld Sanctity and Plantinga's Free Will Defense', *International Journal for the Philosophy of Religion*, 44 (August, 1998), 1–21.

HURD, J. P., 'Hominids in the Garden?', in K. B. Miller (ed.), *Perspectives on an Evolving Creation* (Grand Rapids, Mich.: Eerdmans, 2003).

ICKERT, S., 'Luther and Animals: Subject to Adam's Fall?', in A. Linzey and D. Yamamoto (1998) (eds.).

JOAD, C., and LEWIS, C. S., 'The Pains of Animals', in A. Linzey and T. Regan (eds.), *Animals and Christianity: A Book of Readings* (New York: Crossroad, 1989).

KANT, I., *Lectures on Ethics*, ed. P. Heath and J. Schneewind (Cambridge: Cambridge University Press, 2001).

KARTEN, H. J., and SHIMUZU, T., 'The Origins of Neocortex: Connections and Lamination as Distinct Events in Evolution', *Journal of Cognitive Neuroscience*, 1 (1989), 291–301.

KELLY, J. N. D., *Early Christian Doctrines* (San Francisco, Calif.: HarperCollins, 1978).

KINGSTON, A. R., 'Theodicy and Animal Welfare', *Theology*, 70/569 (1967) 482–8.

LECONTE, JOSEPH, *Evolution: Its Nature, its Evidences, and its Relation to Religious Thought* (New York: Appleton, 1891).

LEIBNIZ, G. W., *Theodicy: Essays on the Goodness of God, the Freedom of Man, and the Origin of Evil*, ed. E. Huggard (LaSalle, Ill.: Open Court, 1988).

—— *Philosophical Essays*, ed. R. Ariew and D. Garber (Indianapolis, Ind.: Hackett, 1989).

—— *The Leibniz–Clarke Correspondence*, ed. H. Alexander (Manchester: Manchester University Press, 1956).

LESLIE, J., *Universes* (New York: Routledge, 1996).

LEWIS, C. S., *The Problem of Pain: How Human Suffering Raises Almost Intolerable Intellectual Problems* (New York: Collier, 1962).

LEWIS, D., 'Mad Pain and Martian Pain', in N. Block (ed.), *Readings in Philosophy of Psychology*, i (Cambridge, Mass.: Harvard University Press, 1980).

—— 'Evil for Freedom's Sake', *Philosophical Papers*, 22 (1993), 149–72, repr. in Lewis, *Papers in Ethics and Social Philosophy* (Cambridge: Cambridge University Press, 2000).

LIBET, B., 'The Neural Time Factor in Conscious and Unconscious Events', in G. Block and J. Marsh (eds.), *Experimental and Theoretical Studies of Consciousness* (CIBA Foundation Symposium 174) (New York: Wiley, 1993).

LINZEY, A., and YAMAMOTO, D. (eds.), *Animals on the Agenda* (Champaign/Urbana, Ill.: University of Illinois Press, 1998).

LYCAN, W., *Conciousness and Experience* (Cambridge, Mass.: MIT Press, 1987).

MCDANIEL, J. B., 'Can Animal Suffering be Reconciled with Belief in an All-Loving God?', in A. Linzey and D. Yamamoto (1998) (eds.).

MACKIE, J. L., 'Evil and Omnipotence', *Mind* 64 (1955), 200–12.

MAHAFFY, J., *Descartes* (London: Blackwood, 1901).

MANN, W. (ed.), *Blackwell Guide to the Philosophy of Religion* (Malden, Mass.: Blackwell, 2005).

MASCALL, E., *Christian Theology and Natural Science* (New York: Ronald, 1956).

MAWSON, T., 'The Possibility of a Free-will Defense for the Problem of Natural Evil', *Religious Studies*, 40 (2004), 23–42.

MEIJSING, M., 'Awareness, Self-awareness and Perception: An Essay on Animal Conciousness', in M. Dol, S. Kasanmoentalib, S. Lijmbach, E. Rivas, and R. van den Bos (1997) (eds.).

MILLER, K., *Finding Darwin's God* (New York: HarperCollins, 1999).

MILLER, K. B. (ed.), *Perspectives on an Evolving Creation* (Grand Rapids, Mich.: Eerdmans, 2003).

MITCHELL, R., THOMPSON, N., and MILES, H. L. (eds.), *Anthropomorphism, Anecdotes, and Animals* (Albany, NY: State University of New York Press, 1997).

MOORE, J. R., *The Post-Darwinian Controversies* (Cambridge: Cambridge University Press, 1979).

MORRIS, H. M. (1973), 'The Day-Age Theory', in K. L. Segraves (ed.), *And God Created* (San Diego, Calif.: Creation Science Research Center, 1973).

MURPHY, NANCEY, and ELLIS, GEORGE E. R., *On the Moral Nature of the Universe* (Minneapolis, Minn.: Fortress, 1996).

MURRAY, M., 'Coercion and the Hiddenness of God', *American Philosophical Quarterly*, 30 (1993), 27–38.

——— (ed.), *Reason for the Hope Within* (Grand Rapids, Mich.: Eerdmans, 1999).

——— 'Deus Absconditus', in D. Howard-Snyder, and P. Moser (eds), *Divine Hiddenness and Human Reason* (Cambridge: Cambridge University Press, 2001).

——— and DUDRICK, DAVID, 'Are Coerced Acts Free?', *American Philosophical Quarterly*, 32 (1995), 147–161.

——— and REA, M., *Introduction to the Philosophy of Religion* (Cambridge: Cambridge University Press, 2008).

NADLER, S., 'Spinoza in the Garden of Good and Evil', in E. Kremer and M. Latzer (eds.), *The Problem of Evil in Early Modern Philosophy* (Toronto: University of Toronto Press, 2001).

ORIGEN, *Origen: Contra Celsum*, ed. and trans. Henry Chadwick (Cambridge: Cambridge University Press, 1980).

PLANTINGA, A., *God, Freedom, and Evil* (Grand Rapids, Mich.: Eerdmans, 1974).

——— *Warranted Christian Belief* (Oxford: Oxford University Press, 2000).

POVINELLI, D. J., *Folk Physics for Apes: The Chimpanzee's Theory of How the World Works* (Oxford: Oxford University Press, 2003).

POWELL, B., *Essays in the Spirit of the Inductive Philosophy, the Unity of Worlds, and the Philosophy of Creation* (London: Longman, Brown, Green, and Longmans, 1855).

PREMACK, D., and PREMACK, A. J., 'Does the Chimpanzee Have a Theory of Mind', *Behavioral Brain Science*, 4 (1978), 515–526.

PUN, P., *Evolution: Nature and Scripture in Conflict?* (Grand Rapids, Mich.: Zondervan, 1982).

RAY, J., *The Wisdom of God Manifested in the Works of Creation* (London: 1691; repr. New York: Garland, 1979).

REICHENBACH, B., *Evil and a Good God* (New York: Fordham University Press, 1982).

ROBERTS, J. H., *Darwinism and the Divine in America: Protestant Intellectuals and Organic Evolution, 1859–1900* (Notre Dame, Ind.: University of Notre Dame Press, 2001).

ROSENTHAL, D., *Consciousness and the Mind* (Oxford: Oxford University Press, 2002).

ROWE, W., 'The Problem of Evil and Some Varieties of Atheism', *American Philosophical Quarterly*, 16 (1979), 335–41.

SANDERS, J., *The God Who Risks: A Theology of Providence* (Downers Grove, HI: InterVarsity Press, 1998).

SCULLY, M., *Dominion* (New York: St Martin's, 2002).

SHUSTER, M., *The Fall and Sin: What We Have Become as Sinners* (Grand Rapids, Mich.: Eerdmans, 2003).

SMITH, Q., 'An Atheological Argument from Evil Natural Laws', *International Journal for the Philosophy of Religion*, 29 (1991), 159–74.

SWINBURNE, R., 'The Argument from Design', *Philosophy*, 43 (1968), 199–212.

—— *Providence and the Problem of Evil* (Oxford: Oxford University Press, 1998).

TENNANT, F. R., *Philosophical Theology, ii*, (Cambridge: Cambridge University Press, 1928).

TILLEY, T., *The Evils of Theodicy* (Washington, DC: Georgetown University Press, 1991).

TONG, F., 'Competing Theories of Binocular Rivalry: A Possible Resolution', *Brain and Mind*, 2/1 (2001), 55–83.

TRAKAKIS, N., *The God Beyond Belief: In Defence of William Rowe's Evidential Argument from Evil* (Netherlands: Springer, 2007).

TRETHOWAN, D. I., *An Essay in Christian Philosophy* (London: Longmans, Green, 1954).

TRIGG, R., *Pain and Emotion* (Oxford: Clarendon, 1970).

VAN INWAGEN, P., 'The Possibility of Resurrection', *International Journal for the Philosophy of Religion*, 9 (1978), 114–21.

—— 'When is the Will Free?', *Philosophical Perspectives*, 3 (1989), 399–422.

—— 'When the Will is Not Free', *Philosophical Studies*, 75 (1994), 95–113.

—— 'The Problem of Evil, the Problem of Air, and the Problem of Silence', in *God, Knowledge, Mystery* (Ithaca, NY: Cornell University Press, 1995).

—— 'The Magnitude, Duration, and Distribution of Evil', in P. van Inwagen (1995).

—— 'The Argument from Particular Horrendous Evils', *Proceedings of the American Catholic Philosophical Association*, 74 (2000), 65–80.

VAN TILL, H. J., 'Basil, Augustine, and the Doctrine of Creation's Functional Integrity', *Science and Christian Belief*, 8 (1996), 21–38.

—— 'The Creation: Intelligently Designed or Optimally Equipped', *Theology Today*, 55 (1998), 344–64.

VARNER, G., *In Nature's Interests? Interests, Animal Rights, and Environmental Ethics* (Oxford: Oxford University Press, 1998).

WARD, K., *Rational Theology and the Creativity of God* (New York: Pilgrim, 1982).

WEISKRANTZ, L., *Consciousness Lost and Found* (Oxford: Oxford University Press, 1997).

WENNBERG, R., 'Animal Suffering and the Problem of Evil', *Christian Scholar's Review*, 21 (1991), 120–40.

—— *God, Humans, and Animals* (Grand Rapids, Mich.: Eerdmans, 2002).

WESLEY, J., 'The General Deliverance', in *The Works of John Wesley, ii*, ed. A. C. Outler (Nashville, Tenn.: Abingdon, 1985).

WHISTON, W., *A New Theory of the Earth* (London: Tooke, 1696).

WILCOX, D., 'Finding Adam: The Genetics of Human Origins', in K. B. Miller (2003).

WILLIAMS, N. P., *The Idea of the Fall and of Original Sin* (London: Longmans, Green, 1927).

WILSON, D. S., and SOBER, E., *Unto Others: The Evolution and Psychology of Unselfish Behavior* (Cambridge, Mass.: Harvard University Press, 1999).

WRIGHT, G. F., *Studies in Science and Religion* (Andover: Draper, 1882).

WYKSTRA, S. J., 'Rowe's Noseeum Arguments from Evil', in D. Howard-Snyder (1996) (ed.).

YANCEY, PHILIP, and BRAND, PAUL, *The Gift of Pain* (Grand Rapids, Mich.: Zondervan, 1997).

YANDELL, K., *The Epistemology of Religious Experience* (Cambridge: Cambridge University Press, 1993).

YOUNG, D. A., *Christianity and the Age of the Earth* (Grand Rapids, Mich.: Zondervan, 1982).

ZIMMERMAN, D., 'The Compatibility of Materialism and Survival: The Jumping Elevator Model', *Faith and Philosophy*, 16 (1999), 194–212.

Index

action
  animal 109–12
  nomic regularity and 136–41, 151–2
  see also free will
Adam and Eve 2, 6–7, 74–80, 83–7, 101–3,
  174
Adams, Marilyn M. 187–91
Adams, Robert M. 26n
Alais, David 65n
Allen, Colin 67 n. 52
Allen, Woody 146
Alston, William 23n, 26 n. 17
Arnauld, Antoine 50
Atheism, Argument from evil for,
  see evil, argument for atheism from
Augustine, of Hippo St. 144, 180–1

Beecher, Henry Ward 3–4, 145–6, 169,
  183–4
Bennett, Jonathan 60
Bergmann, Michael 26 n. 27, 29 n. 22, 30n
Bermond, Bob 62–3, 68 n. 54
best possible world 146–149
big bang 159
binocular rivalry 64–5
Blake, Randolph 65n
blindsight 62
Block, Ned 52 n. 26
Bowne, Borden 3
Boyer, Pascal 120 n. 13
Boyd, Gregory 100–101
Brand, Paul 112–121
Burnet, Thomas 181–2

Calvin, John 79, 124
Capgras syndrome 68–9
Carruthers, Peter 55n
causa dei, definition of 40
Chalmers, Thomas 100
Chaos to Order (CTO) 8, 166–92
  as an intrinsic good 180–6
  divine hiddenness and 175–80
  narrative structure and 170–5
  progress and 168–70
Churchland, Patricia 65
Clark, B. 23n
commensurabilty of goods and evils 153–4,
  185–7
cosmological hypothesis, the 79–80

consciousness
  access 52–4
  animal 41–69
  continuity of 43–69
  creature 52–4
  phenomenal 53–69
Corey, Michael 170 n. 8, 176
creation
  diversity within 115–6, 156–7
  ex nihilo 159
  initial singularities and 159–60
creationism
  divine deception and 91–3
  Gap theory 100–101
  young-universe 88–93, 159–60

Damasio, Antonio 57 n. 33 , 67 n. 51
Damasio, Hanna 57 n. 33
Darwin, Charles 2, 41, 80, 130
Dawkins, Richard 4–5
Descartes, Rene 6, 42, 50–2, 181
  see also, Neo-Cartesianism
divine hiddenness,
  see Hidenness of God
Draper, Paul 12 n. 1, 31–3

Eccles, John Sir 117–8
ethology, cognitive 58–61
evidential argument from evil
  see evil, problem of, evidential argument
evil, problem of
  argument for atheism from 3–4, 12–40
  Darwinian 1–9
  evidential argument 11, 19–33
  logical argument 11–19
  moral 73, 131–4
  natural 7, 73, 131–4
  undefeatable 187–91
evolution 103
  as evidence for non-human animal
    pain 5–66
  and evil 1–9
  and progress 3–4, 168–70

Fall, The 2, 6–7, 74–106
  and the corruption of nature 74–80
  antecedent v. consequent varieties 82
  CD's grounded in 73–106
  fragility objection and 82–3, 92–3, 101

Fall, The *(cont.)*
  Paradisical Motivation Objection to 83–7
  pre-Adamic suffering and 81–2
  precursive conditions and 93–96
  Satanic 96–101, 107–8
Fisher, George Park 116
Fiske, John 4, 182–3
fragility Objection 82–3, 92–3, 101, 104
free will 85
  extent of 104–6
  free choice v. effective choice 136–41
  nomic regularity and 105–6
  non-human animal 108–9
  value of 87–88, 104–6

Gallup, Gordon 61, 156
Galvin, Shelley 72 n. 60
Geivett, Douglas 23n
G.E. Moore shift 21–22
Gosse, Philip 90–3, 155–6
  Law of nature v. law of creation 91–3
Gould, Stephen J. 1
Grant, James 66n
Griffin, David Ray 13 n. 3, 41 n. 1
Guthrie, Stewart 72

Hanson's disease 112–21
Hardcastle, Virginia 68 n. 53, 119n
Hartshorne, Charles 13n
Hasker, William 14 n. 4, 16 n. 8
Harrison, Peter 43, 46–9
Haught, John 170–75
Hawthorne, John 18 n. 21
heaven 77–8, 122–9
Henslow, George 169
Herzog, Harold 72 n. 60
hiddenness of God 162, 175–80
Hirstein, William 68 n. 55
Hurd, James 81n
HOT (higher order thought) 54–6, 58
Howard-Snyder, Daniel 11n, 13n, 24n, 26n,
    30n, 84n, 104 n. 34, 146 n. 21, 149
    n. 23, 197n
Howard-Snyder, Frances 146 n. 21, 197n

immortality, animal 122–9
inscrutability response 25–30, 33–5

Joad, C.E.M. 45, 83

Kant, Immanuel 70, 189
Kitcher, Philip 1–2

Lamarckism 169–70
LeConte, Joseph 169

Leibniz, Gottfried 35, 40, 116, 144–5
Libet, Benjamin 62 n. 41
Logical problem of evil,
  see evil, problem of, logical argument
Lewis, C.S. 43–47
Lewis, David 18 n. 9, 37–8, 57 n. 34
Luther, Martin 124
Lycan, William 52 n. 25

Massive irregularity 158–60
Moral status of animals 69–72
Malebrance, Nicholas 50, 145–6
Mawson, T.J. 140
McDaniel, Jay 106
Meijsing, Monica 53 n. 28
Miller, Kenneth 175–6
Miracles, preventing natural evil and 148–9
Morris, Henry 73, 89–90

neo-Cartesianism 41–72, 107
narrative structure,
  see Chaos to Order, narrative structure and
natural evil, *see* evil, natural
neuroscience, pain and 64–69
Newton, Issac, Sir 144
NOMA 1
noseeum arguments 28–30
nomic regularity 7, 105–6, 115, 128, 131–65
  animal suffering and 149–65
  as intrinsic good 144–6
  created order goods and 143–4, 56–8
  creaturely freedom and 136–41
  definition of 135–6
  free will and 151–2
  intellectual inquiry and 141–3, 153–6
  intentional action and 160–4
noumenalism 34–5
Nyssa, Gregory of 95, 101–3, 180

Omphalos, see Gosse, Philip
order, synchronic and diachronic 167
Origen 95, 101–3

pain 43–69
  and continuity of consciousness 43–9
  dual processing pathways 66–9
  episodic 44–7
  psychological 121
  utility of 112–21
Paradisical Motivation Argument 83–7
Plantinga, Alvin 18, 86–7
Powell, Baden 166
pre-adamic pain and suffering (PAP) 81–2,
    88–93, 94, 99, 102–3
precursive conditions 93–6
Premack, D. 63 n. 45

Premack, A.J. 63 n. 45
Principle of Permissible Deception 156
Progress, evolutionary 3, 5, 168–70
prosopagnosia 68–9
Povinelli, Daniel 64 n. 46
Powers, William 23n
Pun, Pattle 90 n. 18

Ramachandran, V.S. 68 n. 55
Ray, John 80
Rea, Michael 146 n. 21, 149 n. 24
Reichenbach, Bruce 140
Roberts, Jon 80 n. 8, 141
Rosenthal, David 54n, 55n
Rowe, William 5, 12n, 21–2

Sanders, John 13n
Satan 6–7, 96–101, 103–6, 107–8
Scully, Matthew 107
Shuster, Marguerite 93–4
skeptical theism 25–30
soul-making explanations for evil 82, 122–9,
    136–7
Spencer, Herbert 4, 182–3
Sweetman, Brandon 23n
Swinburne, Richard 16 n. 6, 108–112, 156n,
    160–4, 167n

Tennant, F.R. 140
Thomas, Aquinas St. 50 n. 19, 51, 115–6,
    123–4

Tilley, Terrence 35 n. 25
Tong, Frank 65n
Tranel, Daniel 57 n. 33
Trethowan, Dom 98
Trigg, Roger 57 n. 33, 67 n. 30

Unintentional omissions 85–6

Van Inwagen, Peter 13n, 16 n. 8, 38, 85, 124
    n. 21, 146 n. 20, 158–9, 166, 185n, 186,
    188–91
Van Till, Howard 146 n. 20, 183
Varner, Gary 66n

Ward, Keith 122
Wennberg, Robert 49 n. 16, 69, 70 n. 59, 124
    n. 21, 191
Wesley, John 123
Whiston, William 181–2
Wilcox, David 81n
Williams, Norman P. 112–3
World Soul 102
Wright, George F. 141–43, 153–4, 162,
    185
Wykstra, Stephen 28 n. 21

Yandell, Keith 23n
Young, Davis A. 90 n. 18

Zimmerman, Dean 124 n. 21